ZAGREB

Publisher:
MASMEDIA, Baruna Trenka 13, Zagreb
www.masmedia.hr
mm@masmedia.hr

For the publisher: Stjepan Andrašić

Editor: Nikola Štambak

Authors: Bruno Sušanj, Josip Bilić, Dijana Štambak,
Ivana Crljenko, Božica Brkan, Vito Andrić

English translation: Sanja Bingula

Proof-reader: Neda Karlović-Blažeković

Production manager: Vjeran Andrašić

Production: Studio IdeaLab

Production Editor: Danko Gnjidić

Front cover: Jana Jokanović

Data base and index: Marija Geiger

Photographs: Tatjana Bezjak, Boris Hnatjuk, Željko Krčadinac,
Neven Unukić, Goran Vranić, MASMEDIA archives

Illustrations: Krešimir Certić Misch

3D drawings: Zlatko Guzmić, Ivan - Luka Šarić

Maps: Tomislav Kaniški

Promotion of mini-monograph in Croatia and abroad:
Global Media Marketing GMM)

Print: Tiskara Zrinski

Copyright: MASMEDIA

Total number of copies (English, German, Croatian):
14 000 copies

We would like to thank all institutions and individuals who helped
in realization of this project

CIP - Katalogizacija u publikaciji
Nacionalna i sveučilišna knjižnica - Zagreb

UDK 908(497.5 Zagreb)(036)

ZAGREB / <authors Bruno Sušanj ... <et
al.> ; English translation Sanja Bingula ;
photographs Tatjana Bezjak ... <et al.> ;
illustrations Krešimir Certić Misch ; maps
Tomislav Kaniški>. - Zagreb : Masmedia,
2004.

Kazalo.

ISBN 953-157-466-9

1. Sušanj, Bruno
I. Zagreb

441110172

CONTENTS

How to use
the guide **6**

MEETING ZAGREB

STEP BY STEP THROUGH ZAGREB

UPPER TOWN **47**

HOW TO USE THE GUIDE

The passages with headline TOP 10 highlight
the public monuments, architectural monuments, museum exhibits and special places.
There is short description with photograph

Each part of town
has different
colour to help
you find your
way through the
book easily

The most
important mon-
uments that can
be seen during
the walk

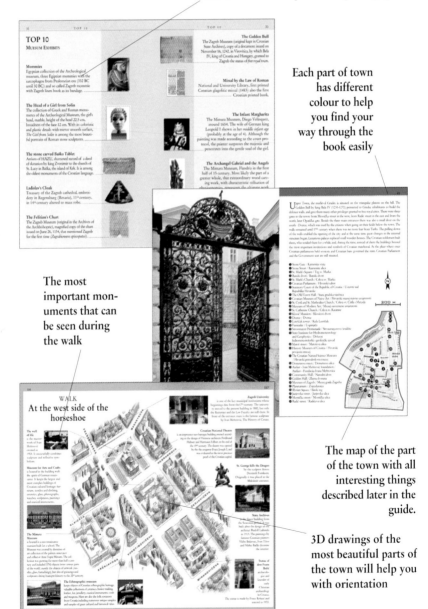

The map of the part
of the town with all
interesting things
described later in the
guide.

3D drawings of the
most beautiful parts of
the town will help you
with orientation

Practical information on addresses, phone numbers and working hours

In highlighted frame there are more extensive data on important persons

List of addresses and phone numbers you may need during your stay in town

Building cut with important details

The most significant museum exhibits

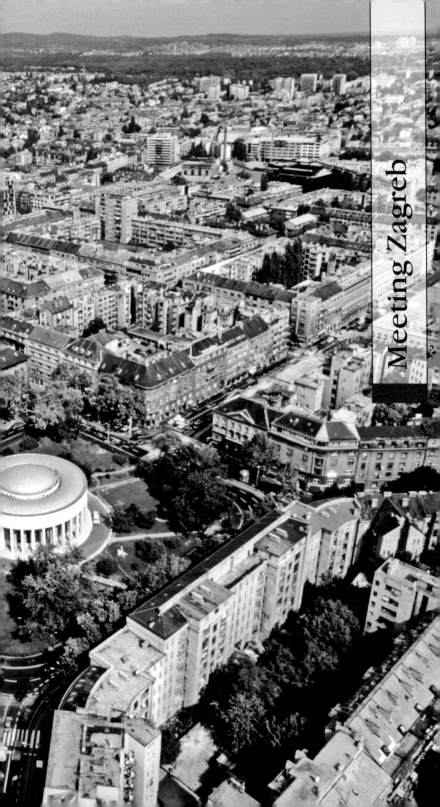

Meeting Zagreb

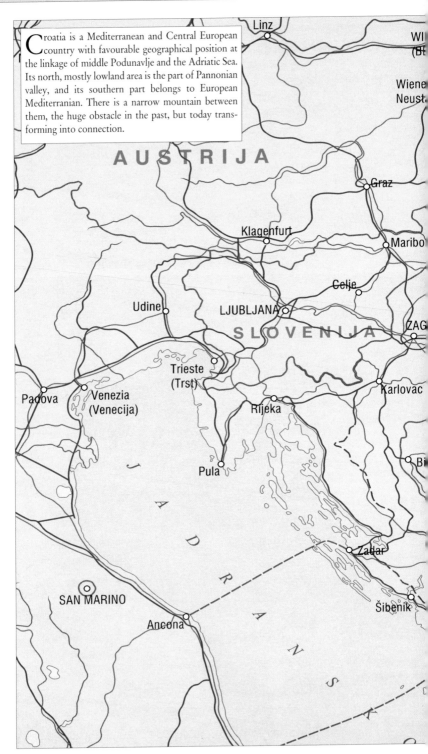

Croatia is a Mediterranean and Central European country with favourable geographical position at the linkage of middle Podunavlje and the Adriatic Sea. Its north, mostly lowland area is the part of Pannonian valley, and its southern part belongs to European Mediterranian. There is a narrow mountain between them, the huge obstacle in the past, but today transforming into connection.

Linz

WI (B

Wiene Neust

AUSTRIJA

Graz

Klagenfurt

Maribo

Celje

Udine

LJUBLJANA

ZAG

SLOVENIJA

Trieste (Trst)

Karlovac

Padova

Venezia (Venecija)

Rijeka

Bi

Pula

J

A

D

Zadar

SAN MARINO

R

A

Ancona

N

Šibenik

S

K

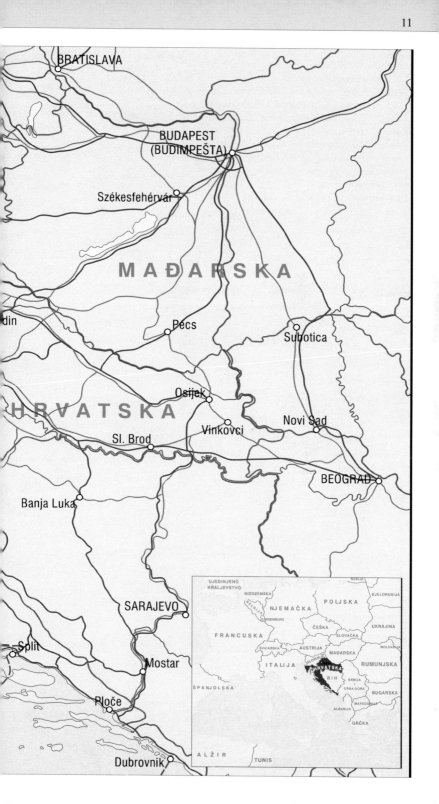

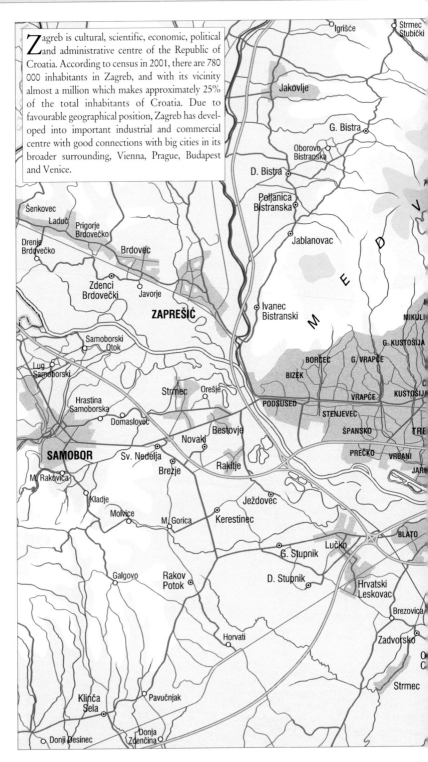

Zagreb is cultural, scientific, economic, political and administrative centre of the Republic of Croatia. According to census in 2001, there are 780 000 inhabitants in Zagreb, and with its vicinity almost a million which makes approximately 25% of the total inhabitants of Croatia. Due to favourable geographical position, Zagreb has developed into important industrial and commercial centre with good connections with big cities in its broader surrounding, Vienna, Prague, Budapest and Venice.

Igrišće
Strmec Stubički
Jakovlje
G. Bistra
Oborovo Bistranska
D. Bistra
Poljanica Bistranska
Jablanovac
Šenkovec
Laduč
Prigorje Brdovečko
Drenje Brdovečko
Brdovec
Zdenci Brdovečki
Javorje
ZAPREŠIĆ
Ivanec Bistranski
MIKULI
G. KUSTOŠIJA
Samoborski Otok
BORČEC
G. VRAPČE
Lug Samoborski
BIZEK
VRAPČE
KUSTOŠIJA
Strmec
Orešje
PODSUSED
Hrastina Samoborska
STENJEVEC
Domaslovec
Bestovje
ŠPANSKO
TRE
Novaki
PREČKO
VRBANI
SAMOBOR
Sv. Nedelja
Brežje
Rakitje
JAR
M. Rakovica
Kladje
Ježdovec
Molvice
M. Gorica
Kerestinec
BLATO
Lučko
G. Stupnik
Galgovo
Rakov Potok
D. Stupnik
Hrvatski Leskovac
Brezovica
Horvati
Zadvorsko
Strmec
Klinča Sela
Pavučnjak
Donji Desinec
Donja Zdenčina

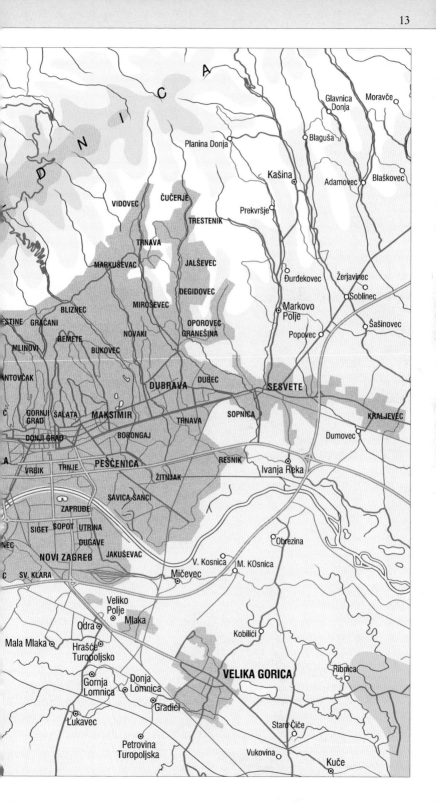

THE HISTORY OF ZAGREB

The Zagreb area has a long and rich history. The beginnings of today's town could be found in two medieval nuclei, Kaptol and Gradec. The year 1094 is considered an official "birthday" when king Ladislav (1040 - 1095) founded on Kaptol the bishopric of Zagreb. The first settlement named Zagreb stretched along the left bank of the stream Crikvenik or Medveščak, from today's Krvavi most (Bloody Bridge) to Drašković street. The significant moment in the town development was the Tatar invasion in the middle of the 13th century. After devastation of Zagreb, king Bella IV (1206-1270) by his 1242 Golden Bull permitted to build the fortified settlement on the hill, on the other side of the stream. The settlement was named Gradec and until the middle of 19th century Gradec lived beside Kaptol. By the end of the Middle Ages this dual town became the most populated in the whole Croatia, and in the period of Turkish invasions, in the middle of 16th century, the political centre of Croatia moved from the south. Intensive development of the town followed the unification in 1850, when strong economic growth also began.

On the wider area of Zagreb there were some findings witnessing the life in this region during the late Stone Age. The ancient hunters lived or passed through this region, finding shelter in caves, mostly on wooded slopes of Medvednica. The richest archeological site is the cave Veternica, on the southwest slopes of Medvednica where numerous places with stones burnt with fire were found and large quantities of ash and burnt coal. There were

Urn with ashes, 1000 years BC

also the sculls found of those ancient inhabitants of the future Zagreb. Around 1300 BC, Indoeuropean tribes settled here, and brought the habit of cremation of the dead. They buried the ashes in *žare*, urns as we found them in the tombs in the Vrapče settlement. Traces of humans from that period were found even in the very heart of Zagreb, in the Upper town, in the cellar of the Town museum.

Stone peaks from Veternica

CHRONOLOGY

The groups of hunters from the late Stone Age strolled the wooded slopes of Medvednica even 35 000 years ago	*Bones and buttons from Veternica*	Unknown people brought the technique of metal processing and built first settlements in the Sava valley at the foot of Medvednica
The scull of cave bear from Veternica	Men used various weapons for hunt and defence	*Golden jewellery, 15th century BC*
35 000 YEARS BC		1000 YEARS BC

Marble head,
3rd century

THE ANTIQUITY

By the end of the 4th century BC, Celtic tribes came from northwest and north, settling along the whole area north of the river Sava. Soon after them, the Romans came from the south. After the conquest, Romans organised the lowland parts of present Croatia into province of Pannonia, with Sisak as its centre. The wider area of Zagreb city had very intensive life during the Romans, and the most important settlement was Andautonia, today Ščitarjevo in the vicinity of Velika Gorica. The

Copper coins,
4th century

remnants of defence walls, sewage, necropolis and river port were found there. Roman settlement was also in the place of Stenjevec, and in present Držićeva street the roman cemetery was found. Roman remnants were found around the cathedral as well.

MIGRATION OF PEOPLES AND CREATION OF THE CROATIAN STATE

The period of peoples' migration brought about great regroupment of the peoples in this area. First the Germanic tribes passed by who did not keep here for long. By the end of 6th century, Avars and Slavs started coming, and Croats were among them. With arrival of new inhabitants, Roman organisation of life, roads and towns slowly disappeared and the old name Pannonia was gradually substituted by the new one - Slavonia. Already by the end of 9th century, the new nomadic people arrived from the east to the lowlands - the Hungarians. Almost simultaneously with their approach, the nucleus of the new Medieval Croatian state was formed along the Adriatic coast. The most famous medieval Croatian king was Tomislav (910-928), who managed to penetrate to the north at the beginning of

Old Croatian
sword,
9th century

10th century and stopped the expansion of Hungarians towards the south, and integrated Slavonia, the land between the rivers Sava and Drava, into Croatian state. There are few data on Zagreb from this period, just a few remnants of jewelry in the tombs found in front of present cathedral.

UNION WITH HUNGARIANS AND FOUNDATION OF BISHROPRIC

At the end of 11th century the last king from the Croatian ruler family died and Hungarian dynasty succeeded due to family relations. In the time of turbulence caused by changes at the top of the state, Hungarian king Ladislas was passing by (1040 -1095) and founded the bishopric of Zagreb at its present place. The exact

The cloak of king
Ladislav, 11th century

year of its foundation is not known, but 1094 is taken as the most likely. By founding the bishropric, the king wanted "those who were driven from the adoration of God by fornication and idolatry to be taken to the path of truth by the bishop of Zagreb". The oldest written record of the existence of the bishropric of Zagreb

Felitian's document

is Felitian's document from 1134, which gives the name of the first bishop of Zagreb - Duh, a priest of Czech origins. The Medieval Zagreb settled along the stream Medveščak that flew through the present Tkalčić street turning over Harmica, along Manduševac towards the present Palmotić street.

A great part of town inhabitants were priests who got some land in the vicinity and wood on Medvednica to use for their own needs. As the influence of bishops of Zagreb increased so did their land. Apart from the priests, merchants and craftsmen lived in Zagreb as well. With their help, in 1217 the bishops managed to finish the building of the first representative cathedral, dedicated to St. Stephen, placed at the same spot as the present cathedral.

INVASION OF TATARS AND THE GOLDEN BULL IN 1242

During the 13th century another nomadic people burst to this region from Asian stepa, the Tatars. King Bela the IV (1206-1270) was hiding from them. Only a year earlier he was almost killed in the battle with Batu khan. Thus he was withdrawing over Zagreb towards the sea, as far as Trogir. The Tatars were following him and arrived at Zagreb, which they looted and burnt. The newly built cathedral was also destroyed, and the majority of inhabitants fled away looking for shelter in the woods of Medvednica. Tatari did not stay long, but continued their pursuit of Bela IV, and the majority of inhabitants subsequently returned to town. Fearing the new attack they decided to fortify the settlement getting permission from Bela IV himself. The most appropriate place was the neighbouring higher hill, surrounded by the streams Medveščak and Tuškanac on the other side.

Except the permission to build the fortifications, the king gave to the inhabitants of Zagreb the Golden Bull, as a token of

Genghis Khan

gratefulness for hiding him in front of the Tatars.

By this document issued in Virovitica on November 16th, 1242, the inhabitants of the new settlement, named Gradec were granted significant benefits: the settlement was proclaimed a free royal city responsible only to the king, not to the authorities of ban or župan.

The Golden Bull

The Golden Bull permitted everyday trading in the town, and great fairs held on Mondays and Thursdays. Furthermore, the King gave rights to town municipality to organize annual Marko's Fair being held a week before and a week after the holiday of St. Mark, and by his chart he put under his protection all traders, domestic and foreign, by freeing them of fee payments.

RECONSTRUCTION AND
BUILDING OF DEFENSE WALLS

New town was quickly erecting the defense walls and in 1257 the settlement was enclosed by the walls. We do not know what it looked

like at the time. According to preserved remnants from the later times we know about the existance of strong town walls and towers, among which the most famous is Lotrščak, built on the south wall.

The Lotrščak tower

The Zagreb canons also contributed to fortification by building a strong tower on the north side, later named Popov toranj. There were four entrances to the town - two at the side, from Mesnička and Radić street and one gate on the north and south side. The only preserved entrance is Stone Gate in somewhat changed appearance (the one from 1760). On the slopes of Medvednica, the bishop Philip with the king's permission built Medvedgrad in 1254, where he stored many church valu-

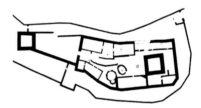

The blueprint of Medvedgrad

ables. During the time, Medvedgrad grew into one of the biggest fortresses in Croatia. The inhabitants of Gradec built a small church on the central town square, though the Golden Bull did not give them right to. They dedicated it to St. Mark to whose honour the annual fair was held. After the departure of Tatars, Kaptol was also reconstructed, and among the priorities was the building of new cathedral, the basic architectural

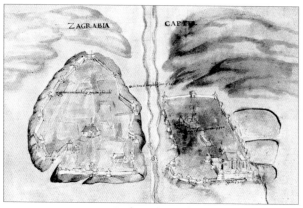

Gradec and Kaptol

nucleus of the present one. Besides the cathedral, in the second half of the 13th century the Bishop's palace on Kaptol was also mentioned. It is the first known residence for ban (vice-roy) in Zagreb recorded in historical documents. But even then the ban spent more time in the neighbouring Gradec than in Kaptol - Gradec was surrounded by defense walls thus it was safer.

EVERYDAY LIFE ON KAPTOL AND GRADEC

Side by side, bishopric Kaptol and Gradec developed, and between them the stream Medveščak over which a canal was dug already in 13th century, so two stream currents flew through Tkalčić street. Numerous mills were built on the canal therefore it was called Mill's canal. There were also two bridges built over the stream - one by the Manduševac spring

Seal of Kaptol
from 1297

where mainly the inhabitants of Kaptol and Vlaška Ves were passing and the other on the place of the present Krvavi most. The inhabitants of two neighbouring settlement were not always living in peace and harmony, so they would pass over the bridges during the attacks to the neighbouring Kaptol, and the canons used the bridges to enter the town area. So the street got its name for those turbulent and hard times, Krvavi most (Bloody bridge). Gradec was a well organized community. Town authorities carefully monitored everything happening in town, especially in the trading area. Great care was taken of the products sold at the market. The mar-

CHRONOLOGY

Second half of the 13th century: Kaptol is reconstructed and the cathedral is rebuilt, Gradec erected defense walls, Medvedgrad was built

1315. Cistercits built the monastery with St. Mary's Church on Dolac

Gradec seal, 14th century

1334. For the first time the church of St. Margaret was mentioned at the foot of Gradec, on the place of present Preradović square

1300

**Back of the Great
Guild tablet**

ket offered various products, from agricultural and cattle products brought from fertile valley beyond the city and numerous villages on mild hills and slopes of Medvednica to various craftsmen products. Often you could find products brought by traders from far regions.

In 14th century, the town court on Gradec held its sessions on Tuesdays and Fridays, immediately after the week's fair, that was held on Mondays and Thursdays, because those were the days with the most conflicts, fights and complaints. Those found guilty were sentenced by fines, caned, branded or thrown out of the city. If the felony was bigger, the sentence for murderers could be death, often in a very cruel manner.

In the 14th century first known census was carried out. There were about three hundred houses, 2810 inhabitants among which 21 shoemaker, six blacksmiths, four jewellers and four pot makers, three butchers and two saddlers. There is also a record of the first pharmacy in town. Houses were also built outside the town walls

**Slavonian banovac, minted in
Gradec in 13th and 14th century**

thus at the foot of Gradec, among others, the street today called Ilica appeared.

THE TERROR OF COUNTS CELJSKI AND DISAPPEARANCE OF MEDVEDGRAD

Life with everyday problems was replaced by hard times during the reign of king Žigmund Luksemburski (1368 - 1437), who did not want to acknowledge to Gradec the benefits granted by its status of royal town. The great supporter of king's politics was the mighy

Remnants of Medvedgrad

feudalist and Croatian ban, Herman II Celjski. Due to good relations with the king, who married his daughter Barbara, he was given Medvedgrad. From there he daily disturbed the nearby inhabitants, and in 1441 he conquered Gradec. Thus Gradec lost all its benefits and rights, and Counts Celjski gave town land and houses to their followers. Because of the terror many inhabitants of Grades fled from their homes. The situation on Gradec did not change until the death of the count

CHRONOLOGY

1345. King Ludovik I acknowledged the tax paying obligation to citizens of Zagreb

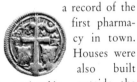

The pharmacy continuing the tradition of the first 14th century pharmacy in Zagreb

1406. Herman II Celjski given the title of ban of Dalmatia, Croatia and Slavonia

1441. Counts Celjski conquered Gradec

| 1350 | 1400 |

Urlich, the last male member of the Celjski family. The town was returned the majority of its freedom and benefits in 1457, and the inhabitants were given back their land and real estate. Soon after the disappearance of the Celjski family, the life on Medvedgrad started to extinct and during 16th century it turned into ruins.

TURKISH THREAT

Despite the disappearance of the counts Celjski, the peace did not last long. Already in the second half of 15th century, there was a new threat on the horizon - the Turks. In September 1469, the Turks penetrated to Sava, close to Zagreb and they would have probably looted it and destroyed if it had not been saved by a flood. Despite fortifications, Gradec could hardly withstand the Turks, who were well armed and trained for conquering of fortifications. Because of the approaching danger from the Turks, king Matijaš Korvin (1458 - 1490) permitted the fortification of Kaptol. The danger of Turks afflicted in 1496 the other parts of Croatia more severely. During 16th century, the Turks gradually conquered the central and south parts of the Croatian countries that caused the nobility from those parts to move to the north. After the great defeat in 1525, Croatian nobility decided to choose

The Kaptol fortress at the beginning of 16th century

The pandzir jacket of Turkish horse rider

the Habsburgs for their rulers, who promised to help them in defense. Despite all misunderstandings the union proved successful and part of the Croatian countries successfully defended themselves. At the end of the 16th century, Croatia was reduced to a narrow belt from Drava to the sea, where Croatian nobility concentrated. Zagreb became the state centre. It was the seat of the ban, and when he was not there, the bishop of Zagreb held his function. What's more, the Croatian nobility gathered here at the meetings.

CHRONOLOGY

1469. The King Matijaš Korvin permitted the erection of fortification around Kaptol

Bishop Tuz's water jug, 15th century

1481. in the field in front of Zagreb Slavonian parliament held its first session

The oldest coat-of-arms of Zagreb, 1499

1450   1500

NORMALISATION OF LIFE AFTER THE DEFEAT OF THE TURKS

From the second half of 16th century, the main part of the Turk army ceased to penetrate into Croatian regions. With organized defense, Military Borderline became effective having a system of fortresses erected along the border towards the Turks. As Croatian nobility did not have money for its financing, the majoritiy of costs was born by the German nobility from the neighbouring Slovenian region, who held commanding positions as

Battle at Sisak, 1593

well. Only the area around Sisak was under the command of Croatian ban, because the majority of costs was covered by the bishop of Zagreb. And the important turning point happened exactly at that place. In June 1593, under the walls of Sisak, Croatian ban Toma Bakač-Erdödy defeated the local men of power Hasan-pasha Predoje-vić. After that Zagreb was not under Turkish threat any more. Unfortunately there were a lot of other misfortunes. The greatest damage was made by fire. In 1624 the roof of the cathedral burnt down, and the

The chart of King Leopold I

fire spread to the neighbouring bishop's palace and several other houses. Disastrous fire destroyed all wooden parts of Stone Gate in 1731, and in the ashes, the story says, only the picture of the Virgin Mary with the Little Jesus was untouched. The fires ravaged until houses started to be built mostly of bricks. During 17th century, the intellectual life in the town grew stronger, and the credit for that went to Jesuits. On the invitation of the town government, they overtook the abandoned monastery on the present Jesuit Square in 1606, and the rich enlightenment activity began. The roots of the Zagreb University, one of the oldest in Europe, stretch to 17th century. That beginning of higher education is linked to Jesuit grammar school, which established the theology classes in 1632. Thirty years later the Academy for the higher philosophy classes started to be built. The king of Croatia and Hungary, Leopold I, by the chart from 1669, gives to that academy the right of university, and the Croatian parliament approved that privilege. Except the important educational institutions, in 1664 the first printing house was established. By the end of the 17th century the Turks were chased from the majority of Croatian countries. Soon, the whole

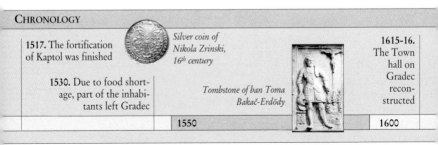

CHRONOLOGY

1517. The fortification of Kaptol was finished

Silver coin of Nikola Zrinski, 16th century

1530. Due to food shortage, part of the inhabitants left Gradec

Tombstone of ban Toma Bakač-Erdödy

1615-16. The Town hall on Gradec reconstructed

1550   1600

Slavonia returned under the authority of ban and Croatian parliament, except the part of Military Border-line that was still under the king's authority. In 18th century during the reign of Maria Theresa (1740-1780) many re-forms in all parts of Habs-burg monarchy were

Zagreb panoramic view, 18th century

implemented. In order to speed them up, the queen tried to avoid agreements with Croatian nobility. Thus she founded the Government in Croatia that she held

The Queen Maria Theresa with family

directly responsible, and she placed it in Varaždin - the center of Military Border-line and strong German point of support in Croatia. Her ideas were not realized, and enlightenment efforts of Maria There-sa and her successor Joseph II (1780-1790) failed. Varaždin was seriously dam-aged in great fire in 1767.

LIFE DURING CROATIAN RENAISSANCE
During 18th century a lot was changed in appearance and manner of work of Kaptol

and Gradec. Because of the work of Par-liament, court and county government, more and more nobility gradually settled in the town area. They left their land in the vicinity and erected their residences in the town. Numerous, still preserved, palaces emerged along the eastern and northwest edge of Gradec - present Demetrova and Opatička streets. At the same time, along with this changes there were some changes in production. In the northern part of town, by the stream Medveščak, first manufactures emerged. Because of the modest results of the manufacture, medieval guilds were pre-served until 19th century. That century was really turbulent. Influenced by the

Main persons of Croatian renaissance

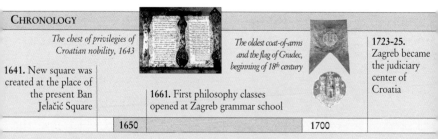

CHRONOLOGY

The chest of privileges of Croatian nobility, 1643

1641. New square was created at the place of the present Ban Jelačić Square

1661. First philosophy classes opened at Zagreb grammar school

The oldest coat-of-arms and the flag of Gradec, beginning of 18th century

1723-25. Zagreb became the judiciary center of Croatia

1650   1700

Ban Jelačić presides the Croatian Parliament in 1848

pressing to introduce Hungarian into public life. Fierce fights of Ilyrians and followers of the Hungarians eventually ended in blood. During elections for the Zagreb County in 1845, the army killed 13 people at St. Mark's square, and several were wounded. Ban Haller had to resign because of the incident. The question of language was finally resolved in Parliament in 1847, when Croatian was chosen to be the official language. That act was an introduction into dramatic year of 1848. Croatian ban Jelačić resisted with his army the Hungarian revolution whose target was also the annexion

Juraj Haulik

French revolution, a group of young intelectuals gathered around Ljudevit Gaj (1809 - 1872), known as Ilyrics, generated a series of changes. At the beginning the Ilyrians were engaged more in cultural issues, but gradually they entered politics as well. In 1835, they initiated the fist newspapers - *Novine horvatske*, in one of the dialects, kajkavian, and only a year later they were printed in stokavian. The question of language was among the crucial ones in the time of creation of the nation. Taking stokavian dialect, Gaj made an enormous step in creation of common language, thus laying the ground for the creation of a unique nation. Soon afterwards, the question of official language arose in the Croatian Parliament. Latin was still the language of Parliament, and Hungarians were

Juraj Haulik

of Croatian countries. Undetermined outcome of the war in 1848, returned Međimurje to Croatia, and under ban's command for the first but short time, Rijeka and Dalmacija were united with the rest of the Croatian countries. It is significant that at that time Zagreb united into one town, and his bishopric became archibishopric. This act made Zagreb "the metropolis of homeland" as cardinal Haulik put it.

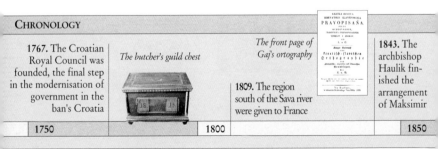
CHRONOLOGY

1767. The Croatian Royal Council was founded, the final step in the modernisation of government in the ban's Croatia

The butcher's guild chest

The front page of Gaj's ortography

1809. The region south of the Sava river were given to France

1843. The archbishop Haulik finished the arrangement of Maksimir

1750   1800   1850

CREATION OF UNIQUE TOWN

The King's patent of September 7th, 1850, free royal town of Gradec, Kaptol, Nova Ves, Vlaška street, suburbs and belonging villages were united into unique town of Zagreb.The first mayor was Josip Kamauf, former town judge of Gradec. The united Zagreb had approximately 16 000 people. It was then when the basis for the development of the modern central European town were created. The new center of municipal life was generated - Downtown, from the Ban Jelačić square in the north to the railway in the south and from the West railway station to the Drašković street in the east. The most representative part of the town was erected among two old roads, Petrinjska and Savska. A series of squares was built there with building of the most important cultural and scientific institutions in town. Due to abundance of plants, the squares were called Green Horseshoe, which became the symbol of modern Zagreb. Simultanously with the development of town in the valley, the wealthier inhabitants of Zagreb

Ilica 1906

built their residences in the north, on the slopes of Medvednica. Unfortunately, on November 9th, 1880, the town was destroyed by an earthquake. Almost all buildings were damaged including cathedral and the surrounding area. For the reconstruction of the destroyed a lot of resources and efforts were needed, and according to what was done obviously there was enough of both. The architect Herman Bollé (1845 - 1926) had an important role in the reconstrucion of town, and his works can be found all over the town. In that period the wider area was urbanized, new houses and new hospitals were built, the cemetery was arranged and the communal issue was raised.Thus the stream Medveščak was re-directed and until the end of the 19th century it went over Ribnjak and the Square of Victims of Fascism towards Držićeva street. The industry, that was increasingly growing, was moved to the outskirts of the town.

Kaptol and the Cathedral before earthquake in 1880.

CHRONOLOGY

1880. Zagreb struck by disastrous earthquake	*One of the first cars in Zagreb*	**1901.** First car in Zagreb
1860. First piece of theater in Croatian language	**1896.** First film shown in Zagreb	**1909.** First great trade exhibition held, named *Gospodarski zbor*
	1900	1918

FAST GROWTH OF ZAGREB

By the end of the World War I, Zagreb declared the separation from the Austro-Hungarian Monarchy. After centuries of joint life the links with Hungarians and Austrians were broken, but newly constituted State of Serbs, Croats and Slovenes did not last long. On the 1st of December 1918, it united with the Kingdom of Serbia and Montenegro into the Kingdom of Serbs,

Funeral of Stjepan Radić

The building of Zagreb Stock Exchange

Croats and Slovenes. The leading role in the political life of Croatia belonged to Croatian Peasants Party (HSS) led by Stjepan Radić (1872 - 1928). He and a few of Croatian representatives were assassinated in Parliament in Belgrade, and the incident was judged by the whole world. It also marked the beginning of the end of the Yugoslav community, but it was also the motive for further bloody retribution.

During the Kingdom, Zagreb was strong economic center and the biggest industrial town. The number of inhabitants in 1918 was around 100 000, and in

twenty year existence of the Kingdom of Yugoslavia, it almost doubled. Due to huge increase of inhabitants the town quickly expanded. Only the eastern part along Zvonimirova street was planned as an urban whole. The entrance into that new part of town was symbolicaly marked by the building of Stock Exchange of Zagreb. Because of the great number of workers, Zagreb was, between the wars, the center of labour movement. Nevertheless, until the beginning of the World War II, HSS had the leading political role in Croatia, led by Vladko Maček (1879 - 1964). After successful negotiations, Maček managed to unite Croatian regions in 1939 and make Banovina Hrvatska with a seat in Zagreb. The efforts to create Croatian autonomy within Yugoslavia were interrupted by the World War II.

Between the two world wars Zagreb had rich artistic life. Especially in the theater that had a long tradition and where two great men worked in those years, its director Branko Gavella

Miroslav Krleža

The arrival of Vladimir Nazor to Zagreb in 1945

gence, especially to Italy, and on the other side atrocities towards opponents and especially toward members of other nations, strengthened the antifascist movement. Only a day before the capitulation of the fascist Germany, first partisan troops entered Zagreb. Troubled period continued in the postwar period. There were a lot of trials and among the sentenced was the archbishop of Zagreb, Cardinal Alojzije Stepinac (1898 - 1960).

(1885 - 1962) and the writer Miroslav Krleža (1893 - 1981). Plastic arts were also important. Already a distinguished sculptor Ivan Meštrović (1883 - 1962) worked in Zagreb, and from time to time there were younger people gathered in numerous associations like *The group of three* or *The Earth*. The first interest for the selfthought peasants-painters in the village Hlebine in Podravina started at that time, and it was Krsto Hegedušić (1901 - 1975) who drew attention to them.

Appeasement of the conditions in the post-war years brought to further expansion of the town that integrated a lot of independent settlements. Finally in 1957, the construction of the first big housing settlements began on the south bank of the river Sava where a year earlier the Zagreb Trade Fair was also moved. The

Cardinal Stepinac at the trial

TURBULENT WARTIME AND POSTWAR PERIOD

At the beginning of June in 1941, under the attacks of fascist countries, the Kingdom of Yugoslavia disappeared and on 10 April the Independent State of Croatia (NDH) was declared in Zagreb. At the front of the regime were the followers of *ustaše* movement. Their politics of indul-

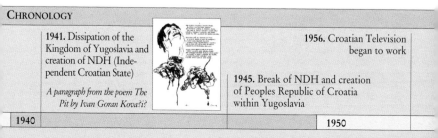

CHRONOLOGY

1941. Dissipation of the Kingdom of Yugoslavia and creation of NDH (Independent Croatian State)

A paragraph from the poem The Pit by Ivan Goran Kovačić?

1956. Croatian Television began to work

1945. Break of NDH and creation of Peoples Republic of Croatia within Yugoslavia

1940   1950

Big flood in 1964.

great moment of town development was once more interrupted by a natural disaster. In 1964, Zagreb was stricken by a horrible flood. In the night between 24th and 25th of October, the risen river Sava flooded the city. Around sixty square kilometers of the town were under the water, and several thousand houses were damaged. It was the last great overspill of Sava since several years later the construction of dikes on the Sava river was finished.

During the democratization process by the end of the 1960's, the cultural and political activities in Z a g r e b strengthened. Political efforts

The Mayor Holjevac with the model of New Zagreb

towards greater independence were interrupted at the end of 1971 with events related to Croatian Spring. Despite slowing of democratization, the life in the city was more dynamic. Film art reached its peak, and especially sucessful was the Zagreb school of animated films that generated the Animafest. At the beginning of 80's the New Wave in Zagreb became the leader of artistic trends among the youth in the whole country. Finally, in the 80's the sport in Zagreb lived its peaks. Dinamo, the football club, once again won the state champi

The opening of University Games in Zagreb

onship and Cibona, with unforgettable Dražen Petrović, climbed to the top of the European basketball. The 1987 University Games that Zagreb hosted closed that period of sport development. Thanks to the games, the town got many new or reconstructed sport terrains, playgrounds and halls, and the whole town was imbellished especially the narrowest center.

CHRONOLOGY

Scene from the animated film, Surrogate, the Oscar winner of 1962

1971. New dike made and future floods prevented

1973. The concert hall *Vatroslav Lisinski* built

1976. The tallest building in town, *Zagrepčanka*, was built

| 1960 | 1970 | | | 1980 |

Celebration of 30th May 1990.

AMONG EUROPEAN METROPOLISES

The changes taking Europe at the end of the 80's did not avoid Zagreb. In 1990 the multi party elections were held in Croatia, and on 30 May 1990, the new, multi party Parliament has been constituted iz Zagreb, electing Franjo Tuđman (1922-1999) for the president of the Republic of Croatia. After a year of unsuccessfull negotiations with other members of Yugoslav federation on reconstruction of Yugoslavia, on 25 June 1991, Croatian parliament proclaimed Croatia independent. At that time, the homeland war lasted for almost a year. During the war, Zagreb was attacked twice. Those two attacks symbolically marked the begin-

The members of UNPROFOR in Zagreb

ning and the end of the homeland war. The Banski dvori were attacked first in autumn 1991, and then the center of the town was showered with missiles in spring 1995, when seven people got killed. Zagreb remained peaceful during the war, which is almost unimaginable having in mind the proximity of battlefields. During wartime, the Holy Father John Paul II visited Zagreb for the first time, in autumn 1994, and held a mass in front of almost a million of believers. After the war activities, at the end of 1995, the situation quickly returned to normal. The ultimate stabilisation of the conditions and acknowledgement of Zagreb as European metropolis was proved by meeting of presidents and prime ministers of the European Union, held in Zagreb at the end of 2000. The process of approachment of Croatia toward the European Union has been especially intensified in the following years. The EU standards have been adopt-

The pope John Paul II on tomb of the cardinal Stepinac

ed and the approximation of legislative carried out at political and economic level. In June 2004, Croatia became an official candidate for the EU membership.

CHRONOLOGY

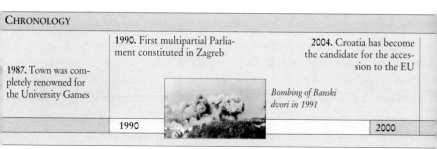

1987. Town was completely renowned for the University Games

1990. First multipartial Parliament constituted in Zagreb

2004. Croatia has become the candidate for the accession to the EU

Bombing of Banski dvori in 1991

1990

2000

TOP 10
Public Monuments

Holy Mary's column with angels and fountain
Anton Dominik Fernkorn, 1865, fountain
by Herman Bollé 1880-1882. Placed in front
of the cathedral - characteristic urbanistic
feature of Kaptol.

Ban Josip Jelačić
Antun dominik Fernkorn, 1866, Ban Josip
Jelačić Square (moved because of ideologi-
cal reasons in 1947, but was returned to the
same place in 1990). First monumental
public sculpture in Zagreb.

Petar Preradović
Ivan Rendić, 1895 at the Strossmayer
Square, since 1954 on Preradović Square.
Realistic approach to naturalistic elements
(especially in details processing).

St. George kills the Dragon
Anton Dominik Fernkorn, 1853, first exhibited in Maksimir in 1867. From 1884 to 1908 at
Strossmayer Square, since 1908 at its present
place - Marshall Tito Square. The monument
inspired by late baroque.

The well of life
Ivan Meštrović, 1905, exhibited in 1912 (architect Ignjat Fischer), in front of Croatian National Theater. Frist monument of the new aesthetic.

Josip Juraj Strossmayer
Ivan Meštrović, 1926, Strossmayer Square. Monument designed as strong plastic sign with prominent outlines.

The Thinkers
Rudolf Valdec, 1937, the entrance stairs to Art Pavillion, Tomislav Square.

King Tomislav
Robert Frangeš-Mihanović, 1927 - 1934, the footage made before the World War II, erected in 1947. Two side reliefs are put much later.

Antun Gustav Matoš
Ivan Kožarić, 1978, Strossmayer promenade. First monument stepping out of traditional trends.

August Šenoa
Marija Ujević, 1987, Vlaška street. Classical experience and modern associations.

TOP 10
MUESUM EXHIBITS

Mommies

Egyptian collection of the Archeological museum, three Egiptian mummies with the sarcophagos from Ptolomeian era (332 BC until 30 BC) and so called Zagreb mommie with Zagreb linen book as its bandage.

The Head of a Girl from Solin

The collection of Greek and Roman monuments of the Archeological Museum, the girl's head, marble, height of the head 22.5 cm, broadness of the face 12 cm. With its coloristic and plastic details with mirror smooth surface, *The Girl from Solin* is among the most beautiful portraits of Roman stone sculptures.

The stone carved Baška Tablet

Atrium of HAZU, shortened record of a deed of donation by king Zvonimir to the church of St. Lucy in Baška, the island of Krk. It is among the oldest monuments of the Croatian language.

Ladislav's Cloak

Treasury of the Zagreb cathedral, embroidery in Regensburg (Bavaria), 11th century, in 14th century altered to mass robe.

The Felitian's Chart

The Zagreb Museum (original in the Archives of the Archbishopric), magnified copy of the chart issued on June 26, 1134, that mentioned Zagreb for the first time (*Zagrabiensem episcopatus*).

The Golden Bull
The Zagreb Museum (original kept in Croatian State Archives), copy of a document issued on November 16, 1242, in Virovitica, by which Bela IV, king of Croatia and Hungary, granted to Zagreb the status of *free royal town*.

Missal by the Law of Roman
National and University Library, first printed Croatian glagolitic missal (1483) also the first Croatian printed book.

The Infant Margharita
The Mimara Museum, Diego Velásquez, around 1654. The wife of German king Leopold I shown in her *middle infant age* (probably at the age of 4). Although the painting was made according to the court protocol, the painter surpasses the majestic and penetrates into the gentle soul of the girl.

The Archangel Gabriel and the Angels
The Mimara Museum, Flandria in the first half of 15 century. Most likely the part of a greater whole, that extraordinary wood carving work, with characteristic stilisation of physiognomies, represents the ultimate work of the Flaman gothics.

The Holy Trinity
The Strossmayer Gallery of Old Masters, the master of the painting *Virgo inter Virgines*, 15th century. The Dutch school of early Renaissance, link to the southern Renaissance.

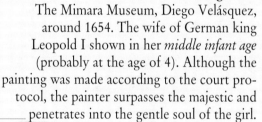

TOP 10
ARCHITECTURAL MONUMENTS

The Zagreb Cathedral
The most monumental and stylistically most eloquent Gothic architectural work in the area southeast of the Alps. _____

St. Francis Church
One navel church, though of impressive measures, carries all simplicity and harmony of the Early Gothic Franciscan churches. _____

St. Mark's Church
Build on Romanesque foundations, finished as a three nave type church makes a unique Gothic whole. The south portal is the most eloquent sculptural achievement in this part of Europe. _____

The Lotrščak Tower
Once the major town tower, today the hallmark of Zagreb and with the cathedral the most attractive town view. _____

The Palace of HAZU
Friedrich Schmidt, 1877 - 1980, built in the forms of Italian Renaissance, adapted to new technical conditions and functional space requirements. It is the only palace (in the real sense of the word) in Zagreb. _____

The Croatian National Theater
Architectural Atelier Fellner and Helmer, 1894-95, first project 1881, neobaroque. Belongs to series of representative theaters built in the historical styles throughout the cities of Central and Eastern Europe.

The State Archives
Rudolf Lubynski, 1913, by the uniqueness of its architecture and ornamentation represents one of the most beautiful examples of Secession (Art Nouveau) architecture in Croatia.

St. Blasius Church
Viktor Kovačić, 1912-1913, constructed on the groundplan scheme of the Greek cross, with strong volume gradation and dominant reinforced concrete dome, the church is the most significant sacral building of modern age in Croatia.

The skyscraper of Napredak
Stjepan Planić, 1936, eight floors (at the time the tallest building in town), with original eleptoid shape and dented top represents the prominent urbanistic accent of Zagreb

The Mestrović Pavillion
Ivan Mestrović, 1938, rotunda, the precursor of well known constructions, even the Guggenheim Museum in New York (1959), masterwork of Croatian architecture.

TOP 10

AMBIANCES

Apsidal stained glass windows of St. Francis church

Stained glass by Ivo Dulčić, inspired by *flowers of St. Francis*, is the most beautiful sacral ambiance in Zagreb.

The Interior of the Croatian National Theater

In the architecture of monumental historicism special attention was paid to the interior: attractive in the function of artistic.

The Interior of the Esplanada Hotel

The atrium of the Esplanada hotel, created under the influence of modified Secession (Art Nouveau), is the most picturesque ambiance of the hotel architecture in Croatia.

The complex of Cathedral and Archbishop's palace

Cathedral with archbishop's palace is the most prominent architectural complex in Zagreb.

The Theater Square (the Marshall Tito Square)

The ambiance of Croatian National Theater - romantic phase marked by the mixture of one or more styles - is among the most beautiful Central European squares.

Zrinjevac
The monument *King Tomislav* by Frangeš and the *Art Pavilion*, first building erected for artistic purposes, and magnificent cathedral are among the most representative Croatian views

Dolac
The central Zagreb market created in the heart of Zagreb pervaded with baroque elements and modern solutions.

St. Mark's Square
The centre of the most picturesque square in Zagreb, the St. Mark's church was town's parish and parliament (Croatian parliament) church.

Park Maksimir with the Viewpoint
Several paths through the woods that spread around the central hill in starlike manner make the view point the important building of the Romantic landscape art.

The Arcades of Mirogoj cemetery
Arcades with domes, the Church of Christ the King and mortuary, make a fine example of urbanistic function in architecture.

DURING THE YEAR

WEATHER

Zagreb is situated in the area of moderate continental climate with warm summers, and climate conditions of the broader town area, as well as of the whole Croatia, are under the significant influence of the Eurasian land, Mediterranean Sea and western air masses from the Atlantic Ocean. At the local level, Zagreb is also influenced by specific topographic position by the Sava river and along sunny slopes of Medvednica. The modifying climate influences of Medvednica are most pronounced along mountain slopes, stream valleys and wooded areas. Stretching in the direction Southwest - Northeast, Medvednica directs winds, thus dominant currents in the majority of town come from the north-east. North-west winds dominate only in the southern parts of Zagreb, over the Sava river. Besides, Medvednica has prominent fen effects, since it warms the air that *passes* over the mountain. Due to differences in the above sea levels or position against Medvednica, some minor climate and weather differences may appear at the broader Zagreb area.

The four seasons are well pronounced in Zagreb and on Medvednica. During the winter, anticyclone dominates over Zagreb, so the weather is calm, cold and cloudy. The average of the lowest January temperatures is - 3°C. The lowest measured temperature in the meteorological station Zagreb-Grič is -22°C (1942). Due to higher height above the sea level, the winter on Sljeme, the peak of Medvednica, is somewhat colder, though temperature inversion is not a rare phenomenon, when weather on Sljeme is clear and warm, while the town is colder and covered with fog. The first three months of the year have the least pre-

Basic information:

- position: 45°10;15'N, 15°30'E
- the above sea level: 122 m
- average annual air temperature is 11,5 °C
- there are 50 cold and 80 sunny days in average
- the sun shines annually around 1600 hours
- the average number of cloudy days is 128
- the average annual precipitation quantity is 883 mm
- the average number of rainy days annually is 133
- the winds are mostly weak (2-3 m/s); only in July and August some scarce stormy winds.

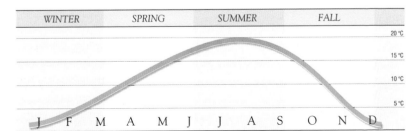

WINTER	SPRING	SUMMER	FALL

J F M A M J J A S O N D

cipitations, when there is less than 60 mm of precipitation per month. The winter months give also the relative air humidity above the average (more than 75‰). The snow is commonplace in Zagreb, and it keeps for around 30 days. Cold winter winds are caused by penetration of cold air masses from the north.

Spring in Zagreb is warm and cosy; the average monthly temperatures are between 8 and 18°C. Frequent short thundershowers bring abundant rains so the major annual precipitation maximum is in June (101 mm). Numerous cyclones bring unstable and very changing weather. The winds are common place for this part of the year; April is the windiest month in the year. Summer months are especially hot and sultry, due to high daily and monthly temperatures and the humidity is around 60‰. The average July temperature is 20-22°C. The highest temperature measured in the meteorological station Zagreb-Grič is +37.3°C (1952). At this time of the year, it is much pleasanter on Medvednica, since the air temperatures on Sljeme are 5-8°C lower than in town. The sunniest month is July with the average of 279 sunny hours. During peaceful summer period, scarce short showers and evening and night breezes from Medvednica bring pleasant refreshment to town inhabitants.

Autumn is a period of changing weather, the nights become colder so the daily temperature amplitude is more pronounced. The early autumn characteristic is calm weather with weak winds (mostly north-west wind). Due to long-lasting rains, the November has secondary precipitation maximum, and relative air humidity reaches its maximum values (79‰).

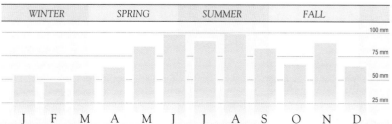

WINTER	SPRING	SUMMER	FALL	
				100 mm
				75 mm
				50 mm
				25 mm
J F	M A M	J J A	S O	N D

DURING THE YEAR

EVENTS

JANUARY

Century of blues; gathers various performers and variants of blues. The festival brings together numerous famous world names, as well as excellent domestic blues performers with international experience.

FEBRUARY

Carnival festivities; traditional festivities that mark the end of winter and coming of spring. The most visited carnival festivity in this part of Croatia is the one in Samobor near Zagreb.

MARCH

Zagreb Auto Show; the most prestigious Auto Show in this part of Europe in attractive exhibition area offers numerous new car models, and the rich side programme. **Springtime Jazz Fever**; jazz festival hosting the

most famous jazz musicians in the world. Good atmosphere spreading from the legendary BP club, for years now shakes Zagreb in the early spring.

APRIL

The St. Mark's Festival; the main purpose of this festival is musical performance of top musicians in concert and sacral ambiances of the Zagreb Upper Town and Down Town. The festival is the meeting place of Croatian musical tradition and presence with European and world musical tradition and performance.
Music Biannual; internationally recognised festival of modern music with tradition of more than four decades. The last Biannual was held in 2003.

MAY

Week of Modern Dance; for more than two decades, it brings to town an overview of modern world dance expression. Great variety of expression forms and aesthetic profiles give context for the development of many new ideas and appearance of new talents.

European short story festival; it is the meeting place of all top European writers of younger generation. Programmes and projects as well as published books leave trace even after the festival. **Zagreb Open ATP Tour Challenger Series**; International tennis championship in Zagreb has been held since 1996, always hosting some famous world tennis players.

JUNE

Cest is d`Best; several day multimedia manifestation in the town centre. Programms are held in the open air, on several small stages or on the pavements. The project consists of various events and activities - musical performances, theatrical events, performances for children, painting events, sport events etc. - designed to include citizens.
Eurokaz; modern European theatre festival where modern theatrical trends are identified and promot-

ed. Many groups at the top of European modern theatre once participated at the festival.

Florart; International flower exhibition showing the achievements of park planning is especially important as a part of today's increased environmental care. The exhibition is thus primarily directed towards the awakening of ecological awareness.

Animafest; meeting point for animators all over the world. Besides the media interest, the festival offers to the world our authentic Croatian product, generated by the Zagreb School of Animated Film. It takes place every second year, and the last was held in 2004.

I. A. A. F. GRAND PRIX II; International athletic meeting also known as *Hanžeković Memorial*. It has been held for over three decades, and in recent years the high jump competition has been especially strong.

JULY

Amadeo - theatre and music; in the space of the Museum of Natural Sciences, during summer evenings offers rich programme of concerts and theatrical performances.

Zagreb Histrionic Summer; offers to citizens of Zagreb spectacular performances during hot summer evenings. Almost all good Croatian actors were once the members of the *Histrioni Ensemble*.

International Folk Festival; the festival has long tradition and once gathered domestic participants showing traditional Croatian culture. At the time of festival, Zagreb is the venue of various peoples and cultures, the stage of their musical, dance and other heritage.

ZABAF; Zagreb Baroque Festival presenting a series of top foreign and Croatian Baroque music performers in the attractive locations of the Upper Town.

AUGUST

PIF; International puppet theatre festival has been held since the end of 1960's. Up to now more than 350 puppet theatres from all continents participated in the festival.

SEPTEMBER

International Zagreb Fair; the greatest trade fair in this part of the Europe. It gathers the participants from all over the world, and each year one of the countries acts as a host.

Samsung nations cup; International Horse Tournament of the highest C.S.I.O. category.

OCTOBER

Zagrebfest; the oldest Croatian festival of popular music.

International Jazz Days; the festival that each year presents the most significant European jazz groups, and beside well-

Folk Festival

known performers there are also some less known younger musicians.

NOVEMBER

The Zagreb Golden Pirouette; International ice skating competition with famous world skaters.

DECEMBER

Christmas Fair; the preChristmas time is marked by shopping and seen at every step. Beside the fair at the Zagreb Fair and in *Boćarski dom*, numerous sellers could be found in the streets, especially Bogovićeva street.

Step By Step Through Zagreb

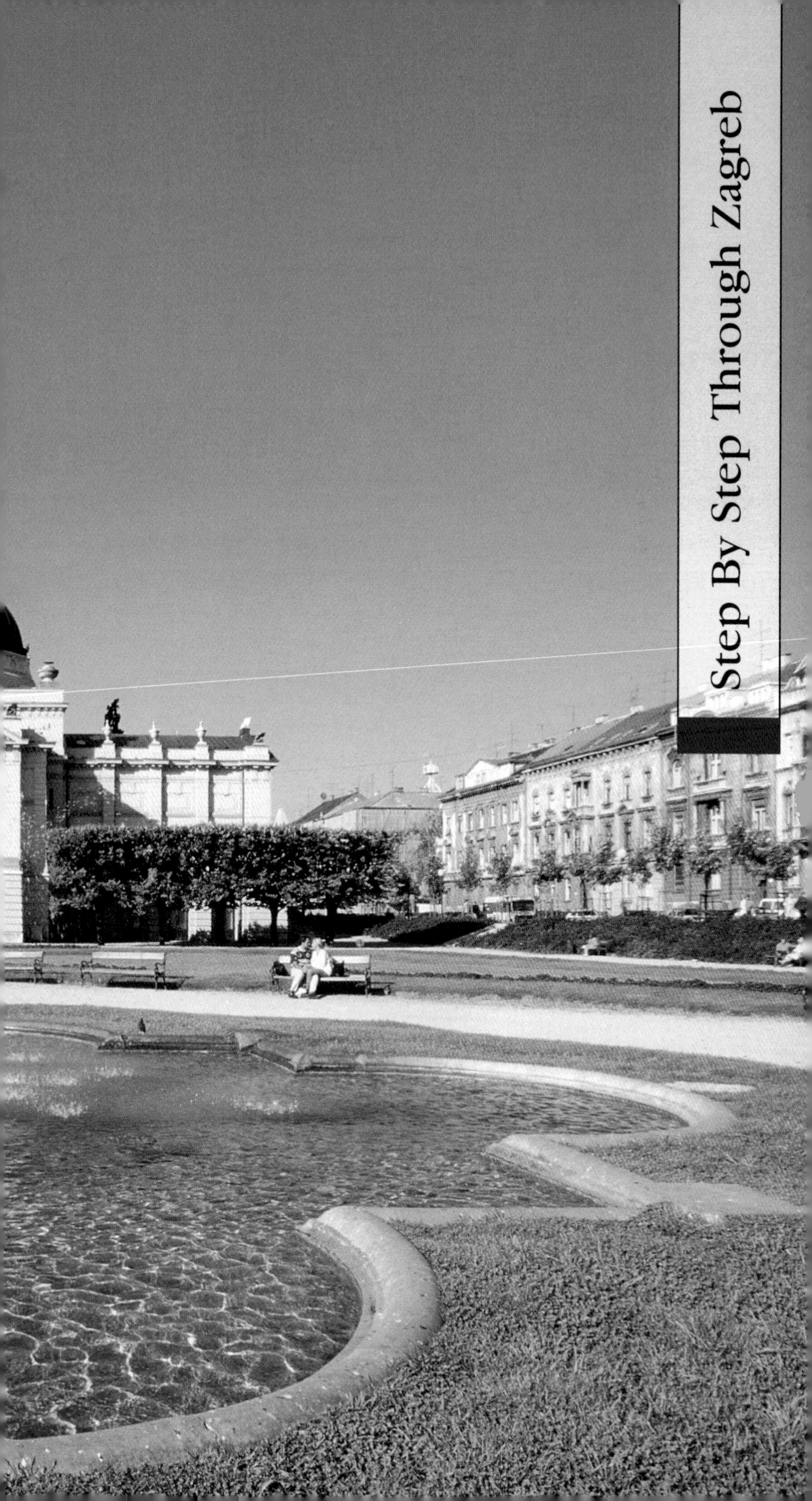

DEVELOPMENT OF ZAGREB

The core of Zagreb consists of three historical wholes. Around them the new town has grown during the 20th century. Until the union in the middle of 19th century there was "dual" town consisting of bishopric Kaptol and Gradec, the present Upper Town. After they united in 1850, in the broad lowland below them the third whole developed - The Down Town, in which many institutions were erected circumscribing Zagreb.

KAPTOL

The settlement in the place of Kaptol had existed even before the foundation of bishopric according to archeological findings. It is likely that a church also existed, serving as cathedral. The first, Romanesque cathedral was consecrated in 1217 in the presence of King Andrew II who travelled through Zagreb to V Crusader War. That cathedral was destroyed in 1242, and nearby the chapel of St. Stephen the First Christian Martyr was built. On the remnants of the cathedral, bishop Timotej (1263 -1287) began the construction of the present cathedral. The work on the cathedral was for some time interrupted, and then it continued with bishop Eberrhard who erected three naves and the bottom part of the north tower. Bishop Osvald Thuza added the belltower and covered the cathedral. In the middle of the 15th century, Kaptol was fortified fearing the Turks, and in the place of canons' gardens the Abbey was built and given to new settlers who were supposed to defend Kaptol. Bishop Luka Baratin initiated the construction of cathedral fortifications that Italian constructors were building from 1512 until 1520. The fortress with six round and two rectangular towers was built, the biggest fortress in Southeast Europe. There is still gothic style monastery church of St. Francis from the 13th century, with side chapels from the 17th century. The church was renowned in neo-gothic style following the project by Hermman Bollé, after the earthquake of 1880. It has valuable stained glass windows presenting the cycle *The Creatures' Song by St. Francis d'Assis*, work of Ivo Dulčić (1960 - 1964). In the series of harmonious canon residences at both sides of Kaptol, *kurija* (house) of Ivan Znika and Toma Kovačević are the most exceptional.

The continuation of Kaptol is the old

street Nova Ves with several outstanding buildings: Alagović's summer residence (at number 87), work of Zagreb builder Bartol Felbinger and the Church of John the Baptist with valuable inventory in baroque-classicist style. The Church of St. Mary on Dolac also belongs to Kaptol. That Gothic church belonged to Cistercian Order, and it was renovated around 1740 into three nave baroque church with nice baroque bell-tower cap. The bishopric Zagreb stretched to Vlaška street that leads to the east, and begins at the south side of the cathedral complex. The row of middle-class one-floor houses at the beginning of the street makes harmonious relation against the cathedral.

UPPER TOWN

The town-planning concept of Gradec is based on triangular plateau on the hill. The settlement developed separately and completely differently from Kaptol. Its history began with the Golden Bull by Bela IV, king of Austria and Hungary, in 1242. The privileges granted by the Bull drew many foreigners, craftsmen and merchants thus the middle-class centre developed here. The town plan of Gradec dates from the Gothic period. Its central part

is regular with the main rectangular square. The outskirts of settlement are adapted to the ground relief. The former fortification and the settlement were destroyed during Tatar's devastation, and the settlement re-fortified afterwards. The walls are partially preserved, and the towers Lortrščak, Stone Gate and the tower called Popov toranj (since 1247 owned by the Zagreb bishop) have been altered during time according to the new needs. There are a lot of chapels and churches on Gradec. The royal chapel was here, then the chapel of St. Mary (later Ursula), chapel at the place of today's St. Catherine Church and the St. Mark's Church. Among them the most important is the latter, erected on the main square in 14 and 15 centuries. Both of its portals are outstanding, especially the south one, made by

The Kaptol settlement Dolac at the beginning of 20th century

Prague masters, possibly the youngest son of Peter Parler, the constructor of the Prague Cathedral. The portal is, despite later damages, the most valuable architectural and sculptural work of the period in Croatia. The St. Catherine Church is among the most monumental baroque achievements in Croatia. It was built by Jesuits (1620 -1631), as one naval early baroque building, and the main façade was renowned after the 1880 earthquake. From the artistic point of view, its interior is of special value with relief and furnishings and big illusionist composition *Saint Catherine among the philosophers and writers of Alexandria* on the wall behind the main altar, made by Anton Jelovšek in 1762. Beside the St. Catherine Church, other important buildings from the 17th century are the Jesuit monastery

ZAGRABIA
SUB FINE SÆCULI XIV.

Zagreb at the end of 14th century

First Zagreb theatre was in the
Upper Town

with representative court-yard, the Zrinski palace (most likely at the place of the former royal palace), Jesuit Academy, nobility boarding-school, the Convent of the Order of St. Clare. The row of late baroque and classicist buildings contributes to the harmony of the Upper Town: Banski dvori, the Magdalenić-Drašković mansion, the Paravić mansion (today Croatian History Institute).

DOWN TOWN

By the decree of the emperor Franz Joseph I from September 10th 1850, the administrative municipalities united into a single town of Zagreb. Since then the town expanded in the lowland. The important document for the life of the town was *The Act on Town Building* issued in 1857. It prescribed that streets must intersect at the right angle, at a distance of 76-95 m, of at least 13.30 m width, the height of houses (at least one floor house with the possibility of adding another floor) etc. Regulatory Plan in 1865 adopted the modern principle of regular blocks of houses. The architecture of the Down Town partially comes from the classicist period (Felbinger's house, 15 Jelačić Square), the Convent and Church of the Sisters of Charity (17 Frankopan Street), the General Hospital building (today the University Rectorate and Law Faculty). The whole blocks were built during historicism, Secession and in manner of modern functional architecture. Though in 1880 an earthquake seriously struck Zagreb, it also initiated many new processes. The Town Building Plan from 1887 envisaged the expansion of town territory applying the same orthogonal grid, but with bigger blocks. Among the most successful urbanistic solutions realised during historicism are the squares of so-called Green Horseshoe, stretching from the main railway station towards the old town cores. Spacious

The Main Railway Station building and the square in front of it

squares with lots of green spread from the neo-classicist building of the Main Railway Station (Franjo Pfaff, 1892) to Ban Jelačić square. In front of the railway station is the exhibition building of the Art Pavilion (1898), and further to the north, Croatian Academy of Arts and Sciences (Friedrich Schmidt, 1880) and Zrinski Square with big plane-trees and fountains. Towards the north, from Botanical Garden (type of English-French garden, 1891) there is a line of squares with public institutions. The most important building of Secession style is the National and University Library (Rudolf Lubinsky, 1913), decorated with works of distinguished Croatian artists of the time. North from it, on a harmoniously arranged square is the neo-baroque building of the Croatian National Theatre (Helmer i Fellner, 1895). Buildings in various styles surround the square: neo-renaissance Crafts School with the Museum of Art and Crafts by Hermman Bollé (1892); functionalist Franck mansion (Viktor Kovačić, 1914). The area of Down Town has also several new sacral buildings: the Orthodox Church of Transfiguration (Franjo Klein, 1866), Jesuit Church (Janko Holjac, 1913), St. Blasius Church (Viktor Kovačić, 1913) etc.

Upper Town, the medieval Gradec is situated on the triangular plateau on the hill. The Golden Bull by king Bela IV (1235-1270) permitted to Gradec inhabitants to build the defence walls, and gave them many other privileges granted to free royal cities. There were three gates to the town: from Mesnička street in the west, from Radić street in the east and from the north, later Opatička gate. Beside the three main entrances there was also a small door on the south - Dverce, which was used by the citizens when going on their fields below the town. The walls remained until 17th century when there was no more fear from Turks. The pulling down of the walls enabled the opening of the city and at the same time great changes in the internal structure began. Luxurious palaces replaced small wooden houses. The Croatian noblemen built them, who resided there for a while, and, during the time, instead of them the buildings housed the most important institutions and symbols of Croatian statehood. At the place where once Croatian parliaments held sessions and Croatian bans governed the state, Croatian Parliament and the Government seat are still situated.

❶ Stone Gate / Kamenita vrata
❷ Stone Street / Kamenita ulica
❸ St. Mark's Square / Trg sv. Marka
❹ Banski dvori / Banski dvori
❺ St. Mark's Church / Crkva sv. Marka
❻ Croatian Parliament / Hrvatski sabor
❼ Statutory Court of the Republic of Croatia / Ustavni sud Republike Hrvatske
❽ The Old Town Hall / Stara gradska vijećnica
❾ Croatian Museum of Naive Art / Hrvatski muzej naivne umjetnosti
❿ St. Cyril and St. Methodius Church / Crkva sv. Cirila i Metoda
⓫ Museum of Modern Art / Muzej suvremene umjetnosti
⓬ St. Catherine Church / Crkva sv. Katarine
⓭ Klović Mansion / Klovićevi dvori
⓮ Dverce / Dverce
⓯ Lotrščak tower / Kula Lotrščak
⓰ Funicular / Uspinjača
⓱ Strossmayer Promenade / Strossmayerovo šetalište
⓲ State Institute for Hydrometeorology and Geophysics / Državni hidrometeorološki i geofizički zavod
⓳ Matoš street / Matoševa ulica
⓴ History Museum of Croatia / Hrvatski povijesni muzej
㉑ The Croatian Natural Science Museum / Hrvatski prirodoslovni muzej
㉒ Demetrova street / Demetrova ulica
㉓ Atelier - Ivan Meštrović foundation / Atelijer - Fundacija Ivana Meštrovića
㉔ Community Hall / Narodni dom
㉕ Golden Hall / Zlatna dvorana
㉖ Museum of Zagreb / Muzej grada Zagreba
㉗ Planetarium / Zvjezdarnica
㉘ Illyrian Square / Ilirski trg
㉙ Jurjevska street / Jurjevska ulica
㉚ Mesnička street / Mesnička ulica
㉛ Radić street / Radićeva ulica

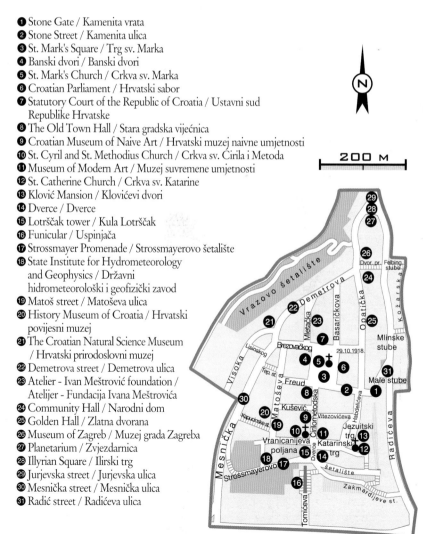

WALK THROUGH THE
Upper Town

Atelier - the Ivan Meštrović Foundation is situated in the house where the famous sculptor lived between the two World Wars. The atelier is a part of Foundation comprising the Meštrović Gallery in Split and Mausoleum of the Meštrović Family in Otavice.

Croatian Parliament is the most important political institution in Croatia with eight-century tradition. During the last hundred years it convened in this palace erected in neo-classicist style. It was here that the decisions on the separation of Croatian countries from Austro-Hungarian Empire in 1918 and on leaving the Yugoslav Federation in 1991 were brought.

Coat-of-arms on the St. Mark's Church, Croatian (left) and Zagreb (right) are made in 19th century. Croatian coat-of-arms consists of three parts symbolising three historical regions: Croatia (top left), Dalmatia (top right) and Slavonia (bottom).

Banski dvori is a long baroque one floor building where once bans resided, and today it is a seat of the Croatian Government.

Community Hall is a neo-classicist palace built in 19th century. It was the centre of all significant social events of the time. The Renaissance hall is where balls were held but political reunions as well. In 1848 the National Demands were declared here, and Josip Jelačić was nominated for Croatian ban.

The Golden Hall is in the palace of Croatian History Institute. It is a big room in baroque style, named after plenty of its gold decorations. There are six paintings on the walls commissioned by Izidor Kršnjavi that illustrate the events from the Croatian history, from the settlement until 19th century. The most valuable among them is the painting by Bela Čikoš-Sesija, The Baptism of Croats.

The Stone Gate is the only preserved gate of the former four town entrances. Its present appearance dates from 1760, after the big fire. The gate houses the Chapel of God's Mother from the Stone gate with valuable baroque grid. In the inner side of the gate is the sculpture of Dora Krupićeva, a character from the novel *The Goldsmith's Treasure* by August Šenoa.

St. Catherine's Church is the finest baroque church in Zagreb. It was erected in the 17th century, and the interior was arranged during the 18th century. The arched ceiling and the walls have luxurious stucco, and above the altar is a big illusionist composition of the Slovenian painter Kristofor Andrija Jelovšek.

KAMENITA

JEZUITSKI TRG

ZOVIĆEVA

KATARININ TRG

The Lotrščak Tower was built in the middle of 13th century and is the best preserved building of the former town defence system. Since 1887 every day the cannons from Lotrščak Tower mark the noon.

The sculpture of Matoš resting on a bench, the work of contemporary Croatian sculptor Ivan Kožarić, dedicated to the great Croatian writer Antun Gustav Matoš (1873-1914).

❶ THE STONE GATE
KAMENITA VRATA

The Stone Gate is the only preserved entrance gate out of the former four. They are

The Stone Gate

mentioned already in medieval times, and their present appearance dates from 1760, when it was renovated after the great fire. According to the legend, all wooden parts of the gate were destroyed by fire except the painting of the Holy Mary and Jesus, found in the ashes, untouched. Since then, the painting is the aim of pilgrims and passing visitors, who pray and light candles as token of gratefulness to the Holy Mary of the Stone gate. The grid in front of the chapel dates from the 1758 and represents the finest example of baroque goldsmith crafts in Croatia. In the inner, west side of the gate, in 1929

Dora Krupićeva

the sculpture of Dora Krupićeva was placed, the goldsmith's daughter from the popular novel by August Šenoa, *The Goldsmith's Treasure*, whose story is situated in the 18th century Zagreb.

❷ THE STONE STREET
KAMENITA ULICA

Steep street leading from the town entrance to the central town square is called the Stone street. Here, at the corner with Habdelićeva street, is the pharmacy with tradition from the distant 1355. At certain period of time, the grandson of the great Italian poet Dante Alighieri, the author of the Divine Comedy, worked here as a pharmacist. The legend says that the chains opposite to the pharmacy come from the war ship of *HSM Victory*. It was the ship of the legendary admiral Horatio Nelson (1758 - 1805) that participated in the famous sea battle at Trafalgar in 1805, where the admiral eventually lost his life. The chains were put at their present place in 1878.

❸ ST. MARK'S SQUARE
TRG SV. MARKA

In the centre of the Upper Town is the rectangular square with parish church of St. Mark in the middle. The finest upper town

The St. Mark's square with the church of the same name in the middle

square was until the mid 19th century the centre of life of the former Gradec. It was trading place and social events place. In front of the vicar of St. Mark's Church, every year on St. Blasius holiday (February 3rd) the newly elected town officials took their oath, as well as Croatian bans.

Since the establishment of the Republic of Croatia, Croatian presidents also take their oath here. In the buildings surrounding the square the key state institutions are placed - the parliament, government and the constitutional court. Thus, St. Mark's square is the symbol of political life in Croatia.

❹ BANSKI DVORI

Trg sv. Marka 2
☎ 01 456 92 22
🖥 www.vlada.hr

Banski dvori is a long one floor baroque building on the west side of St. Mark's Square. Baron Kulmer started to build it at the beginning of 19ᵗʰ century, but in 1808, though it was still unfinished, the Kingdom of Croatia bought it. It houses the archives, parliament room and the courts, and the flat for bans was arranged at the first floor. The one-floor palace at the north side was later annexed to it, so today the whole block houses the highest government offices of Croatia. Many important historical events took place in the complex of Banski dvori, and the legendary Croatian ban Josip Jelačić (1801 - 1859) lived and died here. Today, Banski dvori is the seat of Croatian Government and the Prime Minister office is within.

Croatian bans (vice-roi)

Bans, along with prince, king and Croatian parliament, were the carriers of the Croatian sovereignty throughout the history. The institution of ban existed in Croatian State already in the early medieval time, when ban was the highest ranked official, just after the king. During Austro-Hungarian state union (from 12 until 16 century), ban had a function of prorex - the king's deputy. Under his government all Croatian countries were united - *banus regnorum Dalmatiae et Croatiae et totius Sclauoniae*.

Toma Bakač-Erdödy

Ban governed, judged and instead of the king commanded the army, summoned and adjurned the Parliament, confirmed its decisions, sometimes gave privileges to towns and for some time minted money. Some bans governed completely independently of the king. Thus Croatian people generated the saying: "King reigns, and ban rules".

Especially important role of bans was during the defence from Turks. Many bans were great commanders, e. g. Berislavić, Karlović, Toma Bakač-Erdödy. Ban Jelačić was particularly popular, the commander who in 1848 abolished serfdom in Croatia. First ban who was not noble by birth was Ivan Mažuranić, therefore called *ban from the people*.

The institution of ban remained until the Vidovdan Constitution (1921), and was shortly re-established during the existence of Banovina Hrvatska (1939-1941). The last ban - Ivan Šubašić, left the country at the beginning of World War II in 1941, but as a member of royal government in exile he worked during the whole war.

Ban Mažuranić

On behalf of the Government, in 1944 Šubašić made an agreement with Josip Broz Tito and remained in his government until the end of the war. After the elections and referendum in 1945, only communists remained in power and the institution of ban was abolished.

Banski dvori

❺ ST. MARK'S CHURCH
CRKVA SV. MARKA

Trg sv. Marka 5

Picturesque church of St. Mark is among the oldest buildings in Zagreb and by all means one of its symbols. It was already mentioned in the list of parish churches in Kaptol Statute from 1334. It was built in 13th century, and from that first, Romanesque period only the window in the south wall and the bell-tower foundation are preserved. Gothic vaults and the shrine are built in the second half of the 14th century when the church got its most valuable part - rich gothic south portal. That gothic portal with the richest figuration in Croatia was made in Parler's workhouse, one of the most famous medieval sculptor families. On the north-west wall there is the oldest known coat-of-arms of Zagreb from 1499. The church was thoroughly reconstructed in the second half of the 19th century according to the design of Viennese architects Friedrich Schmidt and Hermann Bollé and then again renovated in the first half of the 20th century. On that occasion the well-known painter Jozo Kljaković (1888 - 1969) painted its walls, and the works of famous sculptor Ivan Meštrović were put on the altar.

During the reconstruction at the end of the 19th century, the interior took neo-gothic features and the west portal was expanded.

The renovation in the middle of 20th century highlighted the gothic features of the space. The big crucifix is the work of the sculptor Ivan Meštrović

The south portal, the richest gothic portal in Continental Croatia

Its present appearance the bell-tower got in the 18th century. It was covered with copper in 1841.

☏ 01 485 16 11
🕐 9 a.m. -12 a.m. and
   5 p.m. -5.45 p.m.

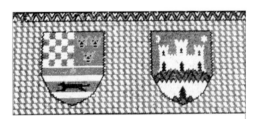

The roof made of multi-coloured tiles with coat-of-arms of Zagreb (right) and Triune Kingdom (left)

❻ CROATIAN PARLIAMENT
HRVATSKI SABOR

Trg sv. Marka 6 i 7
☎ 01 456 93 48
🖥 www.sabor.hr
🕐 8.30 a.m. - 4 p.m. ✍

The palace in which Croatian Parliament holds its sessions is at the east side of St. Mark's square. There were more houses at that place before as well as the baroque mansion in which Sabor convened during the 18th century. At the turn of the 17th to 18th century, one of the houses housed the state printing house lead by a writer Pavao Ritter Vitezović (1652 - 1713). In 1776, it was this place where the high education of law started. Present building of the parliament was erected between 1908 and 1910 in neo-classicist style according to the design of architect Lavoslav Kalda, and for the royal state government of the time. During the 20th century in the parliament building and in front of it many important events of Croatian history took place. From its balcony, in 1918 the separation of Croatian countries from Austro-Hungarian Empire was declared, and since spring

The building of Constitutional Court

1990 new organisation of the Republic of Croatia has been developed.

❼ CONSTITUTIONAL COURT OF THE REPUBLIC OF CROATIA
USTAVNI SUD REPUBLIKE HRVATSKE

Trg sv. Marka 4
☎ 01 455 09 27
🖥 www.usud.hr

Constitutional Court is the highest judicial institution in Croatia. It consists of eleven judges who evaluate the accordance of laws with the Constitution, deal with conflicts of authority between legislative, judicial and executive authorities, monitor working of political parties etc. Constitutional Court, at the Parliament's suggestion determines permanent disability of the president of Croatia to perform his duties, and in particular circumstances Constitutional Court can determine the responsibility of the president of Croatia and that act would then, by the force of Constitution, terminate the president's duties.

❽ THE OLD TOWN HALL
STARA GRADSKA VIJEĆNICA

Ćirilometodska ulica 5

Town Hall is here since Middle Ages. The old building was pulled down in the 19th century, and the first Zagreb theatre was built at its place. In 1839 the premiere of the first play of the modern Croatian literature was held, *Juran and Sophia or Turks at Sisak* by Ivan Kukuljević Sakcinski (1816-1889), and in 1846 the first Croatian opera was put up, *Love and Malice* by Vatroslav Lisinski (1819 - 1854). During the 19th century, Croatian Parliament held its session in the ballroom and in 1847 Croatian language was declared official. After the new theatre was built the old one was rearranged and linked to Town hall, and the sessions continued to be held in the former ballroom. Today it is the place for the Town Assembly meetings and some occasional town meetings.

The entrance to the Parliament building

❾ CROATIAN MUSEUM OF NAÏVE ART

HRVATSKI MUZEJ NAIVNE UMJETNOSTI

Ćirilometodska ulica 3

The baroque mansion built in the 18th century houses the Croatian Museum of Naïve Art. It was the first museum of naïve art in the world, and it has around 1500 works of art. Those are mostly paintings and drawings following the beginnings and development of naïve art in Croatia, and all important masters are represented: Večenaj, Generalić, Mraz, Virius, Rabuzin, Smajić, Skurjeni, Lacković, Feješ, Buktenica and others. The permanent exhibition has been designed under two motos: *Naïve art as the segment of Modern Art* and *They created the history of Croatian Naïve Art*. Some eighty antological paintings and sculptures of twenty naïve art classics have been exhibited, from the beginning of the thirties of the last century until present times, and the focus is on the artists of *Hlebine School* and a few independent artists.

Mirko Virius, *Harvest*

Petar Smajić,
Adam and Eve

Franjo Mraz, *At the grazing*

℡ 01 485 19 11
🖥 www.hmnu.org
🕓 Tue - Fri 10 a.m. - 6 p.m.
   Sat and Sun 10 a.m. -1 p.m.
☞ with prior announcement

Croatian Museum of Naïve Art

Ivan Večenaj, *Cows pulling wood*

Ivan Rabuzin, *Jungle on hills*

Ivan Generalić, *Woodcutters*

Ivan Lacković-Croata,
Suiters

Ivan Generalić
(1914 - 1992)

Ivan Generalić was born in Hlebine near Koprivnica. He preferred painting with oil and tempera on oil, and his motives were village life and still nature. Professor Krsto Hegedušić recognized his talent and organised his first exhibition in Zagreb, in 1931. For some time he lived and worked in Paris where in 1953 he had an exhibition. On the great exhibition in Brussels in 1958 his paintings were among those by Chagall, Picasso, Matisse, Klee and Kandinski. His most important work is *The Deer Wedding* from 1959.

Ivan Rabuzin (1921)

Ivan Rabuzin is among the most important representatives of naive art in Croatia and in the world. With his particular plastic expression, he differs from the features of Hlebine School. He painted mostly landscapes with characteristic round hills overgrown with thick treetops. In his later paintings he preferred the motive of gigantic flower dominating the landscape. He held his exhibitions in many big European cities, and his motives are used for production of numerous items: Rosenthal porcelain, drapes in Tokyo theatre etc.

Ivan Lacković-Croata
(1932-2004)

Ivan Lacković-Croata is the famous Croatian painter and graphic artist, born in village Batinska in Podravina. In his early works he naturally and sincerely expressed his impression of nature and life in native region. Later, he moved to Zagreb and continued painting of poetic scenes from his native region in tempera and oil on glass, very often winter landscapes, and gradually he spent more time on drawings. He had around hundred exhibitions in Croatia and many abroad.

⑩ ST. CYRIL AND ST. METHODIUS CHURCH
CRKVA SV. ĆIRILA I METODA

Ćirilometodska ulica 1
☏ 01 485 17 73
🕐 ring the bell of parish offices

Greek Catholic church of St. Cyril and St. Methodius was erected in 1880 in neo-Byzantine style, following the project of the architect Hermann Bollé (1845 - 1926). It was built on the place of former chapel of St. Basil which was seriously damaged in a disastrous earthquake. The central screen with icons was painted by the Ukrainian artist Epiminondas Bučevski and domestic painter Nikola Mašić, while four spacious paintings on the walls are made by Ivan Tišov (1870 - 1928). There is also Greek Catholic seminary next to the church, founded already in the 17th century.

St. Cyril and Methodius Church

Cyril and Methodius

At request of Moravian prince Rastislav, the Byzantine king sent in 862 the brothers, Constantine (Cyril) and Methodius to spread the Christian religion in Slavic languages. For that purpose, brothers made first Slavic letters - glagolitic script and started translating religious books into the language of Macedonian Slavs from the vicinity of Solun. Thus the first Slavic literary language was created and the foundation to Slavic literacy built. But, German clergy did not like the activities of the two brothers and their followers, so the Slavic clergy eventually had to leave. Constantine went to Rome, where he died, and Method and his students spread to Bulgaria, Macedonia, Raška and Croatia, where they continued their work.

⑪ THE MUSEUM OF CONTEMPORARY ART
MUZEJ SUVREMENE UMJETNOSTI

Katarinski trg 2
☏ 01 485 19 30
🖥 www.mdc.hr/msu

The palace, once the propriety of Counts Kulmer, today houses the Museum of Contemporary Art which follows, documents and promotes contemporary trends in plastic arts.

It keeps the collections of paintings, sculptures and objects, drawings and prints, posters and graphic design, total of around 9 000 works of modern and contemporary art. Most of the Museum's collection covers the works of Croatian and foreign authors, created after 1950, while its minor part consists of works from the first half of the 20th century, whose presence is necessary for the reception of modern and contemporary art. The museum stores several donations (by art collector Benko

The Palace of the Museum of Contemporary Art

Horvat, painter Josip Sissel and architect Vjenceslav Richter - the house architecture with inventory and paintings). For the time being, the museum has no permanent exhibition and the valuables it stores will be more available after the museum moves out into a new building in Novi Zagreb.

⑫ St. Catherine's Church

CRKVA SV. KATARINE

Katarinski trg bb

The St. Catherine's Church is the finest baroque church in Zagreb. It was built by the Jesuits, between 1620 and 1632. It is one-nave church with six side chapels and a shrine. The chapels have five wooden baroque altars (17ᵗʰ century) and one marble altar from 1729. The arc ceiling and the walls are full of rich stucco, dating from 1732. The low main altar is in the shrine, in front of the big illusionist composition *St. Catherine among the Philosophers of Alexandria*, painted by Kristofor Andrija Jelovšek, the painter from Ljubljana in Slovenia. The church was thoroughly reconstructed after the 1880 earthquake, according to the Hermann Bollé's project.

The interior of St. Catherine's Church

The Shrine

The Altar of St. Ignacius

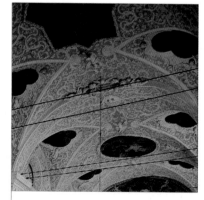

View of the ceiling stucco and paintings

The pulpet

① 01 485 19 59
🕐 10 a.m. - 1 p.m

The monastery rearranged into Museum Gallery Centre

⑬ Klovićevi Dvori

KLOVIĆEVI DVORI

Jezuitski trg 4
☎ 01 485 19 26
🖥 www.galerijaklovic.hr
🕐 Tue - Sun 11 a.m. - 7 p.m.
☞ with prior announcement

The building of former Jesuit monastery dominates the small Jesuit square, housing the Gallery Klovićevi dvori. It is a big four wing complex, erected partially on the tower and eastern part of the ancient Gradec defence walls. The building of the monastery, in the spirit of later Renaissance, started in 1641 and was performed in phases, until 1656. The monastery was burnt down already in 1674, and was reconstructed afterwards. The greatest alterations were made in the period between 1974 and 1983, when the second floor on the west wing was built. The former monastery was transformed

into exhibition premises, intended for the Mimara collection. But the collection was housed in the Down Town, so there are some occasional interesting exhibitions and performances in Klovićevi dvori.

⑭ Dverce

Katarinski trg 6

The town palace Dverce is used for festive receptions and representative occasional meetings hosted by the Town Government and Town Assembly. The palace was built on the south town defence walls, and its present appearance dates from the end of the 19th century. It was named after small town gate - Dverce, that was next to it. The last owner, Klotilda Buratti, by her will left the palace to the town, for representative events.

The Fisherman, work by Simeon Roksandić (1874 - 1942)

⑮ Kula Lotrščak

KULA LOTRŠČAK

Dverce 1
☎ 01 485 17 68
🕐 Tue - Sun 11 a.m. - 8 p.m.
☞ with prior announcement

The Lotrščak Tower erects next to former small town gate Dverce. It was built in the middle of the 13th century and is the best-preserved building of former town defence system. It was named after the bell that was in it, the bell of

The Lotrščak Tower

thief (lat. Campana latronculorum) as it was called, which rang every night before the closing of the town gates. Today, instead of the bell each day at noon the cannon is fired from the tower. This cannon is the most peaceful one in the world, and has been announcing 12 o'clock sharp since 1877. The shot of Zagreb cannon has become one of its traditions. In the Lotrščak Tower there is information and selling place of the Museum Gallery centre.

⑯ FUNICULAR
USPINJAČA

Tomićeva ulica
🕐 every day and holiday 6.30
a.m. - 9 p.m. every ten minutes

The Upper Town and the Down Town are linked by popular Zagreb funicular. It is in the place of the medieval stairs connecting upper and down town. The funicular is the oldest transportation vehicle of the organised public transport of passengers in the town. It started working in 1890, but due to frequent damages, *the old lady* as Zagreb citizens popularly called it, have actually started its permanent, regular transport on April 23rd 1893. Naturally, it was thoroughly reconstructed several times later, and its present appearance dates from 1974. The total length of the steep funicular rails is 66 meters, the height difference is 30.5 meters, and gradient of 52%. It has two gauges and two cabins, two wagons with 16 seats and 12 standing places. The speed is 1.5 m/s and lasts for 55 seconds.

⑰ THE STROSSMAYER PROMENADE
STROSSMAYEROVO ŠETALIŠTE

The promenade is situated along the south defensive wall of former Gradec. There is wonderful view from the promenade on the Down Town, and from its eastern part on Kaptol as well. It was adjusted at the beginning of 19th century thanks to citizens' voluntary contributions. The row of trees was planted, the benches were put and it got its final form at the beginning of the 20th century, when public stairs were added together with fence walls and lamps, following the

Strossmayer promenade

design by Hugo Ehrlich (1879 - 1936). Zagreb citizens, the former as well as the present always like to rest there for a few minutes. They can even sit down with the great Croatian poet and writer Antun Gustav Matoš (1873 - 1914), since a rather unusual but original monument has been put here to his honour - *The statue of Matoš resting on a bench*, work by sculptor Ivan Kožarić (1921).

Antun Gustav Matoš (1873 – 1914)

A.G. Matoš, is among the best Croatian poets and narrators. He was born in Plavna near Vukovar, but already at the age of two came to Zagreb, thus considered as Zagreb citizen by upbringing. He

shortly studied in Vienna, and then went to army in 1893. He deserted the army and was imprisoned in Petrovaradin. He managed to escape and for 13 years he lived as a military fugitive in Belgrade, Geneva and Paris then again in Belgrade. During those years he adopted a second name - Gustav. He came secretly to Croatia on several occasions until the amnesty in 1908 when he returned for good. Matoš was a writer of excellent education, a boem, journalist and lived of his writing (though hardly). In 1910 he passed the exam for the teacher of higher primary school but as nationally aware intellectual and cynical political opponent he could not get permanent position. Severely ill, he diligently worked in the hospital, where he finished his famous poem *Notturno*. He published three collections of narratives, numerous poems, essays, feuilletons, reviews, humorous narratives... He kept a kind of diary of his life and work, famous *Bilježnice*, where numerous working versions of specific works were preserved. Matoš's work as a whole belongs to the greatest works of Croatian literature.

⓲ STATE INSTITUTE FOR HYDROMETEOROLOGY AND GEOPHYSICS
DRŽAVNI HIDROMETEOROLOŠKI I GEOFIZIČKI ZAVOD

Grič 3
☎ 01 456 56 66
🖥 www.tel.hr/dhmz

At the west side of Strossmayer promenade the Capuchin convent was once situated, with the church and the graveyard. Present big building with the yard was erected at the beginning of the 19ᵗʰ century and some time later, the town municipality bought it and rearranged it. For some time it housed a grammar school, and professor Ivan Stožir began there the meteorological observations in 1861. The meteorology station generated the *Observatory Zagreb - Grič*, *Institute for Geophysics, Seismological service and State Institute for hydrometeorology*. The most important events in the history of the building were at the beginning of the 20ᵗʰ century when Andrija

Andrija Mohorovičić (1857 – 1936)

Andrija Mohorovičić is one of the founders of modern seismology. He was the first in the world to reveal the surface of speed discontinuity, on the basis of earthquake waves, the surface dividing the crust from the earth's mantle, and to his honour the phenomenon is called the Mohorovičić discontinuity. He assumed that the speed of earthquake waves in the earth's crust gradually increases as waves enter into greater depth. That assumption was expressed by exponential function, named Mohorovičić discontinuity, and is still applied. He dealt with meteorology as well, and he was in particular interested in the conspicuous meteorological phenomena, as tornado near Novska in 1892 and whirlwind near Čazma in 1898. Many of his ideas were visionary and are only recently appreciated.

Mohorovičić, world famous geophysicist, found out the existence of discontinuity inside the Earth. It is undoubtedly the most important work ever published in Croatian scientific publication.

⓳ MATOŠ STREET
MATOŠEVA ULICA

A picturesque street, stretching from Banski dvori, is interesting not only for its baroque mansion Vojković-

Houses in Matoševa street

Oršić but also for its excellently preserved middle-class houses. At numbers 5 and 7 there are houses of medieval type. They are ground-floor houses, with their narrower side turned towards the street, and the wider towards the inner courtyard entered through street entrance. The house at number 5 is especially interesting; it is made of wood and consists of a room and a kitchen. It was built in 1738, though seems older by the way of building. It is interesting that the 1826 decision aiming at fire protection said that instead of this house another should be built of solid material, but the decision has not been implemented yet.

West facade of the Institute building

Well in the courtyard of Balbi mansion

⑳ HISTORY MUSEUM
HRVATSKI POVIJESNI MUZEJ
See pages 64 - 65

㉑ CROATIAN NATURAL SCIENCE MUSEUM
HRVATSKI PRIRODOSLOVNI MUZEJ
See pages 66-67

㉒ DEMETER STREET
DEMETROVA ULICA
Demeter street is one of the central streets of the Upper Town. Beside the Croatian Natural Science Museum, there is also one of the finest upper-town classicist mansions, the *Jelačić mansion* (at number 7). After it was built, it was rearranged several times, and it carries its name after the last owner Đuro Jelačić, the brother of the ban, Josip Jelačić. At

Facade of Jelačić mansion

number 11, there is the *Balbi mansion* housing the Old Slavic Institute. In the courtyard of the mansion is the last preserved upper-town well, roofed with shingle. It is worth mentioning that the great Croatian opera singer Milka Trnina (1863 - 1941) spend her last days in Demetrova street at number 5.

㉓ ATELIER – THE IVAN MEŠTROVIĆ FOUNDATION
ATELIJER - FUNDACIJA IVANA MEŠTROVIĆA
See pages 68-69

㉔ COMMUNITY HALL
NARODNI DOM
Opatička ulica 18
The neo-classicist mansion known as Community Hall, was built by the end of thirties of the 19th century by count Karlo Drašković. In 1846, the Ilyrians bought the building and in the ground floor placed the National Museum, while the mansion wings housed *Economic Society, Reading Room and Casino*. The most important and the most attractive interior room is the so-called *Renaissance Hall* in the south-east part of the mansion. It was rearranged in 1846 in Biedermeier style. It has a ceiling with the grid, the capitals with Ilyrian coat-of-arms was put on the pillars, the galleries were opened at the sides of the first floor and the mirrors were put around the hall. The place soon became the centre of all important cultural, educational and other social gatherings. The political meetings were held here as

Das Volksheim

well as festive balls. The historical assembly took place in the Renaissance hall, on March 25th 1848, organised by Gaj, Kukuljević and Vranyczany at which Kukuljević declared *National Demands*, and Josip Jelačić was nominated the Croatian ban. Today, the building of Community Hall is owned by Croatian Academy of Arts and Sciences, which was founded in that building in 1866.

㉑ HISTORY MUSEUM

HRVATSKI POVIJESNI MUZEJ

Matoševa ulica 9

The History Museum is housed in the finest upper-town baroque mansion. It was erected in 1763, and was owned by the count families Vojković, Oršić and Rauch. The History Museum developed from the former National Museum, founded in 1846. It collects, stores, museologically processes and presents the Croatian cultural and historical heritage from medieval times to present days. It stores more than 140 000 various museum articles, classified into 15 collections, from the collection of stone monuments, through the collection of everyday life articles, to heraldry, cold and fire weapons and map collection. Though it does not have permanent exhibition, due to lack of museum space, the museum organises occasional exhibitions, showing to the public specific museum collections and prepares theme exhibitions on Croatian social, political, economic and cultural history.

Gerard de Jode, *Map of Croatia*, around 1594

The head of Stephen, the king of Hungary, 13th century

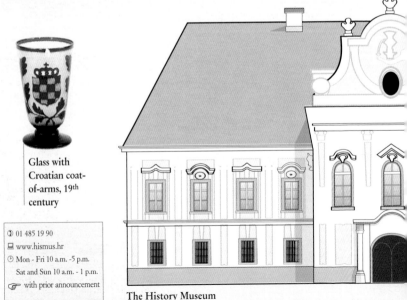

Glass with Croatian coat-of-arms, 19th century

① 01 485 19 90
▢ www.hismus.hr
⏱ Mon - Fri 10 a.m. -5 p.m.
　 Sat and Sun 10 a.m. - 1 p.m.
☞ with prior announcement

The History Museum

Čako of Zagreb National
Guard after 1840.

Armour, 19th
century

Ban Josip
Jelačić flag
from 1848

Wall clock with Kaptol view,
19 century

Michele Canzio, Tommaso da Rin
and Francesco Beda, *Ivan Mažuranić*

㉑ CROATIAN NATURAL SCIENCE MUSEUM

HRVATSKI PRIRODOSLOVNI MUZEJ

Demetrova ulica 1

Croatian Natural Science Museum is in the building where in 1797 the theatre pieces were given, and since in 1807 count Antun Amadeo bought it, the theatre was named after him. In memorial to him the theatre performances are held during the summer in the museum's hall. The Natural Science Museum has geological and paleontological collection, mineralogical and petrographic and zoological collection. In the attractive space one can see numerous remnants from the pre-historic times. Concerning the number of human and animal bones and stone tools, this collection is among the most important in the world. But the most significant museum valuables are the remains of the primitive man from Neanderthal period that a distinguished Croatian scientist Dragutin Gorjanović-Kramberger found near Krapina.

Mediterranean seal

Permanent exhibition

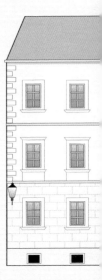

☎ 01 485 17 00
🖳 www.hpm.hr
🕐 Tue-Fri 10 a.m. - 5 p.m.
    Sat and Sun 10 a.m. - 1 p.m.
☞ with prior announcement

The scull of Krapina
primitive man

Reconstruction of primitive man

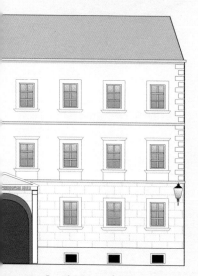

Croatian Natural Science Museum

THE HISTORY OF CROATIAN NATURAL SCIENCE MUSEUM

At the time of awakening of national awareness among Croats, in the period of Croatian National Renaissance, Ljudevit Gaj 1829 directly encourages the foundation of national museum. Croatian Parliament in 1829 suggested the foundation of "The Society of friends of national Ilyrian education", and the museum within. After the foundation of Croatian and Slavonian Economic Society (1841), its first secretary Dragutin Rakovec encourages even more the collection of antiquities and natural articles for the future national museum.

On February 24th 1846, the city of Zagreb bought the mansion of count Drašković Trakošćanski in the present Opatička street 18, turning it into Community Hall dom. In its ground floor there were Economic Society and museum collections. The Committee of the Economic Society appointed Dragutin Rakovac as its secretary. The collections were opened to public and thus the Croatian National museum was established.

In 1849, Mijat Sabljar published the first catalogue of the collections that by 1854 already had 28 000 articles. After multiple requests that National museum publicly became the state institution (1854, 1861), on the suggestion of Croatian Parliamnet and suggestion of its Academy Committee led by the bishop Josip Juraj Stossmayer from 1865, the emperor Franz Joseph I on March 4th 1866 in Budim acknowledged the rules of the Yugoslav Academy of Sciences and Arts and National state museum, subjecting the Museum to Academy's administration on November 29th 1867. The museum was divided into two parts Nature and Archaeology. In 1880, Dragutin Gorjanović Kramberger started working in the museum, and in 1892 Mijo Kišpatić. Since 1893, three National Museum departments have been working independently, zoological, mineralogical and petrographic and geological and paleontological, which are at the same time Institutes of the Zagreb University.

All three Zagreb natural science museums after 1945 have become legally independent. In 1986 all three institutions are united into present Croatian Natural Science Museum.

㉓ ATELIER – IVAN MEŠTROVIĆ FOUNDATION

ATELIJER - FUNDACIJA IVANA MEŠTROVIĆA

Mletačka ulica 8

Atelier Meštrović is in the house built during the 17th century, in which the sculptor lived from 1922 to 1942. Here are the stone, copper, wood and plaster sculptures, pencil drawings, litograph collections, examples of furniture made according to artist's design and others, and all is Meštrović's gift to his homeland. The foundation was established in 1991, and beside atelier in Zagreb and Meštrović Gallery in Split, it comprises the Mausoleum of the Meštrović family in Otavice. In permanent exhibition of Zagreb atelier are also works that Meštrović created during the first 40 years of work. Besides, the street where the Foundation is situated, Mletačka, got its name in medieval times after the Mleci (Venetians) and those were Italians who lived here from the middle of 13th century.

Mother and child, 1942

Vestal, 1915

The facade of the building housing the atelier

① 01 485 11 23
🖳 www.mdc.hr/mestrovic
🕐 Tue-Sat 10 a.m.- 6 p.m.
   Sun 10 a.m. - 2 p.m.
☞ with prior announcement

View of the atrium

Artist at work - Auguste Rodin, 1914

Mary with the child, 1917

Woman beside the sea, 1926

Ivan Meštrović (1883 - 1962)

Ivan Meštrović is the most famous Croatian sculptor and one of the greatest artists of the 20th century. He was born in Vrpolje near Ž u p a n j a , and spent his child-hood in Dalmatinska zagora. At the Vienna Academy he met the great French sculptor Auguste Rodin and befriend-ed him. As a young man, in his head he envisaged the monumental Vidovdan shrine, that could not have been built, but the fragments exhibited in 1911 at the Inter-national Rome Exhibition, made him famous. During the World War I he lived in Rome, London, Geneva, Cannes and Paris and made works of religious themes, mostly in wood. Afterwards he settled in Zagreb, where he was the first rector of the newly founded Art Academy. In the period between the wars, he was impressed by Michelangelo, and made a lot of stone reliefs, nudes and portraits. His works with themes from the national his-tory are very famous as My Mother and monuments like the one to Grgur Ninski in Split. After the World War II, Meštrović moved to USA, and the president Eisenhover personally, in the White House, gave him the decree that made him the American citizen. Meštrović is the only artist that saw his works exhibited in the Metropolitan Museum in New York, and his famous *Indian* is exhibit-ed in Chicago.

㉕ THE GOLDEN HALL
ZLATNA DVORANA
See pages 72-73

㉖ THE ZAGREB CITY MUSEUM
MUZEJ GRADA ZAGREBA
See pages 74-77

㉗ PLANETARIUM
ZVJEZDARNICA

Opatička ulica 22
☎ 01 485 13 55
🖥 www.botanic.hr/ast
🕐 Tue-Fri 8 p.m. - 10 p.m.
☞ with prior announcement

Popov toranj, the tower
on the top of Opatička
street, is the old upper-

Popov toranj with the Planetarium

town fortress, erected in
the middle of 13th century,
after the Tatar invasion,
fearing similar events. The
people called it Popov
toranj (pop=priest)
because it belonged to
Zagreb bishop. When the
tower was incorporated
into town defence walls, in
the middle of 16th century,
its task was to protect the
north town gate. In the
middle of 17th century it
housed the school, and the
second floor was built in

Ljudevit Gaj (1809 – 1872)

Ljudevit Gaj was a writer and politician, and leader of Croatian national revival.
He studied in Vienna, Graz and Pešta where he came in touch with national
youth. In 1830, he published the Short History of Croatian and Slavic
Orthography and gave suggestion of orthographic reform of the Croatian language. Some time later he wrote the poem *Još Hrvatska ni propala* and in 1835
he initiated the newspapers *Croatian Newspaper*, with weekly enclosure
Danica Horvatska, slavonska i dalmatinska, that a year afterwards adopted
stokavian dialect and the new orthography.

Janko Drašković (1770 – 1856)

Count Janko Drašković was in his time among the most educated people in
Croatia. Since Gaj, as a middle class citizen as well as the majority of his followers, did not have any political rights, count Drašković represented Ilyrian aspi-
rations in front of the Parliament. The author of famous *Disertation*, he pointed out the need to replace Latin as an official language. He advocated the
unification of Croatia with Slavonia and Dalmatia and warned of the neces-
sity for higher education level of the people.

Stanko Vraz (1810 – 1851)

Stanko Vraz was the most romantic poet among the Ilyrians. He was born in
the east Styria, and his real name was Jacob Frass. As a law student he translated Classical Latin writers and Slavic poets Mickiewicz and Puskin. In 1833,
he met Ljudevit Gaj in Graz and was thrilled with his revival ideas. He frequently visited Zagreb and started writing in Danica, signing as *Stanko Vraz,
an Ilyrian from Styria*. In 1839 he settled in Zagreb. His most known work
is a collection of love poems *Đulabije* dedicated to Gaj's niece Ljubica
Cantilly.

the first half of the 19th century. Today, one could almost "touch" the stars from Popov toranj. On his top, namely within its dome, there has been Zagreb planetarium for over a century. It was opened on December 5th 1903. Town authorities decided that Popov toranj was an ideal place for planetarium, because it was sufficiently above the town so its telescope could be above the lowest, dirties layers of atmosphere and yet it was virtually in the

Ivan Mažuranić (1814 – 1890)

Ivan Mažuranić, poet and politician was born in Novi Vinodolski. He graduated at the Law Faculty in Zagreb and did his service in the town magistrate in Karlovac, where he wrote all of his major works. He entered literature with his poetry in Hungarian, and from the beginning of Ilyrian movement he was the main Gaj's collaborator and creator in revival spirit. At the invitation of Illyrian Cultural Society, he masterfully completed Osman (XIV and XV poem) by Ivan Gundulić, and ensured his poetical glory by an epic poem of permanent value *The Death of Smail-Agha Čengić*, that was translated to all major world languages. Mažuranić also achieved a great political career and remained remembered as the first ban without noble origins, why he was called *people's ban*.

Ilyrian square and the coffee-house *Palainovka*

centre of Zagreb and had a clear view on it. Planetarium can be reached by pleasant promenade from the nearby town "arteries".

㉘ ILYRIAN SQUARE
ILIRSKI TRG

This beautiful square was created in 1839 when north town gate was pulled down. It was then called the Statue square, after the statue in the chapel in its middle, at the intersection of the three streets, Opatička, Jurjevska and Radićeva streets. The chapel was erected in 1892, according to the design of the architect Hermann Bollé (1845 - 1926). On the south side of the square there was *Palainovka*, one of the oldest and most famous Zagreb coffee-house and today's café at the same place and under the same name has continued the tradition.

㉙ JURJEVSKA STREET
JURJEVSKA ULICA

Jurjevska street connects Upper Town with Cmrok. It got the name after the chapel of St. George (Juraj), that was mentioned for the first time in 1377. The chapel was originally wooden so it was often damaged by fire or lightning, thus in 1729 the new one was built of stone, with a crypt and a graveyard beside. The graveyard was abandoned when Mirogoj was opened in 1876. Besides, Jurjevska street was built after the north Gradec gate was pulled down. The writer Antun Gustav Matoš and *people's ban* Ivan Mažuranić spent the last days of their lives in that street, and Tilla Durieux (1880 - 1971) a great actress and donor of a valuable collection housed in the City Museum, also lived here for some time, at number 27.

Jurjevska street

㉕ GOLDEN HALL
ZLATNA DVORANA

Opatička ulica 10

Among the beautiful mansions in Opatička street one is especially attractive - the one that houses the Croatian History Institute. The mansion is well known for its cast iron entrance, a joint work of Hermann Bollé (1845 - 1926), the architect and Đuro Burić, a master craftsmen. Besides, Izidor Kršnjavi (1845 - 1927) the head of the Department for God Praising and Education had had three rooms arranged. The small one, painted in classic Roman wall painting style, a work room covered with wooden panels carved in the renaissance style and the big room in baroque style, called the Golden Hall due to abundance of gilded decorations. Between 1895 and 1907, its walls were decorated with six paintings illustrating the events from the Croatian history.

Celestin Medović *The Arrival of Croats*

This was the first critical moment, because the Croats came into touch with highly developed urban Roman civilisation. It was the moment when they for the first time stepped off the dusty roads and muddy paths onto the paved roads, they found themselves under the high stone defence walls and strong towers of Roman towns, where they could see palaces, shrines and theatres. From the artistic point of view the most expressive part of the painting is the sunset.

Bela Čikoš-Sesija
Baptism of Croats

From the artistic point of view this is the most valuable piece in the room. It shows a dramatical moment when the priest blesses the people with the cross, in the front plan, and at the same time, in the background, fierce protest of advocators of the Slavic beliefs and gods.

The painting is pervaded with light, and the altar fire with smoke vanishing into the clouds and sky is masterfully painted.

Celestin Medović
Parliament Session in Split in 925

The session was held in the king's mausoleum of the Diocletian palace that was rearranged into a cathedral in the 7th century. The author shows some later works as well, as the altar of St. Staša (left) and gilded wooden vault of the apse (right). The room's equipment and the participants' clothes are from different periods: the chandeliers are from the 14th century, noblemen and church officials' clothing is from baroque period, and the floor pavement is ceramics typical for 19th century Zagreb kitchens and bathrooms. From artistic point of view, the tissues are masterfully presented.

Celestin Medović *The king Zvonimir's engagements*

The engagement of the last ruler of the people's dynasty

with Hungarian princess at the end of the 11th century, are performed in the interior of some Byzantine church with a lot of ornamentation and mosaics on the walls. The painting composition is based on the contrast between the king and his escort in the shadow and brightly lit princess Helena and her father with Hungarian crown on the head. The queen's jewellery is thoroughly painted while the background characters vanish in candle light and incense smoke.

Oton Iveković *The representatives of the Croatian nobility acknowledge Coloman for their king*

The painting shows the meeting of the Croatian noblemen and army with Hungarian king and his escort in front of the battle tents. The painting has a lot of details, precisely drawn, and the author tried to credibly present the clothes and the weapons of the time. The many-coloured, long, unfolded flags and mast-flags give liveliness and mark the whole composition.

Celestin Medović *The coronation of Ladislav of Naples*

The coronation takes place in a western type church, that is only partially seen, and everything else is hidden by curtains and decorative carpets. In the middle of the composition is the king coronated by the Pope's representative, but the main character is the lonely queen in white, sitting in front. Her escort and both of boys (one carries a sceptre, the other a decorative spear) are dressed in renaissance style from the 15th century, when the event took place.

Vlaho Bukovac *Reception of the emperor Franz Joseph I in Zagreb*

This painting differs from the others because it represents a contemporary event but also because the author just returned from Paris and integrated in the picture his significant experience with impressionism. The event is happening at the back of the Mimara museum (at the time School forum, for which the emperor Franz Joseph I put the founda-

tions). Bukovac, the master of portraits, painted the king and his escort and numerous Croatian officials in detail, led by Ban. The most interesting part of the painting is the one with the musicians in the national costume from Šestine (right) and a merry procession of girls accompanied by a young teacher with a nice hat (left). The new painting technique could be best seen on them, where instead of dead, black shades we have light and transparent blue and green shades.

㉖ THE ZAGREB CITY MUSEUM

MUZEJ GRADA ZAGREBA

Opatička ulica 20 - 22

It was initiated by the Society of Croatian Dragon brothers, when in 1907, two important institutions were founded in Zagreb - town museum and the town library. The
first museum space was within Stone Gate. The millennium Cultural and Historical
Exhibition of Zagreb in the Art Pavilion (1925) gave special impetus to it, because it
later provided the Museum with a lot of articles. This was the reason why the new museum exhibition was placed in the ground floor of the Art Pavilion. After many attempts
to find the appropriate space for the Museum, in 1945 it was housed in the Baroque
mansion in Opatička 8, and in 1947 it got its present placement in the renovated former
convent of the order of St. Clare (18th century), in the tower of Popov toranj (13th century) and Zakmardi's granary (17th century). There are three more collections within the
Zagreb City Museum: the apartment of the architect Viktor Kovačić in Masarykova
street 21, the collection by Cata Dujšin and Ivan Ribar in Demetrova street 3, and the
Collection by Rudolf and Margarita Matz in Mesnička street 15.

Reconstruction of the old portal of the Zagreb cathedral that
Kozma Müller made in 1640
on the commission of Bishop
B. Vinković.

Tarok cards with Zagreb motives

☎ 01 485 13 58

🖥 www.mdc.hr/mgz

🕐 Tue-Fri 10 a.m. - 6 p.m.
   Sat-sun 10 a.m. - 1 p.m.

☞ with prior announcement

The Zagreb City Museum

Certificate of an honourable citizen of Zagreb for August Šenoa, 1881

Target from Zagreb shooting gallery

Slavoljub Penkala (1871 - 1922)

Penkala was the engineer, one of the most significant innovators from the beginning of the 20th century. He obtained his doctor degree in Dresden and settled in Zagreb afterwards, where his brilliant career started.

His work consists of 70 to 80 innovations in the fields of mechanics, chemistry, physics, aeronautics (aviation) etc. Already in 1903 he patented "hot-water-bottle" and a few years later the first mechanical pencil in the world and first ink-pen with solid ink. Since the market demand increased, he started working with Edmund Moster and they jointly opened a factory and a joint stock company.

The coat-of-arms of the Ilyrian movement on the Ljudevit Gaj's travel bag, 19th century

The content of the Museum (approximately 74 000 articles) is classified into 12 collections showing the culture and history of Zagreb, and the excavations in the place of the museum (1991-1995) generated the archeological collection.

The collection of pictures and views is the largest in size. The articles connected to life of the dual town (the church Kaptol and civil Gradec) are especially emphasised: the oldest town flag from the end of the 18th century, the town coat-of-arms and the mayor's festive chain from the end of the 19th century, stone sculptures from the portal of the old cathedral, statues and altars from the

The archaeological findings in the Museum cellars

cathedral before Bollé's renovation (1900 - 1902), baroque furnishings from St. Mark's parish church. In the exhibition in 1997 the cultural and historical background of Zagreb was presented chronologically and thematically. There were 45 themes (from rarities to common ones, from artistic to popular) showing the life from the pre-history up to the present. The collections donated to Zagreb make a special whole (the room of the composer Ivan pl. Zajec, part of the August Šenoa's working room, the inheritance of the actress Tilla Durieux, mechanical music machines of the collector Ivan Geresdorfer).

Findings at the site

The archaeological material in situ (on finding site) is a first class sensation and probably the world rarity. By the reconstruction of the findings - the Hallstatt house from the 7th century BC is marked in the groundplan preserved at the site (1.5 m under the level of present floor). The glass showcases exhibit the articles of everyday use (ceramic dishes for food storage and preparation, decorative buckles, pearls, votive items - statuettes). In the vaulted room, former storage, the blacksmith's workshop from the early Iron Age has been reconstructed in site (La Tén culture, 1st century BC),

Felitian's charter from 1134

and the showcases display the original items found at the exact place. The medieval wall has also been preserved (from 679 with visible way of the building of the time). Over the bridge, above the archaeological site, the visitor mounts towards the scheme of the historical period and returns to the found level of the monastery floor from the end of the 18th century.

First trace of Zagreb

The foundation of Zagreb bishopric, as one of the most important events in

The Golden Bull from 1242

The oldest Gradec flag from the beginning of the 18th century

was erected) and to the bishop Kažotić. He was educated Dominican from the noble family from Trogir, who studied at Paris University and worked as professor in Italy, France and Croatia. His picture can be found in the room (Johan Jacobe, 1747).

impressive festive chain of the mayor according to the design of H. Bollé, made by the jeweller Slavoljub Bulvan (1902) and other. The new, blue flag from 1902 with new coat-of-arms (coat of arms

The mask of shame, cast iron, 17th century, used for punishment of market-women

the history of Zagreb, has been noted on the enlarged copy of Felitian's charter (issued on April 26, 1134). This document mentioned Zagreb for the first time in the history (in form of Zagrabiensem episcopatum). Namely, the charter indirectly stated that in 1094 Croatian and Hungarian king Ladislas I Arpadović had founded the Zagreb bishopric.
In the hall there is also the crown of the stone well, erected by the Zagreb bishop Maximilian Vrhovac as memorial to blessed Augustin Kažotić who, at the beginning of the 14th century, during drought years prayed for water from the God, and scratched the soil; that is the most frequent legend about the town's name, linked to that spring (above which the crown

Town signs

The town signs (coat-of-arms, flag, seals, public acknowledgements - certificates) talk about tradition and symbols of town honour of free royal town of Zagreb.
The hall is ornamented with the oldest stone coat-of-arms from 1449, Gradec seal at the turn of 14 to 15 century, the picture of St. Blasius, the protector of Gradec (the town judge, the mayor Adam Ballogh had got it painted at his own cost), and artistically

The mayor's chain of honour, after the design of Herman Bollé, made by the jeweller Slavoljub Bulva

with three towers, crescent moon and star, that appeared already in the 13 century), was confirmed in 1896: on the blue shield there are three towers with the open town gate (the symbol of hospitality and freedom of citizens), on the left is the crescent moon, and on the right the six pointed star. Since then, blue has been the official Zagreb colour.

⑳ MESNIČKA ULICA
MESNIČKA ULICA

Mesnička street on the west side leads to the Upper town. It got its name in the Middle Ages after the butcher shops placed there. At the beginning it stretched to the town gate; until the 19th century was at the intersection with Streljačka street. There was a ditch in front of the gate, so there was a bridge over it, the biggest at the time. After the defence walls had been pulled down, the Pongratz house with the park was built at that place, the masterwork of Janko J. Jambrišak (1834-1892). Some famous people lived and worked in the houses in Mesnička street, as could be seen from the memory plates on the houses' facades. Thus the poet and novelist August Šenoa (1838 -1881) lived at number 34, the historian Tadija Smičiklas (1843 - 1914) at number 35, and from 1871 until 1873, the *father of the homeland* Ante Starčević (1823 - 1896) at number 19. At the intersection of Mesnička street and Ilica

Andrija Kačić Miošić

there is a monument to a Croatian poet, Franciscan priest Andrija Kačić Miošić (1704 - 1760), the author of the most popular national book *The pleasant conversation of the Slavic people*.

㉛ RADIĆEVA ULICA
RADIĆEVA ULICA

Radić street is a nice, slightly steep street leading from the Ban Jelačić Square towards the Upper Town coming from the east. It was named after the Croatian national representative Pavle Radić (1880 - 1928), killed in Belgrade parliament in 1928. Once this street was the business center of the town, with many business institutions. In 1880 the building of the first Croatian savings bank was built (at number 30). From the 18th century the street developed quickly because many settlers came, mostly foreigners. It got its final appearance in the second half of the 19th century. The great Croatian writer Miroslav Krleža (1893 - 1981) was born in this street, at number 7. The most interesting mansion in the street is the Classicist style mansion Domitrović/Demötörfy (at number 32) designed in 1830 by the architect Bartol Felbinger (1785 - 1871).

St. George

View on Radić street

Kaptol

Kaptol, the bishop's seat, is the second part of the medieval core of Zagreb. It is situated on the prolonged hill plateau, east of the Medveščak stream, today's Tkalčić street. Life in this place existed long before Felitian's charter but that document is considered to be the first written trace mentioning the foundation of the diocese during the stay of king Ladislas in the region, most likely in 1904. The first Zagreb cathedral dedicated to St. Stephen the king was built on Kaptol, but was destroyed in 1242 during Tatar invasion. At the same site the new one was built, a representative building modelled on the French cathedrals of the time that changed its appearance during the course of time. In the 16th century, due to the fear from Turks, the defence walls were erected around the cathedral, and the whole Kaptol was fortified. At the outskirts of the settlement the Church of St. Mary was built and the Franciscan monastery, thus the whole looked like a medieval town. When the Turkish threat ceased, Kaptol began to open and change. Its suburbs developed faster, especially those towards the east, towards Budapest and Vienna. Part of the old settlement was pulled down at the beginning of the 20th century and the Dolac market was built instead. The Zagreb bishopric gradually grew into archbishopric and became the leading church institution in Croatia. Its archbishops have been regularly chosen to cardinal assembly since 19th century.

❶ Bakač street / Bakačeva ulica
❷ Kaptol
❸ Cathedral / Katedrala
❹ Comedy Theatre / Kazalište Komedija
❺ Dolac
❻ St. Mary's Church / Crkva sv. Marije
❼ Skalinska street / Skalinska ulica
❽ Opatovina
❾ St. Francis of Assis Church/ Crkva sv. Franje Asiškog
❿ Opatovina park / Park Opatovina
⓫ Tkalčić Street / Tkalčićeva ulica
⓬ Bloody bridge / Krvavi most
⓭ ULUPUH Gallery / Galerija ULUPUH
⓮ Monument to Marija Jurić Zagorka / Spomenik Mariji Jurić Zagorki
⓯ Ribnjak
⓰ Old Vlaška street / Stara Vlaška

200 M

WALK THROUGH
Kaptol

The Comedy Theatre is one of the most popular Zagreb theatres.

The church of St. Francis d'Assis built in gothic style is considered one of the most mature Franciscan sacral buildings of the Central European circle. On its main, neo-gothic altar there is the painting of St. Francis, by Celestin Medović, and in the apses the stained glass windows by Ivo Dulčić.

Opatovina (the Abbey) was named after Cistercian monastery next to the church of St. Mary on Dolac. The street was built with a plan in the 15th century and had kept its pictur-esque appearance for a long time. On its north edge is the park of the same name.

St. Mary Church is at the place of church mentioned already in the 13th century. It is also on the oldest preserved pic-torial presentation of Zagreb (16th century). In the middle of the 18th century, the church was thoroughly reconstructed and broadened, and then the bell tower with baroque top was built. By the end of the 19th century, during the renova-tion of the cathedral, the Zagreb archbish-ops held masses in the church.

OPATOVINA

SKALINSKA

Dolac is the largest and the most popular market in Zagreb. It was opened in 1930, after the great reconstruction of this part of the town. It was on several occa-sions arranged and renovated later, and is considered to be one of the finest and most attractive markets of the European metropolises.

Kaptol is also the square in front of the cathedral and the street leading from the square towards the north. On both sides of Kaptol there is a line of canons' houses, *kurije*, among which the finest is the house of Toma Kovačević, erected in 1710 (at number 8).

The Ribnjak park is named after the bishopric ponds that existed here until the reconstruction in the 19th century. The pond was then transformed into the English type garden, with waterfalls, exotic plants and decorative statues. There is also a monument to the poet Ivan Goran Kovačić.

The Archbishop's palace, the seat of the Zagreb archbishop, in the rearranged part of the fortress around the cathedral.

The Cathedral of the Assumption of the Holy Virgin Mary, its present appearance attained at the end of the 19th century when it was reconstructed in neo-gothic style according to Hermann Bollé's design. Its bell towers are 105 m high and are the tallest constructions in town. They are also one of the symbols of contemporary Zagreb. The walls around the cathedral date from the end of the Middle Ages when they were erected in fear of the Turks.

The statue of the Holy Virgin Mary, the work of sculptor Anton Dominik Fernkorn from 1873.

Petrica Kerempuh, people's tribune and a rogue used in works of many Croatian artists. This statute is the work of the sculptor Vanja Radauš (1906 - 1973).

❶ Bakač Street
Bakačeva ulica

Bakač street is a small street connecting Ban Jelačić Square with Kaptol. Once it ended at Down or South street at the crossing with Vlaška street, pulled down in the 19th century. It was named after the Zagreb bishop Toma Bakač (1435 - 1521) who became bishop of Zagreb in 1511. His main task was to prepare the works around the construction of defence walls around Kaptol. The walls were erected in 1520 and they resisted the two-month attack during the

Kaptol

Bakač street

civil war between the followers of Ferdinand Habsburg and Ivan Zapolja. Toma Bakač governed the bishopric until 1518, soon after the round tower in front of the cathedral was built, named after him. The tower was pulled down in 1906 for the opening of the view to the portal of the neo-goth-ic cathedral, and the stone from the Bakač tower was built in the dike at the left bank of the Sava river. It is interesting that electric tramway was driving through that street connecting the main square with the main town cemetery on Mirogoj.

❷ Kaptol

The name Kaptol today refers to the square in front of the cathedral and the street leading towards the north. In the Middle Ages the church servants, canons and others lived here, thus it was called *Capitulum*, the *Assembly of Canons*. The cathedral dominates Kaptol as well as the whole view on Zagreb. In front of the cathedral, at the Kaptol square, there is the statue of the Holy Virgin Mary with four angels, work of Viennese sculptor Anton Dominik Fernkorn from 1873. Once the square was much smaller because the Bakač tower with the wall was in front of the cathedral. They were pulled down in 1906 in order to open the view on the newly renovated cathedral front. On both sides of the Kaptol street there were canon houses, around thirty smaller mansions belonging to the canons of the Zagreb bishopric. Those preserved date from the period between 15th and 18th century. They are mostly baroque style with gardens and courtyards. The oldest are the *Lector's kurija* from 1498 (at number 27) and the *Prepozit's kurija*, from the end of the 16th century (at number 7).

Detail from the statue of the Holly Virgin Mary

The most beautiful is the house of Toma Kovačević, erected in 1710 (at number 8). In the house is the seat of the most famous Croatian religious paper - *Glas Koncila*.

❸ THE CATHEDRAL OF THE ASSUMPTION OF THE HOLY VIRGIN MARY
KATEDRALA UZNESENJA BLAŽENE DJEVICE MARIJE
See pages 86-91

❹ THE COMEDY THEATRE
KAZALIŠTE KOMEDIJA
Kaptol 9
℡ 01 481 21 79
🖳 www.komedija.com

The *Comedy* theatre was founded in 1950, and its main activities are musical and theatrical performances. The artistic ensemble of the theatre, along with actors and actors-singers, include singers, choir, ballet and orchestra. Among the famous Comedy's hits are a musical Jalta. Jalta and a rock-opera *Gubec beg and The Witch from the Grič*.

The Dolac Market

❺ DOLAC
🕐 6 a.m. - 2 p.m.
Sat 6 a.m. - 3 p.m.
Sun and holidays
6 a.m. - 12 p.m.

Dolac is the largest and the most popular market in Zagreb. It is situated at the place of the former

The *Comedy* Theatre

town settlement of the same name, pulled down in 1925, in order to free the Ban Jelačić Square from the trading function and transform it into town square. The new market on Dolac was opened in 1930, and was afterwards arranged, renovated and reconstructed, so today it is one of the finest and most attractive markets in the European metropolises. Trading on the market is performed indoors and outdoors. The offer is rich and diverse, from fresh sea fish and *frutti di mare*, to quality meat and its products, fresh fruits and vegetables and dairy products, in the indoor space the well known Zagreb speciality fresh cottage cheese and fresh cream. On working days, at least 50 000 people visit the market, and on Saturdays twice as many.

❸ CATHEDRAL OF THE ASSUMPTION OF THE HOLY VIRGIN MARY

KATEDRALA UZNESENJA BLAŽENE DJEVICE MARIJE

Kaptol 31

Cathedral in numbers
- Length 77 m
- Width 46 m
- Towers' height 105 m
- can receive 5 000 believers
- 5 bells (the biggest weighs 5700

The Zagreb cathedral is the most monumental and the richest Gothic style architectural sacral building at the south east of the Alps. The shrine groundplan, slender cross ribbed vaults within the three polygonal apses opened with narrow windows, the cathedral reminds of the French solutions (town of Troyes). With detailed subsequently erected naves of balanced height it corresponds to construction solutions of the contemporary German building, while the imaginative sculpture reflects touches with Czech schools. It all shows not only the early penetration of Gothic style to the north of Croatia and internationalisation of art, but also the importance of Zagreb bishopric of the time and the reputation and power of its bishops.

From its beginnings the cathedral was dedicated to the Holy Virgin Mary, the Assumption of Mary (people call it Velika Gospa). St. Stephen, the Hungarian king, though often pointed out as the primary, actually is the second patron.

① 01 481 47 27
🕐 Mon - Sat 10 a.m. - 5 p.m.
    Sun 1 p.m. - 5 p.m.
☞ with prior announcement

The cathedral of the Assumption of the Holy Virgin Mary (drawing)

The cathedral front with two bell towers (105 m high) constructed according to the design of H. Bollé, is the key orientation point and symbol of Zagreb. The picture was taken before the tower in front was pulled down.

Marble pulpit by Michael Cusse from 1695. It was the first marble furniture of the cathedral, commissioned by canon and curator Ivan Znika.

Wing altar from the sacristy, central composition is the Crucifixion on Golgotha, attributed to young Albrecht Dürer during his stay in Venice in 1495

Fresco from St. Stephen Chapel - the vault fields with scenes of Christ eternal dignity, Rimini school, 14th century

The Zagreb archbishopric is one of the crucial town institutions. For centuries it was a bishopric, and in the middle of 19th century it became the archbishopric. Zagreb cathedral is one of the symbols of the archbishopric and the town.

The history of Zagreb archbishopric

The Zagreb bishopric was founded in the 11th century by king Ladislas, under Ostrogon metropolis. At the end of the 12th century it became a part of the Kalok's metropolis and stayed within it until the independence in the middle of 19th century. Separation from Hungarian metropolis and creation of Croatian and Slavic ecclesiastical region had enormous political significance. After the departure of the Turks in 1699, the bishopric underwent big territorial changes. It lost the Hungarian part of its territory and the western Bosnia, but got Slavonia. Already in Middle Ages the bishops were engaged in social life. In the Middle Ages Kaptol became the centre of high education in Croatia, and even today Catholic Theological Faculty and the Jesuit Faculty of Philosophy are its integral parts.

The history of the cathedral building

It is most likely that King Ladislas (1040 - 1095) did not build the new cathedral after the foundation of

Zagreb bishopric, but nominated the existing one for the cathedral. It was only

The constructor shows the design of the cathedral to King Ladislav

after his death that the construction of the new cathedral began. The cathedral was finished in 1217, and King Andrew II (1205 - 1235) consecrated it on his way to V. Crusade. Already in 1242 the Tatars destroyed the newly built cathedral, so the bishop Stephen II (1225 - 1247) had a chapel of St. Stephen, the First Christian Martyr, erected for cathedral mass service. That building of Romanesque and Gothic forms has been built into the Archbishopric consistory table. Bishop Timothy (1263- 1287) started the construction of the new,

monumental cathedral with integrated remnants of the pre-Tataric cathedral, and was dedicated to St. Stephen the Hungarian king. He managed to build the central and two side apses with altars and the sacristy. The sacristy frescos (the most interesting - St. Kvirin between St. Dominic and St. Francis) are most likely from the time of bishop Augustin Kažotić (1303 - 1322). Bishop Eberhard (1397 - 1406 and 1410 - 1419) has merit for the building of the three church naves (proved by his bishop coat-of-arms on the walls and pillars), and during bishop Osvald Thuz (1466 - 1499) the whole building was roofed. It was at that period that the bell tower on the south side of the front started being built, and was finished only in the 17th century, in renaissance and baroque style. Due to Turkish threat, bishop Thuz began the construction of cathedral fortifications. The construction lasted until 1517 when it was finished by the head of Zagreb bishopric, Ostrogon archbishop Toma Bakač. He erected a tower in front of the cathedral entrance that was named after him, Bakač tower. It was pulled down during the last reconstruction of the cathedral in 1906. During the 17th century, the cathedral was destroyed by fire on several

The drawing of the old cathedral front

occasions, but during each reconstruction its interior was enriched with valuable inventory. For example, baroque altars (wooden and marble) and pulpit by sculptor Mihael Cusse which is still in the central nave. The cathedral interior was decorated later as well. Bishop Aleksandar Alagović (1829 - 1837) provided the painting of the Assumption of Mary that was placed on the main altar, and the choir. Archbishop Juraj Haulik (1837 - 1869) removed the altar painting (he sold it to parish church in Pregrada), and erected the neo-gothic style altar instead. Besides he procured church-organs in 1855 (three manuals and a pedal, and 53 registers), made by Walcker company from Ludwigsburg. The architecture of the organ closet has neo-gothic traits. Finally, Haulik got the shrine windows painted. Those are the oldest stained-glass windows in Croatia. In the attempt to

return to the cathedral its primary appearance, Viennese professor of Architecture Friedrich Schmidt was invited to Zagreb who took his student Hermann Bollé with him. However, the disastrous earthquake in 1880 severely damaged the cathedral. Thus the Cathedral was not only reconstructed but was also given some interior neo-gothic characteristics, according to the Hermann Bollé's design. It was especially obvious in the shape of the façade and two neo-gothic bell towers (105 m high), in 1902 they defined the present appearance of the cathedral. During the last 30 years, many comprehensive construction works on the cathedral were performed. Because the non-quality stone (from Zagreb quarries Vrapče and Bizek) was used for Bollé's reconstruction (due to economic reasons and proximity of quarry) mostly for new bell towers and west front, soon they started dilapidating under atmospheric influence, particularly air pollution (smog and chemicals). It was primarily observed on the cathedral front and stone plastic (e. g. small towers) that gradually became unrecognisable. The first reconstruction of the part of the south belltower started in 1938 (The Communists interrupted it); it was continued in

1968 when the top of the north bell tower was reconstructed, and then, mostly with donations by Croatian emigrants, the ruined roof was completely replaced with copper plates. In 1987, Archbishop Franjo Kuharić founded the Zagreb Archbishop Committee for the reconstruction of the cathedral, and a narrower working team of chosen experts. Soon the Committee for Reconstruction Progress was founded as well and included science and art institutions, municipal and state authorities. After the choice of architects and performers of reconstruction and preservation

Herman Bollé next to the completed cathedral bell-tower

works, the renovation started in 1990. Since then it has been carried out in phases and according to the priorities, and since 1999 the Committee occasionally issues the journal Our Cathedral, reporting on complex reconstruction works.

*C*athedral Treasury, old as the bishopric, the world significant cultural institution, among the most famous world institutions of the type (with Treasuries in Köln, Reims and Milan). Former cathedral defence wall has been rearranged into archbishop hall and is among the most interesting bishop seats in Europe.

14th century Gylay's mitre; refurbished in 1549 for the bishop W. Bylay. Silk background, pearls and precious stones in gold, golden panels with relief scenes. Origin: Croatia or Salzburg area.

The Cathedral Treasury

The treasury has been formed during eight centuries, collecting and carefully keeping its treasure. It is an important cultural and historical source for research of Croatian history. The Treasury objects consist of church clothing and vessels, liturgy codex and other church books and historical documents. The placement of the treasury during pre-Tataric period was not known. The historical documents were moved to Rab, while many were ruined, and since bishop Timothy and the construction of Zagreb cathedral, the treasury has been kept in the so-called inner sacristy. Some more valuable codex and archives are placed in the same room, with the treasury. In 1870, the canon-curator had had a special room arranged above the inner sacristy, where it still exists. Inappropriate space, old and unpractical closets and the lack of all technical standards of modern museology practice needed a better placement of the most important Zagreb collection. The Cathedral Inventories are of particular importance for the learning about treasury objects. Those are official lists of all objects in the cathedral and all its property. They were regularly created when the duty was passed to another canon - curator. Thus the lists show us what cathedral, and treasury possessed at particular time. The oldest preserved inventory dates from 1394 (published in 1951). From the later inventories those created up to 1526 (John the Baptist Tkalčić) have been published while the rest waits for its turn. Fabric valuables of the cathedral treasury consist of sacral clothing from the 11th century (Ladislav's cloak) up to domestic monastery works stretching to contemporary period (work of Sisters of Charity and order of St. Ursula) which give modern artistic expression to the field of textile art. The cathedral treasury has also a large number of objects of church golden decorations created in the 12th century (small cross of bishop Mathian), historicism style objects (crucifixes, eternal lights, ciborium) created after the design by Hermann Bollé from the end of the 19th century. The Metropolitan Library dates from the 11th century

God's Tomb by J. W. Stoll from 1659. The sarcophagus frame is covered with wooden plates covered with embroidered silk (158x204x80). Relief golden embroidery and multy-colored silk embroidery

when the first bishop, Duh, of Czech origins, brought the necessary liturgical books. It is difficult to say when it became the library in its proper sense but already in the first preserved Cathedral Inventory from 1394 more than 100 manuscripts was registered. It flourished during the bishop Aleksandar Mikulić (1688 - 1694) when the foundation for book purchase was established and the valuable library of Johann Wikhard Valvasor was bought. Motropolitana keeps the largest number of incunabulas in Croatia (253).

The festive Bible of the Zagreb cathedral, illuminated manuscript from the 14th century, parchment, 369x246 mm, Gothic letters. It is decorated with 156 miniatures and initials and marginal golden decorations

The Archbishop Hall

In Middle Ages the stone building pulled down at the beginning of the 16th century was used as Bishop's palace, and afterwards it was moved to south fortification tower. The hall was renovated by bishop Šimun Bratulić (1603 - 1611), and bishop Petar Domitrović built in 1619 a new wing to the old hall up to southwest tower called Nebojan. This renaissance palace was destroyed by fires in 1624 and 1645. In 1729 bishop Juraj Branjug built new wings to the existing palace, in the place of St. Stephen chapel and the old hall towards the east up to southeast tower and along the east defence wall up to the big rectangular tower. By additional building the palace became the biggest baroque castle in Croatia. The palace walls were opened with rows of baroque windows, the existing old towers were rearranged for living, and the new building included the two new wings by a row of pilasters. At the courtyard side the palace is opened by arcades in the ground floor, and the arcades on the first and second floor are closed. The interior has a lot of rooms and halls and the representative baroque stairs next to St. Stephen

Monstrance, Hans Georg Pfisterer, Graz, 1738. Baroque shaped - gilded silver, cast, beaten, engraved, precious stones, enamel (height 70cm). The upper part is richly decorated and made in sunny monstrance manner

chapel. The last additional building of the bishop palace was made by the bishop Aleksandar Alagović in 1833, by prolonging the palace on the east side up to the northeast tower. On the south side of the castle, the ponds are transformed into the Bishop's garden.

Missal of Juraj Topuski, illuminated manuscript. Zagreb around 1495, seventeen pages illustrated by Ioannes-Hans Alemanus (two signatures preserved), some of 35 renaissance miniatures are thought to be made by J. Klović

6 ST. MARY'S CHURCH
CRKVA SV. MARIJE

Dolac 2
☎ 01 481 49 59
🕐 7.30 a.m. - 12.p.m.

It was at first a monastery church then from the beginning of 16th century, a parish church. It was built on a plateau that in terraces descends towards the former Kaptol suburbs. The chapel at the same place and of the same name was mentioned already in 13th century, which is the church that belonged to Cistercian Order, who had a monastery and bathing place on their own land near the Potok (today's Tkalčić Street). At the beginning of the 16th

The interior of St. Mary's Church

The front of St. Mary's Church

century, the Cistercian order disappeared, and the church of St. Mary became a parish church. In the oldest preserved view of Zagreb (16th century) the church was near the west Kaptol wall and was rather small compared to the cathedral. The small gothic a church with tower on east side was gradually broadened in the middle of the 18th century into three nave building with bell tower on the north side. The west

entrance to the church with the stairs was made at the end of the18th century, but the smaller entrance with baroque portal on the east side was mainly used. The main marble altar with statues of St. Peter and St. Paul and angels was placed in 1768. The fresco behind it in the shrine was painted by Slovene painters, father and son, Franc and Krištof Jelovšek. On the four altars in the naves (1772 - 1773) next to marble saints statues, there were altar paintings of the Slovene painter Anton Cebej, but only one has been preserved, *Reverence of the three Holly Kings*. The statues on all altars and the relief on the pulpit are made by the painter and builder Franjo Rottman from Ljubljana. The pulpit is decorated with big relief showing the preaching of St. John the Baptist. The church was spared during the big fire in 1880, so it was used for mass services instead of the severely damaged cathedral, during its reparations. At present, St. Mary church is

surrounded by modern buildings, built after the arrangement of Dolac in 1925, when Cistercian monastery was also pulled down.

7 SKALINSKA STREET
SKALINSKA ULICA

Skalinska street is a short, lively street connecting Opatovina and Tkalčić street. It gives a wonderful view on the Cathedral towers, the sight captured by many artists. It got its name after the stairs (scalarum) that led to Small gate, which was used as exit from Kaptol to

Skalinska street

Potok and Upper Town. Beside the gate, placed in the middle of the street, there was a tower, pulled down in the second half of the 19th century. The gate and the stairs also disappeared but the name of the street has been preserved.

❽ OPATOVINA

Opatovina (the Abbey) was named after the abbot of Cistercian monastery, who lived by St. Mary Church on Dolac. From the 15th century the settlement was planned here with houses leaning to the west Kaptol wall. Wooden houses were severely damaged in the great fire in 1731 and thereafter only the houses of bricks or stone were built. For a long time Opatovina kept

Petrica Kerempuh

its medieval street appearance, with baroque houses but a part of the buildings was pulled down for the new market dolac. On the south part of Opatovina, at Dolac, there is a statue of Petrica Kerempuh, by sculptor Vanja Radauš (1906 - 1973). Petrica Kerempuh was people's tribune, a rogue and cynical comedian described by many Croatian artists. The most famous are *The Ballads by Petrica*

Kerempuh by Miroslav Krleža (1893 - 1981).

❾ CHURCH OF ST. FRANCIS OF ASSISI
CRKVA SV. FRANJE ASIŠKOG

Kaptol 9
☎ 01 481 11 25
🕐 6 a.m.-12 p.m.and
  5 p.m. - 8 p.m.

The monastery church and the church of the same name are situated at the northwest side of the Kaptol square, at the place where the street narrows and goes further to the north. The monumental church was built in the 13th century, but it is possible that Franciscans had had their residence at that place even earlier. The interior Gothic structure of one nave church with a long choir stalls and elongated shrine has not been significantly changed and is considered in spatial terms one of the most mature Franciscan sacral buildings of the Central European circle. It has cross ribbed vaults. The chapel of St. Francis of Assisi is decorated with painted cartouche with scenes from saints' lives and plastically expressed plant motives and angels. The early baroque cycle of stuc-

The Church of St. Francis
d'Assisi

co-decorations with mannerism mixtures was made in 1683. The church and the monastery were thoroughly renovated after the 1880 earthquake when the original gothic character was tried to be achieved. The church then got the new high bell tower with pointed roof. During the renovation from the Kaptol side of the church, the open chapel of Crucified Jesus was also arranged. At the south side of the monastery, between Kaptol and Opatovina, the construction of so-called Franciscan hall started in 1936 (today, the Comedy Theatre). In the church, there was the painting of St. Francis on the main neo-gothic altar, by Celestin Medović. The apse stained-glass windows with motives inspired by St. Francis's flowers are the work of the painter Ivo Dulčić from 1960.

❿ Opatovina Park

Six gardens, belonging to canon houses on Kaptol, stretched to the west Kaptol wall, and after the World War II they were transformed into the public promenade. The west Kaptol wall is well seen in this park. It is built of irregular stones, and it is 65-70 cm thick. In the north-west corner of the park there is the best preserved four side Kaptol tower, called the Prišlin tower. It belonged to house at num-

Tkalčić Street

The Prišlin tower

ber 15 on Kaptol. From the Prišlin tower, the north Kaptol wall stretches to the Kaptol street. During the summer the stage is put in the park where theatrical performances are held.

⓫ Tkalčić Street
Tkalčićeva ulica

The ancient Tkalčić street, *the old Tkalča*, as Zagreb citizens popularly call it, today pulses with contemporary city life. Numerous cafes, restaurants and inns in the old, lovely houses make special atmosphere particularly during hot summer evenings when numerous terraces are fully alive. Once the stream Medveščak flew through the present street, whose bed divided Gradec and Kaptol. In the middle of the 17th century, the Gradec inhabitants were allowed to build houses on the west bank of the stream but not on the east one yet, belonging to Kaptol. Once the channel was digged up by the Medveščak stream. The mills worked on it. By the end of the 19th century, the stream was moved from the street and the street was left to ruins until gradual but complete reconstruction in the second half of the 20th century.

⓬ Bloody Bridge
Krvavi most

Bloody bridge is the short and lovely street with a terrifying name, evoking its troubled history. On the stream Medveščak, that divided citizens' Gradec and Bishopric Kaptol, once there was Pisani bridge. During centuries many claimants to the throne fiercely struggled, and since Gradec and Kaptol usually were on the oppo-

Bloody Bridge

site sides, it was the ideal point of attack or defence. But the exact moment of Pisani bridge turning into Bloody bridge is not known, because there were many occasions for changing its name, due to frequent fights. After the regulation of the Medveščak stream, Bloody bridge was pulled down in 1899, and the only reminder is the name of the small street connecting Radić and Tkalčić streets. It is worth mentioning that in the house at number 2, in

The ULUPUH Gallery

1887, the first Zagreb telephone exchange started working.

⑬ ULUPUH GALLERY

Tkalčićeva ulica 14
☎ 01 481 37 46
🖥 www.ulupuh.hr
🕐 Mon - Fri 10 a.m - 1 p.m.
   and 5 p.m. - 8 p.m.
   Sat 10 a.m. - 2 p.m.

ULUPUH is the Croatian Association of Applied Arts gathering the most important

artists in seventeen different sections: ceramics, graphic design, photography, industrial design, textile design, fashion design, theatrical and cinema art, jewellery design, architecture, horticulture, applied painting, caricature and animated film study, renovation and multi-media section. Each year ULUPUH organises about twenty exhibitions and Zagreb Salon, the annual exhibition of modern Croatin plastic art creations. Besides, every three years ULUPUH organises the International Graphic design and visual Communication Exhibition - ZGRAF and *The International Small Ceramics Triennial*, the largest contemporary ceramics exhibition in the world according to number of countries represented at the exhibition.

⑭ THE STATUE OF MARIJA JURIĆ ZAGORKA
SPOMENIK MARIJI JURIĆ ZAGORKI

Marija Jurić Zagorka (1873 - 1957) peacefully observes the liveliness of today's Tkalčić Street. The sculptor Stjepan

The statue of Zagorka

Gračan is the author of the statue of the popular writer, the author of many exciting novels from the history of Zagreb and Croatia and the first female journalist in Croatia.

⑮ RIBNJAK (POND)

Ribnjak is the park stretching along the east walls of Kaptol. It was named after the bishopric ponds that existed here until the 19th

---

Marija Jurić Zagorka (1873 – 1957)

Marija Jurić (Zagorka is her pen-name) was the first Croatian female journalist and thus had to prove herself all her life. She was born in w e a l t h y

family, and at school excelled with her intelligence and talent. On recommendation of bishop Strossmayer, she became the member of editorial board of the paper *Obzor*, and she initiated and edited the first Croatian journal exclusively for women, *Woman's Paper* and later *The Croatian Woman*. As a writer she created novels with love plots and national themes. *The Witch of Grich*, *Gordana* and other Zagorka's novels were extremely popular at that time, but even today are well read.

The Ribnjak Park

century. Then the whole area was transformed into an English type garden, with waterfalls, exotic plants and decorative statues. It was bishop Alagović who, in 1829, initiated the arrangement of the park. Ribnjak was to become the park of sculptures as well but the idea was never fully realised. At the moment it has only two monuments, *Shame* by Antun Augustinčić, and the monument to Croatian poet Ivan Goran Kovačić. Today, the park covers the area of almost 40 000 square meters and has thirty year old yew, old plant of Atlas cedar-tree, many magnolia trees and liquidambars. The street along the east side of the park Ribnjak bears the same name.

August Šenoa (1838 – 1881)

August Šenoa was a poet, short-story writer and novelist. He was born in middle class-craft family. His father was Czech, and mother Slovaque. He started writing songs when he was in primary school, but in German. He started studying in Zagreb, and then in 1859, supported by bishop Strossmayer continued his law studies in Prague, but he never finished them. He returned to Zagreb in 1866 and soon became the editor of Vijenac, vice president of the Croatian Cultural Society and town senator. In 1871 Šenoa wrote the first modern Croatian artistic novel The Goldsmith's Treasure, and later he wrote *The Peasant's Revolt, The Curse, Beggar Luka* and others. Exhausted by public and literary work, after the 1880 earthquake he got sick and died, at his creative peak.

⓰ THE OLD VLAŠKA STREET
STARA VLAŠKA

Vlaška is among the oldest streets in town. In its way it shows how Zagreb grew and developed. The west part of the street, the Old Vlaška, is among the oldest in Zagreb, while the part going towards the east is a modern traffic and trade *artery*. Its name (Vicus Latinorum) reveals its inhabitants of Roman origins who settled the Kaptol hill in the Middle Ages. At that time, the Italians were called Vlahi, Vlaki or Laki, and Vlah in general meant every foreigner. There are several old houses preserved in Old Vlaška street. Once the Home for Poor Students was there, situated by former bishopric almshouse, and warm water bathing place (at number 47), getting the water from thermal source in Ribnjak. At the crossing of old part of Vlaška street and Branjug street there is a statue erected to Croatian writer August Šenoa (1838 - 1881), a work by sculptor Marija Ujević Galetović.

Statue of Šenoa

Old Vlaška street

Down Town

ARHEOLOG
DON FRANE BULI

Down Town is the third part of the historical core of Zagreb, built according to the plan in the second half of the 19th century. The citizens of Zagreb had at their disposal a huge empty area with a road here and there connecting the town with the Sava river and villages on its banks. That favourable situation was well used, and the town grew there with regular blocks of buildings and orthogonal streets successfully interpolated into the existent communication net. Care was taken of integral town parts, therefore numerous parks were created, representative palaces and culture shrines. The north border of the Down Town was Ban Jelačić Square with its extensions, Ilica street to the west and Jurišić street to the east, while it stretched to the south up to railway trails. The west and the east outskirts of Down Town were present Drašković street and the Republic of Austria street. They were planned for the military barracks, but only one on the west was built, the Rudolf's barracks. The central part of the Down Town was reserved for the *Green Horseshoe*, line of squares-parks gradually filled with mansions where the most important cultural and scientific institutions of the town and state were housed.

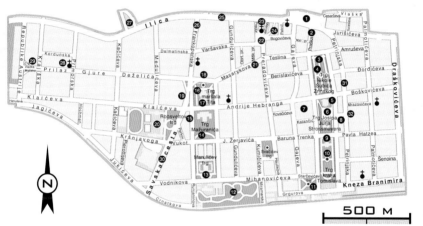

❶ Ban Jelačić Square / Trg bana Josipa Jelačića
❷ Praška street / Praška ulica
❸ Nikola Šubić Zrinski square / Trg Nikole Šubića Zrinskog
❹ Archaeological museum / Arheološki muzej
❺ Croatian Academy of Arts and Sciences / HAZU
❻ The Josip Juraj Strosmayer Square / Trg Josipa Jurja Strossmayera
❼ Modern Gallery / Moderna galerija
❽ Croatian Cultural Society / Matica Hrvatska
❾ Art Pavilion / Umjetnički paviljon
❿ King Tomislav Square / Trg kralja Tomislava
⓫ Ante Starčević Square / Trg Ante Starčevića
⓬ Botanical Garden / Botanički vrt
⓭ State Archives / Državni arhiv
⓮ Mažuranić Square / Trg Mažuranića
⓯ Ethnographic museum / Etnografski muzej
⓰ Marshall Tito Square / Trg maršala Tita
⓱ Croatian National Theatre / Hrvatsko narodno kazalište
⓲ Zagreb University / Zagrebačko sveučilište
⓳ Museum for Arts and Crafts / Muzej za umjetnost i obrt
⓴ The Mimara Museum / Muzej Mimara
㉑ Masaryk street / Masarykova ulica
㉒ Petar Preradović Square - Flower Square / Trg Petra Preradovića - Cvjetni trg
㉓ St. Transfiguration church / Crkva sv. Preobraženja
㉔ Octogon / Oktogon
㉕ Ilica / Ilica
㉖ Frankopan street / Frankopanska ulica
㉗ Britain Square / Britanski trg
㉘ St. Blasius Church / Crkva sv. Blaža
㉙ Rudolf's barracks / Rudolfova vojarna
㉚ Savska street / Savska cesta
㉛ Petrinja street / Petrinjska ulica
㉜ Basilica of Jesus Heart / Bazilika Srca Isusova

❶ BAN JOSIP JELAČIĆ SQUARE

TRG BANA JOSIPA JELAČIĆA

The most popular and the most spacious town square. At first it was called Manduševac (after the spring at its east side, at the place of a fountain), and then Harmica. Until the middle of the 19th century, it was the place of provincial fair and market, with a hospital and an inn at the south Side and a line of small houses at the north side. St. Mark's Square was always the centre of social and political events where in 1845 first victims fell. In the subsequent decades the situation changed fast. Ban Jelačić Square got three representative buildings on the north side, and in 1866 the monumental equestrian statue of the popular ban Josip Jelačić, work by Anton Dominik Fernkorn (1813 - 1878). The square named after the ban became the centre of social and political life, and nothing changed even when the monument was removed and divided into pieces during the World War II, and the square renamed in the Republic Square. The status of special place was confirmed in 1989 when the petition for return of the monument and the pop concert announced the arrival of changes.

The building of Croatia Insurance Company, the oldest insurance company in Zagreb

One of the first two-floor buildings that the architect Bartol Felbinger built for himself between 1827 and 1829

The building housing The European House was built in 1905-1906 by the architect Vjekoslav Bastl for the pharmacist Feller, innovator of the famous Elsa-fluid. The architect Peter Behrens (1869-1940) reshaped the front in 1928

The building of Assicurazioni Generali erected in Italian modernist style, work by the architect Marcello Piacentini (1881 - 1960). Today, besides apartments it houses many associations, the most famous being the Architect's Society

Josip Jelačić (1801 - 1859)

Josip Jelačić was very popular among the people because he advocated the key Croatian objectives: freedom, unity of Croatian provinces and equality among nations. He was appointed the Croatian ban in 1848. In that same year he abolished serfdom. When Hungarian hegemonists refused to accept Croatians as political nation, he went to war with his army. The war was undecided, but Međimurje was returned to Croatia. Austrian ruler Franz Joseph I, appointed him the governor of Osijek and Dalmatia so after a long time Croatia united under his rule. In 1849, together with Windischgratz he entered Budapest and terminated the Hungarian revolution threatening all non-Hungarian nations in Hungary. He also helped with foundation of Zagreb archbishopric, unification of Zagreb and opening of Croatian Theatre.

The Foundation block (Ilica, Gaj street, Bogović street and Petrić street) the special place of Croatian modernist movement to which the controversial skyscraper was later added. The first municipal hospital was at that place until 1931.

Popović House built in 1907 decorated with figural relief according to the project by Ivan Meštrović. It was his first public exhibit in Zagreb.

This building was built in 1889 by Đuro Gavella, the grandfather of famous theatre director Branko Gavella.

WALK THROUGH
Zrinjevac

Archaeological Museum is the most important museum in town. Its rich exhibits are presented in five collections. Especially valuable Egyptian collection should be pointed out as well as the longest written Etruscan inscription in the world and the extremely valuable numismatic collection.

Croatian Academy of Arts and Sciences is one of the basic municipal and state institutions. Housed in the only neo-renaissance palace in town. In the palace hall the Baška Tablet is kept, one of the oldest stone records in Croatian language written in glagolic script.

The monument to Josip Juraj Strossmayer erected in 1926, work by great Croatian sculptor Ivan Meštrović. Dedicated to bishop Strossmayer (1815-1905) the creator and patron of the Academy of Arts and Sciences.

Modern Gallery keeps the valuable collection of the Croatian works of art created between 1850 and 1950. Its holdings are based on several larger donations and purchase of important works of art, mostly of Croatian artists.

Statue of Starčević, Croatian politician who, following the break of Bach's absolutism, in 1861 declared in Rijeka his famous principles. They later became the basis of politics of the Right in Croatia and procured him the title of *Father of Homeland*.

The Esplanade Hotel
One of the finest Secession style buildings in Zagreb. It was built in 1925 and since then is known for its high service and famous guests. Among the others, the famous film directors Orson Welles, Francis Ford Copolla and the actor Kirk Douglas stayed in it.

The Gallery of Croats of merit on Zrinjevac, In the front plan is the bust of Ivan Mažuranić.

Croatian Cultural Society is the oldest Croatian cultural institution founded in the middle of the 19th century. It had enormous influence on social events during the 19th and 20th centuries. Numerous important persons were at the head of it, starting with its first president, count Janko Drašković (1770 1856).

The Art Pavilion the oldest exhibition facility in this part of Europe. It was built for big, representative exhibitions. The history of the pavilion is in a way the history of plastic art in Croatia, from the end of the 19th century up to the present. It was erected for the Croatian pavilion at the Millennium Exhibition in Budapest in 1896. After the exhibition the iron construction was moved to Zagreb, adjusted and opened in 1898.

Statue of king Tomislav by Croatian sculptor Robert Frangeš Mihanović (1872 - 1940). It was erected in 1947, and dedicated to medieval Croatian ruler Tomislav (910 - 928) who opposed the Hungarians and annexed these regions to his state, declaring himself a king.

Main Railway Station Built according to the design of Hungarian architect Ferenc Pfaff in 1892. The neo-classicist front is decorated with numerous sculptures and ornamentation.

❷ PRAŠKA STREET
PRAŠKA ULICA

Praška is a short street connecting the Ban Jelačić Square with Zrinjevac. At the time it was created in 1866, it was an elite street named after Mary Valerie, the daughter of the emperor Franz Joseph I, and later named after the Czech capital. In 1867 the synagogue was built in the street following the design of the architect Franjo Klein. During the fascist regime it was destroyed by order of municipal authorities. From Praška street one could reach the Gaj street through the passage built in 1938, and named Marić passage after the first oil family in Zagreb, the Mayer (Marić) family, who lived here.

The Zrinjevac fountain

❸ NIKOLA ŠUBIĆ ZRINSKI SQUARE
TRG NIKOLE ŠUBIĆA ZRINSKOG

The square was founded in 1826 as the public space for cattle fair. On occasion of celebration of 300 years from the defence of Siget from the Turks and of death of Croatian ban Nikola Šubić Zrinski (1508 - 1566), the square was transformed into public garden with neo-renaissance style characteristics and was named Zrinski Square. On the wall of the building at number 20 there is a painting of Siget defender, work of Croatian painter Oton Iveković (1869 - 1939). The citizens of Zagreb consider this square and the remaining two in line to the Main Railway Station as a whole and popularly call them all Zrinjevac. It is the favoured promenade with special charm and atmosphere of fountains and a lovely music pavilion, built in 1895. On the north side of the square is the meteorology column, a gift from military physician Adolph Holzer, made of Istrian marble according to the design of Hermann Bollé. In the green of Zrinjevac, in front of the Academy palace, there are the busts of famous and meritorious Croats placed in semi-circle: Ivan Mažuranić, Juraj Julije Klović, Andrija Medulić, Ivan Kukuljević Sakcinski, Nikola Jurišić and Krsto Frankopan.

❹ ARCHAEOLOGICAL MUSEUM
ARHEOLOŠKI MUZEJ

See pages 106-109

❺ CROATIAN ACADEMY OF ART AND SCIENCE HAZU

See pages 110-111

Josip Juraj Strossmayer (1815 – 1905)

Josip Juraj Strossmayer was the bishop of Đakovo, but also a great educator, politician and patron. He entered politics as a yound student becoming enthusiastic over the idea os Slavic mutuality so during the 1848 revolution he supported ban Jelačić. He was against the regime and fought for federalism of Monarchy. He had the famous Đakovo cathedral built, and with financial donation he founded the Zagreb University. Besides he was the creator and patron of the Academy of Sciences and Arts. Ecclesiastical circles remembered Josip Juraj Strossmayer by his daring thoughts, because he openly opposed the dogma of the Pope's infallibility.

❻ JOSIP JURAJ STROSSMAYER SQUARE
TRG JOSIPA JURJA STROSSMAYERA

Behind the Academy palace there is the square once called the Academy Square, because the Academy building is actually placed at it. Its shape and size was defined by the Academy palace and Chemical Laboratory (1882). The monumental statue of Josip Juraj Strossmayer was placed on the square in 1926, work of Ivan Meštrović, and only two years later the square was renamed. Beside the statue to the Academy founder, there are several smaller statues around. On the east is the bust of August Šenoa, by Rudolf Valdec, and on the west side the bust of the poet Dragutin Domjanić. Behind the Chemistry Laboratory is the monument by Frane Kršinić, *The Shot*, erected to memory of the victims of the anti-fascism war. At the square rims, in the Secession style mansion from 1891, at the beginning of the 20th century the first Zagreb hotel was opened, *Palace Hotel*, which still exists.

Josip Juraj Strossmayer

❼ GALLERY OF MODERN ART
MODERNA GALERIJA
See pages 112 - 113

❽ CROATIAN CULTURAL SOCIETY
MATICA HRVATSKA

Strossmayerov trg 4
☎ 01 487 83 60
🖳 www.matica.hr

Croatian Cultural Society was founded in 1842 under the name of Illyrian Cultural Society. Its first president was the oldest Croatian renaissance follower count Janko Drašković (1770 - 1856). It soon became the important publishing institution that initiated the first Croatian literary magazines Književnik and Vijenac. Between the two world wars, Croatian Cultural Society published the most important works of Croatian writers. Even during the World War II, Croatian Cultural Society became the central publishing house in the country due to its historical merits. Even under the circumstances it did not betray its principles of justice and freedom, art and humanity. Thus it continued its activities after the war, and the peak of its post-war work was the initiation of the edition Five Centuries of Croatian Literature, in anthology form presenting the historical and cultural development of Croatian written word from its beginnings to the present. In 1967 the Society wrote the *Declaration on name and position of Croatian literary language* that was the announcement of its future activity. During the 1970's, strong group of Croatian writers and intellectuals tried to make it the central national institution. But, due to its activities, the Society was dismissed in 1972 and only the Publishing House continued to work. The work of the Society was re-established in 1989 and today it has more than 120 branches in Croatia and abroad. Today, the Society publishes around twenty central regular editions, bi-weekly magazine *Vijenac*, and literary magazine *Kolo* and *Hrvatska revija*. The hundred existing branches of the Croatian Cultural Society publish some twenty literary magazines. Due to their rich cultural activity, the branches are in some places the unavoidable carriers of cultural life if not the only one.

The building of Croatian Cultural Society

❹ ARCHAEOLOGICAL MUSEUM

ARHEOLOŠKI MUZEJ

Trg Nikole Šubića Zrinskog 19

Archaeological Museum is housed in a luxury historicism style mansion of baron Dragan Vranyczany-Dobrinović, designed by Zagreb builder Ferdinand Kondrat (1878), and the present interior design is made by the architect Mario Beusan (1999). The museum foundation was encouraged by collaborators and members of the Croatian renaissance institutions (Croatian Cultural Society, Zagreb Reading-room) who wanted to promote national and cultural identity and prevent cultural heritage from being taken away from the country. It was founded within the National museum in 1846, and became independent in 1939. One of the most interesting and most significant town institutions keeps the famous bandages of Zagreb mummy that are actually linen book with the world longest Etruscan inscription. Within the Museum is one of the richest specialised archaeological libraries in Croatia. The garden has an attractive collection of antique stone monuments, from 1st to 4th century.

The stone collection, sarcophagus

Vespazian coins from Erdut

The Vučedol dove

Archaeological museum

① 01 487 31 02
🖳 www.amz.hr
🕐 Tu-Fri 10 a.m. - 5 p.m.
  Sat-Sun 10 a.m. - 1 p.m.
☞ with prior
  announcement

Prince Branimir inscription, 888

Egyptian collection sarcophagus

Head of a Solin girl,
2nd century

A sign on greek
from Korčula,
3. BC

The rich museum holdings (more than 4000 000 objects) have been represented in five collections. The important collections are pre-historic, antiquity and medieval as well as numismatic collection. The Egyptian collection is very attractive, the only of the kind in this region.

Dish with lid decorated with modernised bull's heads, 6th century BC

Pre-historic collection

includes mostly the objects from continental Croatia. Especially attractive are the Vučedol dove and askos from Dalj, from 2000 BC.

Antiquity

along with known Greek stone monument from Lumbarda (4th century BC) and Greek painted vase, the collection has numerous Roman findings from Croatia, and broader Ancient Mediterranean area. Among the many extraordinary findings (stone monuments, glass, metal…) the most attractive is the finest portrait in Roman art, named after the finding site - *the Head of a girl from Solin* (2nd century)

Medieval collection

beside the findings from early Peoples migration period, there are also those from the later period, as is the outstanding inscription of prince Branimir from 888 (the oldest dated inscription from the early Croatian period) and various types of early Croatian earrings from the broader Croatian region (e. g. Zagreb town quarter Stenjevec).

Earring from the Stenjevec tomb

Egyptian collection

has more than 2100 objects, and is considered important for Europe as well by the diversity of its holdings. The collection was purchased from the family of Austrian vice marshall Franz Koller (for the procurement of the collection the most credit was given to bishop of Đakovo, J.J. trossmayer). The majority of objects dates from the late old Egyptian period (from 1070 BC to 30 AD). The

most famous exhibits are the mummies with painted wooden sarcophaguses and so-called Zagreb mummy bandaged in famous Zagreb linen book.

Sarcophagus and inscription of Kaipamau mummy was found in Assasif, and from the period of 22nd dynasty (945 - 715 BC) it belonged to Amon Ra's priests. The sarcophagus has two parts - bottom and the cover; it is painted in the upper part, to the level of necklace. In the presentation of dead woman the wig is painted in blue, and on her head is the figure in shape of the Mut goddess. At the front side, hieroglyphic inscription stretches along the sarcophagus (it is written on white stitch bordered with red line). The text contains usual invocation formulae to gods in relation to the

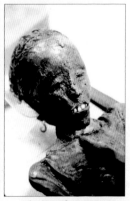

The *Zagreb* mummy

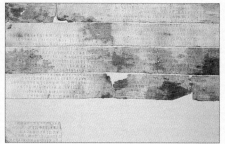

Zagreb linen book is the longest extant text in Etruscan script

dead person. At the bottom of the lower sarcophagus part, there is the figure of goddess Isis in red dress. The iconography of the inscription (the bird as a symbol of soul that liberates from the body) was typical for the period when the monument was created and shows the elements of the official cult (goddesses Isis and Nephty in shape of women protect the symbol of Osiris stretching along the middle of the inscription.)

Zagreb linen book (Liber linteus Zagrabiensis) is actually the manuscript with the longest preserved text in the Etruscan script (around 1130 words), the only preserved copy of linen book from antiquity. The canvas that bandaged the Egyptian mummy was bought by Mihael pl. Barić probably in Egypt, for his exhibition in Vienna. Based on Barić's will, in 1859 the mummy was given to the National Museum in Zagreb. The Book's text contains a

Sestercium of the emperor Trajan from Mirogoj

sequel of ritual regulations on feast of the gods of Etruscan pantheon. It is actually a kind of liturgical calendar, in codex shape (book with pages arranged like harmonium). The book is 340 cm long, and the width varies up to 35 cm. After many guesses and attempts to identify the bandage text, Viennoese Egyptologist Jakob Krall revealed its Etruscan origins in 1892. The text is usually put in the period between 3rd and 1st century BC.

Numismatic collection

is of particular cultural and scientific importance. It is one of the most important in Europe, and together with Zagreb Treasury it is by all means the most significant monument of cul-

tural heritage in Zagreb. It has more than 260 000 pieces of metal money, paper money, medals, plaques, coins etc. The collection is divided into three basic periods: Greek (autonomous money of Greek and Roman towns and Celtic) money, Roman Republican, Roman

Coins from numismatic collection

Imperial and Byzantine money, Middle and New Age money and medals. Of special value are the collection of Celtic money, Ilyrian and Greek, medal collection and several group findings, the so-called depots from all temporal periods.

❺ CROATIAN ADACEMY OF SCIENCES AND ARTS
HRVATSKA AKADEMIJA ZNANOSTI I UMJETNOSTI

Trg Nikole Šubića Zrinskog 11

In 1860 bishop Strossmayer initiated and financed the foundation of Academy. It was officially opened in 1860, and its first president was Franjo Rački. The first 14 regular members were elected. Today the Academy has 155 full right members, 90 members-collaborators and 143 corresponding members. The purpose of Academy is autonomous research and comprehensive promotion of science and art. It is divided into 9 classes, and research and art work is organised within several units (Glyptotheca, Print and drawings department . . .) Within the Academy are the Academy's Archives, Oriental collection, foundation and the Library, as well as numerous Departments and centres. The Academy building was erected on Zrinjevac on the initiative of bishop Strossmayer in 1880. Friedrich Schmidt designed the mansion in Italian neo-renaissance style. The Academy entrance is decorated with Baška Tablet, one of the oldest stone records in the Croatian language written in glagolic script. On the top of the building is the Gallery of Old Masters founded by Strossmayer as well, who donated the collection of valuable works of European painting from the period between 14th and 19th century.

Andrija Medulić,
Story about Tobias

Federiko Benković,
The Abraham's Sacrifice

☎ 01 489 51 11
🖥 www.hazu.hr
🕐 Tu 10 a.m. - 1 p.m.,
   5 p.m. - 7 p.m.
   We-Sun 10 a.m. -7 p.m.
☞ with prior
   announcement

Croatian Academy of Sciences and Arts

Fra Angelico, *St. Francis Stigmatisation and Death of St. Peter*

Jean Antoine Gros,
Madame Récamier

Jacob van Ruisdael,
*Crossing the
river*, 1665

Baška Tablet, 11th century

Breviar of Alfonso I. D'Este

❼ GALLERY OF MODERN ART

GALERIJA MODERNE UMJETNOSTI

Trg Nikole Šubića Zrinskog 19

The Society for Art founded the Gallery of Modern Art in 1919, as national institution for modern Croatian art. At first it was opened in the premises of the Museum for Art and Craft, then in Strossmayer Gallery and in 1934 it was moved to baron Ljudevit Vranyczany mansion where it still is. The foundation of collection was made in 1905, when the *Society* bought three works of art (I. Meštrović, F. Rački, F. Bilak) and the holdings were enriched by larger donations (works from the Strossmayer Gallery of Old Masters, first half of the 19th and 20th centuries) and purchase of important works of art (mostly of Croatian artists). Thus the collection at present has more than 9500 objects, paintings, sculptures, prints, posters, medals and etc. The new permanent exhibition from the 1990 discusses the temporal context of the works creation and includes Croatian art between 1850 and 1950. Modern Gallery has numerous anthology works of all relevant Croatian artists. The outstanding works are by: Vjekoslav Karas, Nikola Mašić, Vlaho Bukovac, Celestin Mate Medović, Mencije Klement Crnčić, Slava Raškaj, Rudolf Valdec, Robert Frangeš-Mihanović, Ivan Meštrović, Josip Račić, Miroslav Kraljević, Ljubo Babić, Zltako Šulentić, Krsto Hegedušić, Miljenko Stančić, Ferdinand Kulmer, Ljubo Ivančić, Julije Knifer etc.

Vlaho Bukovac,
Japanese Woman

Menci Klement
Crnčić, Calm sea

Ferdo Kovačević, *Bura*

Vladimir Becić,
Girl with flowers

☎ 01 492 23 68
🕐 Tu-Sat 10 a.m. - 6 p.m.,
  Sun-Mo 10 a.m. - 1 p.m.
☞ with prior
  announcement

Gallery of Modern Art

Josip Račić
(1885 - 1908)

Josip Račić is one of the greatest painters from the beginning of the 20th century. He studied in Munich where he revealed drawing with coal, soft drawing material that suited his sensibility. After Munich, Račić went to Paris and met the town at time of cubism and fauvism beginnings, but he was primarily interested in Goya and his refined nuance scale founded on black colour use. The most famous Račić paintings are Mother and child, Girl in front of the mirror, Portrait of the Woman in Black and Self-portrait. In his Paris room he committed suicide at the age of 23.

Slava Raškaj
(1877 - 1906)

Slava Raškaj was born in Ozalj near Karlovac, deaf and mute, she was withdrawing to solitude since her childhood. Her gift for painting was early recognised in the Institution for deaf and mute children in Vienna. She practised drawing and upon arrival to Zagreb in 1895 she started to attend the School for Painters. Her favourite motives were landscapes around her homeland, Ozalj, interiors, portraits and still nature. She preferred water colours and her most valuable works are Spring in Ozalj, Winter Landscape, Tree in the Snow and Waterlilies.

Miroslav Kraljević
(1885 - 1913)

Miroslav Kraljević is one of the fathers of modern painting in Croatia. He started studying law in Vienna, but after some time he opted for painting at the Munich Academy. In 1911 he left to Paris where he made his best works: Self-portrait with a pipe and Small self-portrait with PALETA. His portraits of his father and mother, Portrait of Aunt Luika and Girl with the Doll are among anthological works of Croatian painting. Due to his illness he had to return to Croatia where he prepared his only autonomous exhibition.

Josip Račić,
Woman in black

Oton Gliha,
Gromače on Krk (1957)

9 THE ART PAVILION
UMJETNIČKI PAVILJON

Trg kralja Tomislava 22
☎ 01 484 10 70
🖥 www.umjetnicki-paviljon.hr
🕐 Mo-Sat 11 a.m. - 7 p.m.
   Sun 10 a.m. - 2 p.m.
☞ with prior announcement

The Art Pavilion is the oldest exhibition facility in this region. It was intentionally built for big, representative exhibitions. Almost all exhibitions that surpassed the borders of Zagreb by their significance were held in it. It housed group exhibitions, movement and currents. The history of the pavilion is in a way the history of plastic art in Croatia, from the end of the 19th century up to the present. The Art Pavilion is among the finest Zagreb facilities situated within the Green Horseshoe. At the end of the 19th century the space for large exhibitions was needed. The idea and initiative for the building of the Art Pavilion came from the painter Vlaho Bukovac in 1895, and the opportunity of realisation appeared during the preparations for the Millennium Exhibition in Budapest in 1896 where Croatia actively participated. Persuaded by Bukovac, Croatian artists ask for a special prefabricated pavilion whose iron structure would be transported to Zagreb after the Exhibition. So it was, and the construction designed by the architects Korb and Giergl came to Zagreb. The work on its completion was given to Viennese architects Hellmer and Fellner. The first exhibition was held in 1898 - The Croatian Salon.

Milan Lenuci (1849 – 1924)

Milan Lenuci was an engineer and physical planner who marked the urbanistic development of Zagreb at the end of the 19th and the beginning of the 20th century. He graduated at the High Technical School in Graz and subsequently performed various functions within Zagreb City Government. He is given credit for the design of the Green Horseshoe, the best quality European physical planning solution at the turn of the centuries. Lenuci left trace in the whole town not only with his wooden stairs to the Upper Town, but also with numerous studies and projects for representative parts of the town.

---

10 KING TOMISLAV SQUARE
TRG KRALJA TOMISLAVA

The last square in line of *Green Horseshoe*, at the east side bears the name of the Croatian king Tomislav, whose monument, work of Robert Frangeš Mihanović (1872 - 1940) was erected in 1947. The adjustment of the park behind the monument started on occasion of arrival of the emperor Franz Joseph I to Zagreb, in 1895. The arrangement was finished ten years later. The square is dominated by the building of the Main Railway Station, built according to the design of Hungarian architect Ferenc Pfaff. The front has been made in neo-classicist style decorated with sculptures

King Tomislav

The Art Pavilion

and ornaments. The building was opened on July 1st 1892.

❶ ANTE STARČEVIĆ SQUARE
TRG ANTE STARČEVIĆA

The present square is only the half of the former South park, adjusted in 1903. It was envisaged as a link between the two parts of the *Green Horseshoe*, and shaped according to the ideas of the gardener Franjo Jaržabek. After 1925 when on his west side the Hotel *Esplanade* was built, it became its decorative surface. It was named after the Croatian politician Ante Starčević (1823 - 1896), the founder of Croatian Party of the Right and fighter for freedom and independent Croatia. The monument to Ante Starčević is placed on the building of Starčević Hall that houses Town Library. The modern busi-

The Main Railway Station

ness and shopping centre has been recently built just above the square - *Importanne*, including the underground parking place.

❷ BOTANICAL GARDEN
BOTANIČKI VRT

Trg Marka Marulića 9a
☎ 01 484 40 02
🖥 www.hirc.botnic/hr/vrt
🕐 Mon and Tu 9 a.m. - 2 p.m.
  Wed-Sun 9 a.m. - 7 p.m.

Botanical garden stretches along the Mihanović street and makes the integral part of the Zagreb Green Horseshoe. It extends at a surface of around 4.7 ha and has ten thousand plant species from Croatia and the whole world including some endangered ones. The Faculty of Nature and Mathematics owns the garden, and Antun Heinz (1861 - 1919) was its

Botanical Garden

founder. The first plants were planted in 1892, after some preparatory work. Already by the end of that year, the garden was completed: it got ponds, artificial hills, bridges, and even some artificial caves. The majority of the garden is the park - arboretum. It was made in English garden style, and the flower floor in the central and west part of the garden shaped in historical style, with strictly symmetrical lines.

Ante Starčević (1823 – 1896)

Ante Starčević returned to his homeland after his study in Budapest, where he got a doctor's degree in philosophy. On return he became enthusiastic over the Ilyrian ideas and got in touch with Eugen Kvaternik. He contributed to Danica with his poetry and prose work and pleaded for the preservation of Croatian language and exalted Croatian history and culture. After the fall of Bach's absolutism, in 1861 in Rijeka he declared the famous principles the basis for later right movement in Croatia that procured him the title of the Father of Homeland. He was great opponent to Monarchy and advocated the interruption of connections with Vienna and Pešta and autonomy of Croatia. Because of his activity he lost his post and was imprisoned for several times.

WALK
At the west side of the horseshoe

The well of life

is the master-work of Ivan Meštrović created in 1905. It successfully combines sculpture and reflective symbolism.

Museum for Arts and Crafts
is housed in the building with the spirit of German renaissance. It keeps the largest and most complex holdings of Croatian cultural heritage: furniture, textiles and clothing, ceramics, glass, photographs, watches, sculptures, paintings and musical instruments.

The Mimara Museum
is housed in a neo-renaissance mansion built for a school. The Museum was created by donation of art collection of the painter, renovator and collector Ante Topić Mimara. The collection was growing for more than half a century and included 3750 objects from various parts of the world, mostly the objects of artwork (textiles, glass, furnishings), but also of paintings and sculptures dating from pre-history to the 20th century.

The Ethnographic museum
keeps objects of Croatian ethnographic heritage, valuable collections of ceramics, basket making, leather, fur, jewellery, musical instruments, tools and weapons. Here are also the folk costumes from Croatia including numerous unique samples and samples of great cultural and historical value.

Zagreb University
is one of the key municipal institutions whose beginnings date from the 17th century. The university moved to the present building in 1882, but only the Rectorate and the Law Faculty are still there. In front of the entrance stairs is the famous sculpture by Ivan Meštrović, The History of Croats.

Croatian National Theatre
is an impressive neo-baroque building erected according to the design of Viennese architects Ferdinand Helmer and Hermann Fellner, at the end of the 19th century. The theatre was opened by the the emperor Franz Joseph I, and was evaluated as the most precious pearl of the Croatian capital.

St. George kills the Dragon
by the sculptor Anton Dominik Fernkorn. Originally it was placed at the Maksimir entrance.

State Archives
is the finest building from the Secession period. It was built after the design of the architect Rudolf Lubinski in 1913. The paintings by famous Croatian painters Vlaho Bukovac, Ivan Tišov and Mirko Rački decorate the interior.

Statue of don Frane Bulić
archaeologist and founder of early Christian archaeology in Croatia.
The statue is made by Frane Kršinić and erected in 1935.

HEBRANGOVA

ŽERJAVIĆEVA

MIHANOVIĆEVA

⑬ STATE ARCHIVES IN ZAGREB
DRŽAVNI ARHIV

Marulićev trg 21

Croatian State Archives is a central and primary state archives that keeps, protects, professionally processes and gives to use archive and register records about state bodies, state and public institutions and organisations and legal persons, families and individuals whose activities covered or cover the entire or larger part of the area of the Republic of Croatia, or are of importance to the Republic of Croatia as a whole.

1916 Cover of Coronation Oath Book of Charles IV (taking an oath in the Croatian Parliament after the death of the emperor and king Franz Joseph) with coat-of-arms of the Austro-Hungarian Monarchy and pending seal in a metal box with relief of St. Stephen's crown

1631 Coat-of-arms of the Drašković Family - the Emperor Ferdinand II makes Gašpar Drašković of Trakošćan the count of German Empire and grants him the right to use the title of Count of Luttenberg and Baron of Trakošćan and Klenovnik

1669 Emperor and king Leopold I grants to Zagreb Jesuit Academy university rights for doctor's degree

1848 Zagreb - Ban Jelačić's announcement on abolition of serfdom

1643 the Ban's key - one of the three keys (belonging to ban, vice-ban, and notary) that opened the Chest of Privileges of the Kingdom of Dalmatia, Croatia and Slavonia

① 01 480 19 99; 01 482 92 44
🖳 http://zagreb.arhiv.hr/hr/hda
☞ with prior announcement

⑭ THE MAŽURANIĆ SQUARE
TRG MAŽURANIĆA

The square is named after the three writers from the famous Mažuranić Family. It was the place of the first artificial skating ring in the middle of the 19th century. The ice was made of water from the Tuškanac stream that flew here. The north side of the square was defined in 1883 with the historicism style building housing the Singing Society *Kolo* and the Society for gymnastics and patriotism *Croatian*

View to the Square with Croatan National Theatre and the Museum of Art and Crafts

⑮ ETHNOGRAPHIC MUSEUM
ETNOGRAFSKI MUZEJ
See pages 120 - 121

⑯ THE MARSHALL TITO SQUARE
TRG MARŠALA TITA

The present Marshall Tito Square was in the middle of the 19th century still a moor ground at the outskirts of town. Then the buildings started growing: first the University building then the neo-renaissance block of the Craft School and the Teacher's Hall. And finally the most representative building - The Croatian National Theatre, placed at that site by insistence of the ban Hedervary himself. The square was called The University Square at the beginning, and since 1946 bears the name of

Josip Broz Tito (1892 - 1980), leader of the antifascist battle and the president of the former Federation of Socialist Republics of Yugoslavia. In front of the theatre, at the north side, is the master-peace by Ivan Meštrović, *The Well of Life* from 1905. It is a successful combination of sculpture and reflective symbolism, attracting the passenger's attention. In the south west corner of the square, there is equestrian monument *St. George Kills the Dragon*, by Anton Dominik Fernkorn.

St. George Kills the Dragon

Falcon. Today the building houses the Academy of Acting and includes the premises of the famous folk ensemble *Lado*. The other buildings worth mentioning are the Franck mansion (at number 1), work of architect Viktor Kovačić.

The Well of Life

⑮ ETHNOGRAPHIC MUSEUM

ETNOGRAFSKI MUZEJ

Mažuranićev trg 14

This is the only building in Zagreb built for museum. It was designed by Vjekoslav Bastl for the Trade and craft museum. Thus at the top of central cantilever there are allegoric figures of trade and craft, and in front of the dome is a group of figures showing Croatia as protector of trade and craft. Ethnographic museum was founded in 1919. It keeps and exhibits numerous objects of Croatian ethnographic heritage, valuable collections of ceramics, basket making, leather, fur, jewellery, musical instruments, tools and weapons. Here are also various national costumes including numerous unique samples and samples of great cultural and historical value. They impress with their choice of material, sewing technique, colours, ornaments and decorations. The outstanding examples are the samples of famous lace from the island of Pag, Slavonian national costume decorated with golden embroidery, silk embroidery on the woman costume from Konavli etc. The museum has the collection of non-European indigenous cultures.

Jewellery from Ravni kotari

Head cover from Croatian posavina

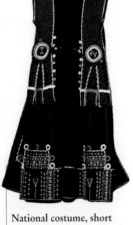

National costume, short peasant coat from Dalmatia

Ethnographic Museum

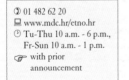

☎ 01 482 62 20
🖳 www.mdc.hr/etno.hr
🕐 Tu-Thu 10 a.m. - 6 p.m.,
   Fr-Sun 10 a.m. - 1 p.m.
☞ with prior
   announcement

National costume, short peasant coat from Vugrovec, beginning of the 20th century

Permanent exhibition, collection of objects of non-European traditional cultures

Permanent exhibition, the village house, 20th century

ETNOGRAFSKI MUZEJ

⑰ CROATIAN NATIONAL THEATRE

HRVATSKO NARODNO KAZALIŠTE

Trg maršala Tita 15

The view of the Marshall Tito square is dominated by the shrine of Croatian Thalia, impressive neo-baroque building of the Croatian National Theatre. Erected according to the design of the Viennese architects Ferdinand Helmer and Hermann Fellner, specialised in design of representative theatre and concert houses. The Theatre was opened on October 14th 1895 by the emperor Franz Joseph I himself. Thrilled city historians then wrote that the Theatre building was the most precious pearl of the Croatian capital. Indeed, Croatian National Theatre has become the central theatre house in Croatia, and the most significant Croatian actors and directors have been working in it.

The stage of the Croatian National Theatre

The box of honours

The festive curtain, work by Vlaho Bukovac

The hammer with which the emperor Franz Joseph I finished the building of the theatre

First floor hall with busts of important theatre people

☎ 01 482 69 20
🖥 www.hnk.hr

⓲ ZAGREB UNIVERSITY
ZAGREBAČKO SVEUČILIŠTE

Trg maršala Tita 14
☎ 01/456 41 11
🖥 www.unizg.hr

The beginnings of the high education in Zagreb date from 1669. After the university grew and divided into several faculties, the building in the Upper Town became too small. Thus in 1882 it was moved to the oldest building on this square, built as a hospital in 1855. With the expansion of the University, new buildings spread around the town housing individual faculties. In the building at Marshall Tito square only the Rectorate and the Law Faculty remained. In front of the entrance stairs there is the famous sculpture by Ivan Meštrović *The History of Croats*. Today, Zagreb University has around 1 000 regular professors, and 50 000 students allocated to 30 faculties and 3 art academies. 7-8 thousand students graduate each year and the University promotes 200 - 350 doctor's degrees.

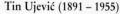

Tin Ujević (1891 – 1955)

Tin Ujević, actually Augustin, was born in Vrgorac, and he studied Croatian language and literature, classical philology and philosophy at Zagreb University. He stayed for several months in Belgrade, Dubrovnik, Šibenik, Zadar, Rijeka and especially Split. At the end of 1913 he went to Paris and returned a few years later, psychically and physically completely changed and ruined. That was the beginning of the period of drinking and rejection of middle class oppression. He was poet-intellectual and lived on relation library - pub. He published his first poems and articles in 1909 and soon confirmed himself as one of the most talented poets of the so-called Matoš circle. Ujević's poems represent the best Croatian poetry, and are published in collections *Lelek sebra*, *Kolajna*, *Auto na korzu*, *Žedan kamen na studencu* and others. His style echoes the renaissance and minstrel poetry, in modern and wordly form influenced by Matoš, Kranjčević, Rimbaud and Baudelaire.

⓳ MUSEUM FOR ARTS AND CRAFTS
MUZEJ ZA UMJETNOST I OBRT
See pages 124-127

⓴ THE MIMARA MUSEUM
MUZEJ MIMARA
See pages 128 -131

㉑ MASARYK STREET
MASARYKOVA ULICA

The street named after the first president of former Czechoslovakia, Tomaš Masaryk (1850 - 1937), started to be built in the second half of the 19th century. Viktor Kovačić built in it the building (at number 21-23) where he arranged his own appartement that is opened to public today, and at the time was considered the peak of the rationalised dwelling. Besides this building, the other interesting ones are Huth-Zorac mansion (at number 11) and Donner (at number 7), built by Rudolf Lubynski and the first Zagreb skyscraper at the corner with Gundulić street. But the Masaryk street is notable also for its restaurants where generations of Croatian artists used to gather. At the corner with Marshall Tito square is the famous Theatre coffee-house, legendary *Kavkaz*, the meeting place of cultural and intellectual "cream". Near it, at number 23, in the *Zvečka* pattiserie the generation of Zagreb New Vawe gathered, and in *Blato* inn (corner of Masaryk and Gundulić streets) Zagreb poets Tin Ujević, Vjekoslav Majer and others spent their time.

Masaryk street

⑲ MUSEUM FOR ARTS AND CRAFTS
MUZEJ ZA UMJETNOST I OBRT

Trg maršala Tita 10

The museum for Arts and Crafts is housed in the classicist style building made according to the design by Hermann Bollé from 1888. The Museum was founded in 1880 on the initiative of the *Society for Art* especially its president Izidor Kršnjavi. That museum was supposed to be the *collection of samples for masters, crafts and artists*. The first collections were created in the early years of its existence through purchase, gifts and exchange with related European museums and private collections. The Museum collected during the years the largest and most complex holdings of Croatian cultural heritage (more than 160 000 objects). In the Museum some representative thematic exhibitions were held: *The Pavlin Culture* in 1989, *The Holy Trace*, 1994, *Classicism in Croatia* in 2000 and *Secession in Croatia*, 2004.

Plate with the picture of Zagreb cathedral, around 1885

Detail from the tapestry from Tournai, 15th century

☎ 01 482 69 22
🖥 www.muo.hr
🕐 Tu-Fr 10 a.m. - 7 p.m.
☞ with prior announcement

Museum for Arts and Crafts

Festive dress

Sofa made in Varaždin
around 1835

Secession
vase

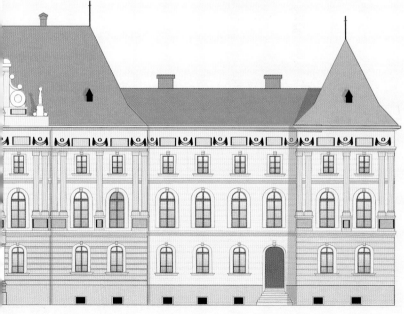

The museum holdings is divided into numerous collections among which the collection of furniture, textiles and clothing, ceramics, glass, photograph, watches, Gothic and Baroque sculpture, home and European painting and print drawings (15-20th century), portrait miniatures (17-19th century), ivory, printing, musical instruments, graphic and industrial design are worth mentioning.

The collection of sacral art

has an important place within the Museum. It contains domestic works of art (Varaždin, Zagreb, Drivenik in Vinodol), with domination of polychrome wooden sculptures from 15th to 18th centuries. The altar of the God's Mother from Remetica near Varaždin is an outstanding work, showing two styles: gothic, in the altar's core from the 15th century and mannerist, in the frame from the 17th century. The altar of St. Stephen the First Christian Martyr from Drivenik in Vinodol is a typical example of 17th century art. Specific whole is the late gothic middle European sculpture with Tirolian circle statues. The art of Order of St. Pauline is presented with chosen paintings and sculptures; to works by Gabrijel Tallera from the end of the 18th century are of special value (The reverence of kings and The reverence of shepherds). Domestic art are presented by fragmentarily preserved altars (with sculptures by Ivan Komersteiner) from the Zagreb cathedral (St. Mary and St. Ladislas) dating from the end of the 17th century. The other works are those by Valentin Metzinger (altar painting with St. Joseph and the Jesus) and Anton Ceberj (Death of St. Joseph), created in the 18th century in Varaždin area. The collection contains important liturgical objects: made of metal (from 14th until the 20th century), the older belonging to the Dalmatian workshops, but the majority is from central Croatia and neighbouring Middle European countries; made of textile (15th to 18th century), with casula as the most valuable objects, the oldest from 15th century Italy.

The Picture Gallery

contains the European baroque paintings presented by various painting schools. Among the Italian works two authors are outstanding - Guido Reni (Eneid and Didona, mature author's work from the first half of he 17th century) and Il guercino (King David with harph and David, works of high baroque period). French baroque is represented by Charles Le Brun (Bachanal, high baroque work), a painter who beside N.

The collection of sacral art

Poussin determined the French art of the 17th century. Dutch baroque is represented by several works of Rembrandt's painting school. Ferdinand Bol was one of the most famous Rembrandt students (the Pharaoh's daughter gives Moses to the nurse, high baroque work from 1660), and Jan Victors (Diogen - hominem quero) achieved outstanding work using the combination of antiquity motive and genre scene (some Dutch town).

The Watch Collection

It has around 400 clocks and around 200 pocket and wrist watches as well as larger number of elementary time measurers (solar watches, sand watches and oil watches) dating from the 17th century to the present time. The watches are mostly of foreign make, and the most numerous are the samples of the Middle European, especially Viennese production. The collection has all characteristic types of European watchmaking, from floor watches, standing, portal, mantelpiece, tabernacle, table, wall (e. g. framed watches or picture watches), as well as watches typical of particular

milieu, e. g. Viennese Telleruhr, Schwarzwald watch, Viennese Zappler and so on. Among pocket watches the watches made in the 18th and 19th century in England for the Turkish market are of special value. The most numerous and the most quality are pocket watches from the end of the 18th and first half of the 19th century, mostly made in France or Switzerland. Cases are decorated by beating, engraving, by insertion of pearls and glass paste, enamel, by use of several hues of gold.

The Photograph Collection

The holdings is made by systematic collection of photographs and photographic equipment including the samples of the first dagerotypes from the first half of the 19th century up to the works of recent photographers.

The collection has also the samples of early calotype, ferrotype i ambrotype, of the often unknown travel-

Juraj Drašković, *The Drašković Family on the castle terrace*

Pocket watch, mid 18th century

ling authors, and the works of the first known Croatian photo amateur, count Juraj Drašković. From the historical development of Croatian photography the exhibits from the first international photograph exhibitions organised in Zagreb in 1910 and 1913 are preserved, and some documentary photographs from the World War I with counter balance of idyllic scenes of mountaineers' exhibitions in Zagreb in 1919.

The Collection of Musical Instruments

This is a rather modest collection, but contains several objects of great importance, for example Tafelklavir of the brand Franz Xaver Christoph from Vienna, from the end of the 18th century, then clavichord, and piano of the Rijeka master Baraga from the beginning of the 19th century. Here are also several violins, interesting wind instruments, guitars and two harps.

㉓ THE ART COLLECTION OF ANTE AND WILTRUD TOPIĆ MIMARA
ZBIRKA UMJETNINA ANTE I WILTRUD TOPIĆ MIMARA

Rooseveltov trg 5

The Mimara museum, the youngest Zagreb museum, is situated in the rearranged part of the former school building. That neo-renaissance building dates from 1898 and was just a part of the foreseen block. The foundation stone for its construction was laid by the emperor and king Franz Joseph I during his visit to Zagreb a year earlier. The credit for the collection of works of art belongs to Ante Topić Mimara, collector, born in 1898 in the small village Korušce in Dalmatian Zagora. During the World War I, Mimara was recruited and afterwards, as a genuine cosmopolitan, travelled around the world, procuring the works of art for his collection. At the end of his life together with his wife Wiltrud he donated the whole collection to Croatian people.

Jan van de Cappelle (Amsterdam, 1626 - Amsterdam, 1679); *Dordrecht port*, around 1665, oil on wood

Carl Schuch, (Vienna 1846 - Vienna, 1903); *Still Nature*, end of the 19th century; oil on cardboard

☎ 01 482 81 00
🖳 www.mimara.hr
🕐 Tu, Wed, Fr, Sat 10 a.m. - 7 p.m.
    Thu 10 a.m. - 7 p.m.
    Sun 10 a.m. - 2 p.m.
☞ with prior announcement

The Pharaoh's Head, Egypt; end of the Middle Empire, 2040 - 1640 BC; granite

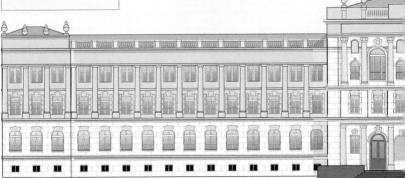

The art collection of Ante and Wiltrud Topić Mimara

Pierre Reymond, around 1513 - after 1584); *Jewellery Box*; Limoges, around 1540; wood, gilded bronze, copper, enamel

Pierre Auguste Renoir (Limoges, 1841 - Cagnes-sur-mer, 1919); *The bather*, around 1868; oil on canvas

Camille Corot (Paris, 1796 - Paris, 1875); *A girl*, around 1868 - 1879; oil on canvas

Showcase with metal exhibits

The collection has around 3 700 various works of art. The permanent exhibition of the Museum exhibits more than 1500 objects ranging from the pre-history to the 20th century

The Holy Trinity, Venetian and Byzantine icon; 15th century; tempera on wood

THE COLLECTION OF TEXTILE

is quite rich (80 carpets and 20 tapestries); the countries of their origin (Persia, Turkey, Morocco) and the date of origin (16th -19th century) tell enough about the importance of the collection, and numerous European tapestries (carpet from Spain from the beginning of the 17th century) show the mingling of textile crafts in the broader European area.

Praying carpet, Constantinople; 17th century

characteristic for the covering of dishes with soft glaze of iron mixture. Special technological achievement happened during the Song dynasty (960 - 1279) when the famous Chinese stone dish

THE ICON COLLECTION

Beside the icons from the early Middle Ages, there are also icons from Palestine, Antioch (6 - 13th century).

THE GLASS COLLECTION

is among the richest (550 objects), and depicts the technological development of that important art from the ancient Egypt to the 19th century (Czech glass); the objects of particular value are the exhibits of engraved glass from Germany.

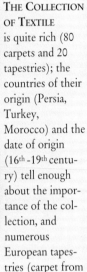

Winchester Reliquary; end of the 10th century, transparent glass; multi coloured enamel and gild

THE COLLECTION OF CHINESE ART

has more than 300 objects.
Cultural and historical dimension are best shown by ceramics and early porcelain, preserved as tomb objects. The ceramics technique during Han dynasty (206 BE-220) was

Ritual wine chalice ZunKin, Shang dynasty; 16-11th century BC, bronze

reaches its peak due to controlled oxygen quantity in the ceramic stove. From the beginning of the Ming dynasty (14th century) the history of ceramics turned into the history of porcelain.

The processing of jade is a Chinese speciality and since Neolithic it has been the example of Chinese culture continuity. Due to its alleged magical powers, it was mostly used for the production of ritual objects and tomb objects (clothes for the dead made of jade plates from Han dynasty).

The oldest Chinese art is confirmed with bronze plates and belongs to the peak of the world Bronze age art - dynasties Shang and Zhu; first ritual vessels gradually developed into utility dishes of various use, for the court and state administrators. Early Chinese enamel (14th century) was made with cloisonné technique, and from the 17th century the painted enamel dominated. Chinese engraving in various materials (ivory, wood, horn) shows the

Vase, China, Ming Guo; around 1911; porcelain

outstanding skill (shrine sculpture, home altars). From the 14th century the technique of carved varnish developed (the varnish was put in 80 or 100 thin layers, with inter-layers of varnish and ash, for the insulation). Late Chinese porcelain, produced from the middle of the 17th century as state monitored industry, was centred in Jingdezhen. Due to rich taste of imperial court the porcelain was of high quality, and innovation and quality of baking always brought new decoration ways; large quantities were exported to Europe. At the end of the 19th century the manufacture and factory production began and is still working.

COLLECTION OF ARTWORK

has more than 1000 objects of mostly European furnishings from various periods (early Middle Ages until the 19th century) produced in various historical styles.

Pyx, with royal coat of arms of Jan III Sobieski, Middle Europe (Poland ?); 18th century, ivory

SCULPTURE AND PAINTING

Sculpture mostly includes the Europe region and dates from antiquity to impressionism, while some of the paintings (more than 600) have been attributed to the famous world artists (Raffael, Veronese, Van der Weyden, Rubens, Rembrandt, Gainsborough, Goya, Manet, Renoir, Degas . .).

Diego Velasquez (Sevilla, 1599 - Madrid, 1660) The Infant Marie Therese around 1653 - 1654, oil on paper glued to the wood

Vessel, China, Quing dynasty; 18th century; porcelain

WALK
Around Ban Jelačić Square

Statue of Petar Preradović
(1818 - 1872), work of sculptor Ivan Rendić (1849 - 1932).

Croatian Musical Institute
together with Lisinski Concenrt Hall the most important con-

cert hall in Zagreb. It is housed in the same building with the Academy of Music.

Flower Square
established at the end of the 19th century by pulling down the row of houses. The square soon got representative appearance and due to numerous flower sellers it is popularly called the Flower square.

Statue of Tin Ujević
(1891 - 1955) one of the most talented poets of the so-called Matoš circle. His poems make the best Croatian poetry.

The skyscraper of "Napredak"
The building designed by the architect Stjepan Planić, for the HKD Napredak (Progress) from Sarajevo.

Octogon

the finest Zagreb passage, adjusted at the end of the 19th century. A beautiful glass stained dome, originally made in Vienna roofs his most attractive central part.

Foundation block

A block of business-housing and trade-housing buildings constructed between 1932 and 1937. Many notable architects of the time participated in its building, from Hugo Ehrlich to Stjepan Planić.

The landed Sun

sculpture by Ivan Kožarić

Mandušević

spring at the east side of the Ban Jelačić Square, according to the legend determined the name of the town. Namely, a ban passing by, once said to a girl standing by the spring: "Mandušo, ZAGRABI!", and the spring was named Mandušević, and the settlement Zagreb.

RADIĆEVA

CA

SPLAVNICA

POD ZIDOM

PETRIĆEVA

TRG BANA JELAČIĆA

BAKAČEVA

JURIŠIĆEVA

GAJEVA

PRAŠKA

㉒ Petar Preradović Square - The Flower Square
Trg Petra Preradovića - Cvjetni trg

In the Middle Ages, at this place was the square by St. Margaret Church. At the end of the 18th century, the land with the church was sold to "municipality of Greek Catholic citizens". The land of the church was already built on so the church was in a row of buildings. At the end of the 19th century it was decided that this line of house should be pulled down and that a square by the Orthodox Church should be adjusted. At the beginning of the 20th century the fruit and vbegetables market was plänned there but the idea was abandoned and it got a representative appearance. It was named after the Croatian poet Petar Preradović (1818 - 1872), but is better known as Flower Square due to a long tradition of selling flowers on it.

㉓ The Transfiguration Church
Crkva sv. Preobraženja

Preobraženska ulica bb
☎ 01/481 95 06
🕐 9 a.m. - 12 a.m. and
　 4 p.m. - 7 p.m.

The Orthodox Church was erected in 1866, at the place of the medieval St. Margharet Church, by which the Margharet Fair was held in the past. During

Flower shops that gave name to the square

the 16th century, the church ceased to be the parish church and became the subsidiary church of St. Mark parish, and the fair was moved to Harmica (Ban Jelačić Square) in 1641. The Jesuits took care of the church during the 17th and 18th century. From 1779 it did not have the sacral purpose so the town authorities sold it, in 1794, together with the surrrounding land to orthodox merchants (mostly Greeks) who became the citizens of

Zagreb. The Orthodox community *Communitas Graeci non uniti* re-adjusted the church and named it the Holy Transfiguration. It the place of St. Margharet Church's cemetery in 1882, the orthodox municipality built a three-floor building according to Bartol Felbinger's design (today Ilica 7). The ruined church was replaced with the new one in 1866 built by Franjo Klein, in round vault style (*rundbiges style*). The church is one nave building with central ground plan and semi-round apse, dome and the bell tower at the front. The screen with icons was designed by Hermann Bollé, while the Ukrainian painter Epiminondas Bučevski made the paintings in 1884. The project of representative church by Hermann Bollé from 1897 was not implemented but was used only for the recon-

The screen of icons in the Transfiguration Church

struction of the bell tower. In the eve of the World War I, its interior was changed in neo-byzantine style finally giving to the church its appropriate style and symbolic identity.

㉔ OCTOGON

Octogon is the finest Zagreb passage and the oldest of the kind in this part of Europe. It is arranged in the building from the end of the 19th century, and was named after the octogonal shape of its central part where the passage turns making a lovely widening. That central part is roofed by glass stained dome, originally made in Vienna. The passage stretches through the ground floor of a rich building of former First Croatian Savings Bank that played an important role in the economic development of Zagreb and Croatia. Today here is the subsidiary of Privredna Banka Zagreb. There is a saying above the bank entrance: "Grain by grain makes bread, stone by stone makes a palace".

Vlaho Paljetak (1893 – 1944)

In the passage through skyscraper there is a statue of well known Croatian composer and chanson writer Vlaho Paljetak. He was born in Dubrovnik, and his art career started in 1919 when he got a job as a prompter, actor and musician. The post awakened in him a wish for creation and composing. He found himself in the cabaret culture that in the 1930's came from Germany, and thus his famous songs were created, Adio Mare, Fala, Popevke sem slagal, Tri palme na otoku sreće, Marijana and others. He recorded several songs that were performed also in foreign languages: German, Czech, and Japanese. He always carried a guitar with him.

㉕ ILICA

Ilica is the longest Zagreb street and the business and social center of the town. It was named after the stream next to which it developed. Ilica grew with the town. In the second half of the 18th century it did not go further than the Britain Square, and at the beginning of the 20th century it reached Črnomerec. Until the end of the 19th century it was the street of small and modest houses, and then the huge bank buildings were built and a famous hotel "To the Austrian Emperor". One of

View of Ilica

the oldest Zagreb restaurants *The Hunting Horn* (Lovački rog - at number 14) is in Ilica and long time ago the notable coffee-houses *Corso* and *Medulić* were also there. In the courtyard of the house at number 31, at the place of present *Satirical Theatre Kerempuh*, in 1911 the famous cinema *Apolo* was opened. Somewhere in the middle of present Ilica is the seat of Zagreb brewery, founded in 1892. Its first product launched a year later was the well known *Ožujsko* beer (*March beer*).

The interior of the central part of Octogon

26 FRANKOPAN STREET
FRANKOPANSKA ULICA

Frankopan Street connects Ilica and the Marshall Tito Square. It was named after the notable Croatian Frankopan family. The *Church of St. Vinko Paulski* and the convent of the *Sister's of Charity* are placed here. This monumental classicist architectural block was finished in 1861. The painting of St.Vinko by Huber is kept here, and the clock on the bell tower is the work of the skilful watchmaker from Innsbruck. The theatre Gavella is also situated in Frankopan Street, founded by prominent theoretician and director Branko Gavella (1885 - 1962). The theatre is housed in the building erected at the beginning of the 20th century, and during the digging of the foundations, the bone of woolly mammoth was found, old around 15 000 years, therefore this is one of the oldest archaeological sites in Zagreb. At the end of the street there is the seat of the *Lexicographic Institute Miroslav Krleža*. Notable Zagreb architect Kuno Waidmann built it in high Italian renaissance style with dominant south portal and interesting dome. The Lexicographic Institute was founded in 1950, and since then it prepares and publishes encyclopaedias, lexicons, guides and other lexicographic and specialised editions.

Miroslav Krleža (1893 – 1981)

Miroslav Krleža was the most prolific and versatile Croatian writer. He was educated at the military academy in Budapest, and during the World War I he was at the battlefield in Galicia. At the end of the war he came to Skopje where he volunteered in Serbian army, but was captured under suspicion of being an Austrian spy. After returning to Zagreb he devoted himself to literary work and attained high artistic achievements in all literary kinds. He was also the editor of several magazines and for many years the head of the Lexicographic Institute. In 1936, on the occasion of centennial of the victory of stokavian over kajkavian dialect, he published the kajkavian poem *Ballads of Petrica Kerempuh* that many consider his best work. From the rich literary work the novels *The Return of Philip Latinovicz*, drama *The Glembaj Family* and the short story collection *Croatian God Mars* could be highlighted.

27 BRITAIN SQUARE
BRITANSKI TRG

The square got its present shape in the 80's of the 19th century. Since then it changed its name for several times, until 1946 when it got its present one. Zagreb citizens popularly call it *Small market*. In the past the stream Kraljevec was flowing under it, and after the square got arranged, at the beginning of the 20th century the stream was roofed. Then the majority of present houses were built. In the extension of Britain Square there is a street and a residential quarter called Pantovčak, known for its beautiful houses and villas. Among other houses, here

The building of the Lexicographic Institute Miroslav Krleža

㉘ St Blasius Church

Crkva sv. Blaža

Deželićev prilaz 64

St. Blasius church is in the Prilaz Đure Deželića. It was built between 1912 and 1915 according to the project of the architect Viktor Kovačić. It has a large reinforced concrete dome, with around 18 meters in diameter, the first of the kind in this region. The World War I enabled the completion of the church, especially its interior, according to the original idea. Since Kovačić died in 1924, Albini and Hribar started finishing the interior, following his design, but it is still not finished. The four church bells were made by Antun Blazina, the last bell moulder in Zagreb.

Nativity scene by Vojta Braniša

☎ 01/377 01 02
🕐 6.30 a.m. - 7.30 a.m.
5.30 p.m. - 7.30 p.m.

The main altar made according to the design of architect Viktor Kovačić and sculptor Ivo Kerdić

is the working residence of the president of Croatia.

㉙ The Rudolf's Barracks

Rudolfova vojarna

At the former west town rim, in the 19th century the military block named Rudolf's barracks was built. It was erected in 1899, but despite planned town building gradually started a negative influence on the town expansion. During the 20th century the army moved out, and in 1978 the majority of the block was pulled down. The remaining buildings house a part of state administration. Rudolf's barracks, together with the French Republic Square make the largest public green surface in the west part of Zagreb.

The commanding building of former Rudolf's barracks

㉚ Savska Street

Savska cesta

Savska street is a road leading diagonally from the most favourable crossing over the river Sava towards St. Mark's square. Its natural flow was interrupted by the University Rectorate building and later square adjustments. Recently, Savska is notable for its high buildings. The business towers of *Cibona* and *HOTO* are here, and a slender business building, popularly called *Zagrepčanka*. Worth mentioning is the Vjesnik building housing the editorial boards of the most important Croatian daily and weekly papers.

View to cathedral towers from Petrinjska street

③① PETRINJSKA STREET
PETRINJSKA ULICA

Only fifty meters eastward from the Green Horseshoe, Petrinjska street stretches towards the south and the Sava river. It openes the view towards the cathedral thus marking the target point, at the same way Savska road pointed to St. Mark' Church. The municipal government of Gradec built in 1830 a military barracks. That building later housed police government thus the whole street has become the synonym for police investigations. Petrinjska street is interesting also because at number 3, the stone head of a Roman was found, made in 3rd century. Since many other objects from antiquity were found around it was rightly presumed that this area was once a Roman settlement.

③② THE BASILICA OF THE SACRED HEART
BAZILIKA SRCA ISUSOVA

Palmotićeva ulica 33
☎ 01/480 30 00
🕐 6 a.m. - 12 a.m. and 4 p.m. - 6 p.m.
☞ ring the office

The late historicism style church was built in 1902 according to the design of Zagreb architect Janko Holjac and is a perfect example of neo-baroque ecclesiastical building. It was erected by means of advocating and foundation of 60 000 forints from the archbishop Juraj Haulik. To the largest church in Zagreb, apart from the cathedral, the monastery was added. The Basilica is situated in the downtown core. Since the micro-urbanistic regulation with appropriate street widths (small square and a view to Zrinjevac) has not been followed, the integrity of the building in the space has been reduced. Spacious nave is vaulted and lit through high side chapels. Plastic baroque and neo-classicist decoration is harmonised with modern space concept dominated by width and light. The church front is highlighted by bell towers that in the upper part turn from square into hexagon and finish with domes. The church was furnished by domestic masters, and the main altar was made according to the design of Hermann Bollé. The honourable title, *basilica minor*, was given to the Church of the Sacred Heart in 1941 by Pope Pio XII.

Basilica of the Sacred Heart

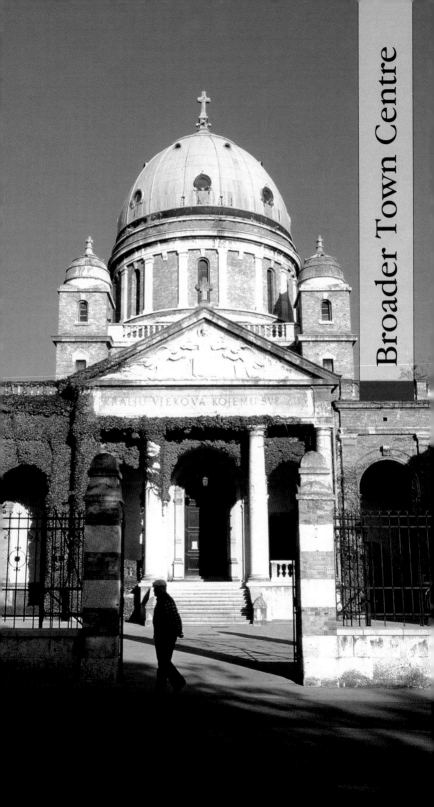

BROADER TOWN CENTRE

The Town continued to develop between the two World Wars. Since the railway tracks hindered the expansion towards the south, the main development axis was the east-west direction. Eastwards from the Down Town the new ideas on physical planning appeared. The regular grid of downtown streets was not continued, but the diagonal streets were made and extraordinary blocks of trapezoid shapes. On the contrary, the west part of the town was not carefully planned. In the period after the World War II, the development in the mentioned direction continued and the outskirts were moved to Dubrava and Gajnice, but at that time the expansion in the direction north south was also initiated. The town crossed the river Sava for the first time, and Novi Zagreb was created. Recently, the town development spread to the footings of Medvednica as well. In the 19th century wealthier citizens of Zagreb built their summer residences there and now the area of former villages has become the most attractive part of the town.

❶ Tuškanac
❷ Memorial collection of Miroslav and Bela Krleža / Memorijalna zbirka Miroslava i Bele Krleže
❸ Glyptotheca / Gliptoteka
❹ Croatian Great's Square / Trg hrvatskih velikana
❺ Zagreb film
❻ Croatian Artists Centre / Dom hrvatskih likovnih umjetnika
❼ St. Peter Church / Petrova crkva
❽ Square of the King Peter Krešimir IV / Trg kralja Petra Krešimira IV
❾ Maksimir
❿ Mirogoj
⓫ Vatroslav Lisinski / Vatroslav Lisinski
⓬ Statue of Većeslav Holjevac / Spomenik Većeslavu Holjevcu
⓭ National and University Library / Nacionalna i sveučilišna knjižnica
⓮ Sport and business centre Cibona / Sportsko-poslovni centar Cibona
⓯ Technical Museum / Tehnički muzej
⓰ The Mosque / Džamija
⓱ Sport park "Mladost"
⓲ Jarun Sports Center / Rekreacijsko-sportski centar Jarun
⓳ New Zagreb / Novi Zagreb
⓴ Park of the Newlyweds / Park mladenaca
㉑ Zagreb Fair / Zagrebački velesajam
㉒ Hippodrome Zagreb / Hipodrom Zagreb

❶ TUŠKANAC

The *Tuškanac* woods stretches on 30 ha of surface and as a green wedge cutting into the narrowest center of the town, close to Ilica. With his green "tentacles" it extends towards Rokov perivoj and Upper Town, and on the north side ends with a big meadow Cmrok. In the Middle Ages the witches were burnt at a stake at the

A statue of Vladimir Nazor

entrance to Tuškanac, while from the 19th century Tuškanac was considered a noble quarter, with rare summer residences. At the time the *Shooting Gallery* was built here (today *Tuškanac* cinema), for the citizens' leisure and it was often a meeting place for the Ilyrians. There was also a basketball playground built in Tuškanac where later Europe champions, the Cibona basketball players, played their first seasons. Thus they are still popularly called *The Tuškanac wolves*. After their departure from the hall, the famous Zagreb discotheque Saloon was opened.

Miroslav Krleža 's working room

❷ MEMORIAL COLLECTION OF MIROSLAV AND BELA KRLEŽA
MEMORIJALNA ZBIRKA MIROSLAVA I BELE KRLEŽE

Krležin Gvozd 23
☎ 01/483 49 22
🕐 Tu and Fri 11 a.m. - 5 p.m.

Miroslav Krleža and his wife Bela lived at this address from 1952 until their death. The representative apartment consisting of a dining room, Bela's small drawing room, Bela's bedroom and Krleža's working room and bedroom, is opened today to the public. The period of life the great writer spent here was not marked with significant literary achievement but is important because Krleža held many meetings and gatherings here, with important participants of the social events of the time. Two decades after his death, his whole heritage was listed with more than 5000 objects, many personal things, documents, albums, letters and manuscripts. His library is also important having around 4 500 volumes.

❹ CROATIAN GREAT MEN SQUARE
TRG HRVATSKIH VELIKANA

The Croatian Great Men Square is situated at the

Viktor Kovačić (1874 - 1924)

Viktor Kovačić, the architect, is one of the most significant Zagreb architects. He became famous by winning the awards for the design of St. Blasius Church. Here is the anecdote connected with it: they predicted him that the dome will collapse as soon as the supporting pillars were removed, and he, in order to refute it, sat in the centre of the dome and ordered to remove the supporting pillars. Thus he sat the whole night and many curious people with him, but of course outside the church . . . Kovačić is the author of remarkable project of Kaptol renovation, that was unfortunately never realised. His last big work was the renovation of the Zagreb Stock Exchange - the finest neo-classicist building in town, but he didn't live up to its completion.

❸ GLYPTOTHECA
GLIPTOTEKA

Medvedgradska ulica 2

In the building of former leather factory, the Glyptotheca of the Croatian Academy of Arts and Sciences was housed. It is unique museum institution in Croatia and one of several similar in Europe. It was founded in 1937, according to the idea of Antun Bauer. Its mission was to collect valuable sculptural works of art, and exhibit the important cultural and historical Croatian monuments as plaster casts. The holdings have 13000 exhibits, divided into nine collections. They are exhibited in chronological order from 5th century BC to the contemporary sculpture. Among the collections, the outstanding is the Collection of Croatian Historical Monuments, and Glyptotheca is an organiser of *Triennial of Croatian sculpture*.

The atmosphere of former factory architecture

Permanent exhibition

Part of the altar partition from St. Marin's church in Split

Lunnete from Trogir Cathedral, work of the Master Radovan

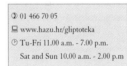
℺ 01 466 70 05
🖳 www.hazu.hr/gliptoteka
🕘 Tu-Fri 11.00 a.m. - 7.00 p.m.
Sat and Sun 10.00 a.m. - 2.00 p.m

crossing of Jurišić and Drašković street. Until the end of the World War I that area was not built and was used as a fair. At the beginning of the 20th century, the citizens of Zagreb watched the first movie projections, in a tent. In the middle of the 1920's the space started to be arranged, and the central part in the triangular square was given to impressive palace of the Zagreb Stock Exchange. Therefore the square was twice named after it, the Stock Exchange Square. The building was designed

Front of the Croatian National Bank

by architect Viktor Kovačić and erected in 1927. After his death, the work was finished by Hugo Erlich. Today the building houses the seat of the Croatian National Bank.

❺ ZAGREB FILM

Vlaška ulica 70
☎ 01/ 455 04 89
🖳 www.zagrebfilm.hr

After the World War II, the Czechs, the Americans and the Canadians had the leading role in the development of the modern animation. By the end of the 1950's, the films from Zagreb joined them because at the Cannes Film Festival in 1958 they were very successful. Because of the film, but also due to variety and richness of genres and styles produced by Zagreb film, French reviewers Geroge Sadoul and Andre Martin launched the sintagm *Zagreb school of animated film*. For the success of the film the most credit goes to Zagreb film, founded in 1953. In the 1960's it specialised in documentaries and short feature films that made it famous at world festivals. Among more than 400 awards, the special place is reserved for Oscar Award for the best animated film in 1962, *The Surrogate* by Dušan Vukotić. Dušan Vukotić was the first author outside the USA who was awarded that prize. Beside art films, Zagreb film produces feature films, documentaries and cartoons. The most famous animated film is *Inspector Mask*, *Small flying bears*, *Maxi Cat* and the unavoidable *Professor Balthazar*.

❻ CROATIAN ARTISTS CENTRE
DOM HRVATSKIH LIKOVNIH UMJETNIKA

This building was erected in the eve of the World War II, and was designed by Ivan Meštrović. It has particular circular shape differing from the surrounding houses and roofs. Stone columns placed in shape of a cylinder with their classical clarity and regular rhythm will impress every Zagreb visitor.

Circular exhibition space of the Centre, Meštrović conceived as the studio with steady diffuse light of the glass dome

The Centre was built of stone from Brač, and the fountain rotunda shows the monumentality of the building.

❼ ST PETER'S CHURCH
PETROVA CRKVA

Vlaška ulica 93
☎ 01/463 35 33
🕐 after 6 p.m.

St. Peter's Church erects in Vlaška Street, in its newer part towards Kvaternik Square. Its front looks at Vlaška street, while the back is in Peter's street, named after the church. At that place, there was St. Anthony Church, mentioned for the first time in the 15th century. After it crumbled, the baroque

The front of St. Peter's Church

style St. Peter's Church was built in1770. Since then it was renovated and extended on several occasions, and its present appearance dates from 1931.

❽ SQUARE OF THE KING PETER KREŠIMIR IV
TRG KRALJA PETRA KREŠIMIRA IV

The square is situated the eastern part of the town and is one of the finest

---

Hermann Bollé (1845 - 1926)

Hermann Bollé was German who lived and worked in Zagreb. He came to Zagreb with his master Schmidt, for the renovation of the cathedral that he had to entirely reconstruct after the 1880 earthquake. It remained his most known work in Zagreb although he embellished Zagreb with numerous buildings since he lived in it for the rest of his life. Bollé had an important role in physical planning of Zagreb in the second half of the 19th century. Besides the building for the Museum of Art and Craft, the neo-renaissance architecture of Mirogoj is of extraordinary significance since it gave to town its hallmark and made it a unity.

---

squares. It was named after the medieval Croatian ruler Petar Krešimir IV (1058 - 1074). Under his rule Croatia reached the peak of its power. In the middle of the square is a small little park, decorated with famous monument Kršinić, *The Rose Gardener*. At the north side of the square is a big block of former foundation of Croatian worker, at present the Ministry of Defence and Main Headquarters of the Croatian Army. At the rim of the square (at number 2) in 1937 the interesting building of the Labour Centre was erected, with library and reading room.

❾ MAKSIMIR
See pages 146 - 147

❿ MIROGOJ
Cemetery and the park *Mirogoj*, situated in the north part of the town on the slopes of Medvednica. It was named after the medieval land of Miroslav

Hercule Mirogojski, where in the 13th century the vineyards were grown surrounded by groves. By the present mortuary in the second half of the 19th century there was summerhouse of the Illyrian Ljudevit Gaj. After Gaj's death, the town purchased the whole land and arranged the central Zagreb cemetery. Great credit for its appearance goes to Hermann Bollé who shaped it with monumental composition of arcades, pavilions and domes, intertwined with rich vegetation. Within the cemetery there is a real gallery of works of art of Croatian sculptors as Rendić, Frangeš-Mihanović, Meštrović, Radauš, Augustinčić and others.

The Mirogoj Arcades

❾ MAKSIMIR

Maksimir perivoj bb

Maksimir park is situated in the eastern part of the town. It was open to public in 1794 and was the first public promenade in this part of the Europe. It was named after its founder, the Zagreb bishop Maksimilian Vrhovec (1752 - 1827) who, apart from the archbishop Haulik, took the credit for its arrangement. Maksimir is arranged in the place of part of the oak woods in the middle of the19th century. In the new park the paths were arranged surrounded by meadows and clearings full of decorative flowers and bushes. The park was enriched with monuments and various style buildings. The Swiss house, the Viewpoint, The Doorman hut and the Echo Pavilion have been preserved as well as several park sculptures.

The Echo Pavilion is the only preserved Maksimir pavilion. It was built after 1840. It has stone foundation and wooden walls. The  interior almost perfectly echoes the sounds, thus its popular name.

Portal - the main entrance gate in their present appearance date from the 1914. It consists of four columns - two bigger, with large street entrance between them and two smaller at each side, where the pedestrian entrances are. Big columns are connected with arch bearing the carved lines of great Croatian poet Ivan Gundulić.

Mogila - made in 1925 of the soil brought from 155 places in Croatia - all the places where some important cultural or historical event took place. The foundations of this hilloc store the valuable objects of Croatian cultural heritage in completely closed space - embroidery, flasques, handmade objects, scientific works, books - gifts from Academy of sience and art, Croatian Cultural Society and other institutions. At the hillock top is the block of stone slabs - a big stone with Croatian historical coat of arms and a falcon.

THE ZOO

Maksimirski perivoj bb

In the finest part of the park, by the Down lake in 1925 the Zoo was arranged. Its founder and first head was professor Mijo Filipović, natural scientist and lover of animal world. Today the surface of 7 ha displays animals from all meridians and parallels. The Zagreb Zoo is among middle size zoos in Europe.

☎ 01 230 21 98
01 230 21 99
🖳 www.zoo.hr
🕘 9 a.m. - 8 p.m. (1.5. - 30.9.)
9 a.m. - 7 p.m. (1.10. - 30.4)

MAKSIMIR TOWN STADIUM

Maksimirska cesta 128

The Maksimir Town Stadium is at the south rim of Maksimir Woods. It was officially opened on May 5th 1912, and since then the HAŠK played on it. After the World War II and creation of Dinamo, "Zagreb Blue Boys" moved here. The stadium was rearranged on several occassions. During 1998 the north side was pulled down, and the new one was built together with glass wall on the offices looking at Maksimir road. The working on Maksimir stadium is close to end, and its present capacity is around 40000 seats.

The Viewpoint - three floor tower 17 m high, built in 1843. It has a square groundplan, and the winding interior stairs and the terraces are built of wood. It gives wonderful view to First and Second lake and the main promenade.

⓫ **VATROSLAV LISINSKI CONCERT HALL**
KONCERTNA DVORANA VATROSLAV LISINSKI

Medvedgradska ulica 2
① 01 466 70 05
🖥 www.hazu.hr/gliptoteka
⏲ Tue - Fri 11 a.m. - 7 p.m.
Sat and Sun 10 a.m. - 2 p.m.

The musical centre *Vatroslav Lisinski* is situated on the south side of the railway track, on a kind of extension of *Green Horseshoe*, on the way to New Zagreb. It was built in 1973 close to hotels *Esplanade* and *International*. Since then it has turned into a genuine musical temple. It was named after the composer Vatroslav Lisinski, the author of the first Croatian opera *Love and Malice* (1846). The centre consists of the Big Hall, perfectly shaped aesthetically and accoustically that can take 2000 visitors, and the Small Hall. Many famous symfony orchestras performed here with famous conductors and soloists, and beside concerts at this place many international meetings were held, as well as congresses and sym-

Vatroslav Lisinski (1819. - 1854.)
His life and work were closely connected to the Illyrian movement. He was the son of a German craftsman, born as ignac Fuchs. He was carried by the Illyirain movement and even changed his own name. The first opera in Croatian language, *Love and Malice* was widely acclaimed, and he went to Prague for further musical education, with libreto for the newo opera - *Porin*. He was not admitted to Prague conservatory because of the prescribed age of the students so he privately studied music for three years and then returned to native Zagreb. In the meantime, Croatia lost its Illyrian enhusiasm so the "foreigner" Lisinski was received with distrust. Serious lack of means of living made forced him to work as a clerk, but he soon got sick and died, lonely and forgotten at the age of 34. His second opera *Porin* was performed for the first time at the end of the 19th century.

posiums, while the Small Hall is appropriate for theatrical performances and Chamber concerts, jazz and chanson. Apart from the halls, the centre has four meeting halls.The big glass hall with exhibition surfaces as well as the *Lisinski café* contribute to the atmosphere.

⓬ **STATUE OF VEĆESLAV HOLJEVAC**
SPOMENIK VEĆESLAVU HOLJEVCU
On the way to New Zagreb just before one of

Statue of Holjevac

the bridges, there is a statue of the popular Zagreb mayor Većeslav Holjevac (1917 - 1970). He was a prominent Croatian politician and one of the organisers of antifascist uprise, and between 1952 and 1963 he strongly contributed to the development of the town across the Sava river. Thus his statue is at the place full of symbolism, at the "gate" connecting the two parts of town.

Lisinski Concert Hall at night

⓭ NATIONAL AND UNIVERSITY LIBRARY
NACIONALNA I SVEUČILIŠNA KNJIŽNICA

Hrvatske bratske zajednice 4
☎ 01 616 41 11
🖥 www.nsk.hr

National and University Library

In harmonious and functional building of National and University Library the priceless valuables, manuscripts and books have been kept from the first Croatian printed book to the most recent editions. The library, as institution, was founded at the beginning of the 17th century, and was situated at present Jesuit square, in the Upper Town. During the 20th century for some time it was at Marulić square, and moved to this building in 1995. Croatia has erected two buildings for national library during only one century. Beside storage of valuable collections, National and University Library is necessary for any study, research and writing of scientific papers. In the hall some occasioanl concerts, exhibitions, book presentations and similar are held, while it has important place in the Zagreb and Croatia cultural and artistic stage.

Particularly valuable Library articles

The most valuable part of the Library are the collections: *The collection of manuscripts and rare and old books, Graphic collection, Collection of musical instruments and audio material and Colletion of geographic maps and world maps.* In the collection of manuscripts and rare old books of especial importance are the following manuscripts: *Vinodolski zakonik* (transcription from the beginning of the 16th century, parchment, glagolitic script); *Mavrov Brevijar*, 1460 (parchement, glagolitic constitution); *Istarski razvod* (transcription form the 16th century, paper, glagolic script); *Statut poljički* (17th century, paper, Croatian Cyrillic script); *Adriai tengernek syrenaya* (first half of the 17th cenutry, paper, original manuscript), *Elegia in mortem filii* (17th century, original manuscript) both by Nikola Zrinski; *Smrt Smail-age Čengića* (before 1847, original manuscript) by Ivan Mažuranić; manuscript heritage by Pavao Ritter Vitezović, Baltazar Adam Krčelić, Ljudevit Gaj, Vatroslav Jagić, Family Brlić Maćuranić, Eugen Kumičić, Eugen Kvaternik, Miroslav Krleža. Among the oldest Craotian books pritned in glagolic scripte here are the following: *Misal po zakonu rimskoga dvora* (1483) and *Brevijar po zakonu rimskoga dvora* (1493). Here are also the works of great writers: Marko Marulić, Hanibal Lucić, Marin Držić, Ivan Gundulić, Bartol Kašić, Andrija Kačić Miošić, Croatian renaissance members etc, works of Croatian scientists: Antun and Faust Vrančić, Matija Vlačić Ilirik, Marin Getaldić, Ivan Lucić, Ruđer Josip Bošković, Baltazar Adma Krčelić and others. The Graphic Collection keeps the works of Croatian graphic artists. Andrija Medulić Schavone (1500 - 1563) and Martin Rota Kolunić (1532 - 1582), drawings and prints by Miroslav Kraljević, Josip Račić, Ljubo Babić, Tomislav Krizman, Menci Clement Crnčić, Krsto Hegedušić, Vladimir Becić and many others, and from foreign graphic artists of special value are the works of Rembrant Harmensz van Rijn (1600 - 1637), Sadeler Egidias (1570 - 1629), Caesa Dominicus (1550 - ?), Fischer von Erlach (1656 - 1723), Toulouse-Lautrec (1864 - 1901), Georg Grosz (1893 - 1959), Max Pechstein (1881 1955), Gustav Klimt (1862 - 1918) and Kaethe Kollwitz (1867 - 1945).

⑭ TECHNICAL MUSEUM
TEHNIČKI MUZEJ

Savska cesta 18

Technical museum in Zagreb is housed in the buildings constructed in 1948 for Zagreb Fair. After the Fair moved to the present location, the premises were used for various social and sports activities. The museum was founded on the model of the existant big scientific and technical museums in the world, as a complex museum of science and technology. The idea for such museum dates from the end of the 19th century, but the real history of that musum began in 1954 when the decision for its foundation was made. The conceiver was Božo Težak, and the one who actually made it and was its first head was Predrag Grdenić. The first departments of Technical Museum (Energy Transformation, Transport Vehicles and Mining) were opened to the public in 1963, and then the collection on Oil was opened (1964), Planetarium (1965) and demonstration cabinet Nikola Tesla (1976), department of Basic agriculture (1981), Fire-fighting (1992), Apiary (1994) and *Muzeorama* geodesia - land-registry (1994).

Aircrafts exhibits

Samoborček (train to Samobor) in the courtyard of Technical Museum

First Zagreb tramway pulled by horses (model) from 1891 when tramway transport in Zagreb began; the coach was made by Austrian company Weittzer

① 01/484 40 50
🖥 www.mdc.hr/tehnicki
🕐 Mon–Fri 9 a.m. - 5 p.m.
   Sat and Sun 9 a.m. - 1 p.m.
☞ with prior announcement

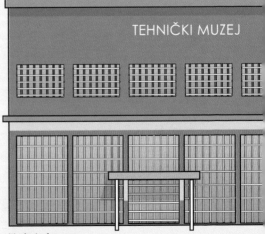

Technical museum

Exhibits in transport department

Nikola Tesla (1856 - 1943)

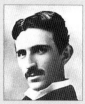

Nikola Tesla was born in Smiljane near Gospić, and after staying in several European cities he went to USA. He became famous for his numerous inventions, to mention only the most important related to the use and transmission of alternating current. He experimented with wireless transmission of electrical energy, and for long time persistently worked on radio waves. He invented the radio, as we know today that was eventually acknowledged by the USA Supreme Court. His comment on the injustices that were done to him was: "The present belongs to them (sceptics), but the future, to which I devoted my work, belongs to me." Besides the known inventions, public is still interested in his heritage that, allegedly, contains some extraordinary inventions. During his stay in the USA, Tesla gained a lot of popularity, he associated with famous persons of the social life of the time, like the writer Mark Twain, and in 1979 the Tesla Memorial Society was opened in New York.

Nikola Tesla Cabinet with copies of his most important machines and devices

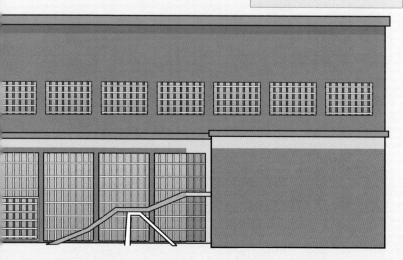

The museum treasure is more than 5600 objects from various technical fields. The holdings are divided in eight departments; first departments (Energy Transformation, Transport vehicles and Mining) were opened in 1963, and those related to contemporary scientific trends (land registry) in 1994. The permanent exhibition is conceived didactically (the museum is included in regular education programme) and shows the systematic development of specific technical achievements.

Mine model with total corridor length of more than 300 meters

Department of agriculture

The department shows the basic notions related to farming and basic tools for it. The predecessors

Historical and technical development of ploughing and digging devices and tools

of the present digging tools could be found in the far away past when the ordinary pointed stick or animal horn was used for the primary primitive farming. Mastering the technology of metal processing the people add to those primitive tools some metal pieces thus making the first digging devices, the predecessors of present spade and hoe. By further perfection, adding of parts to digging tools, the first tilling devices were made - plough and ploughshare. *Apiary* - demonstration beehives consisting of three glass hives with live bees. Here in a direct way one can watch the work and life of bee community. Each hive is linked to the environment by a passage enabling bees to go to the nature and collect pollen and nectar. The speciality of Apiary is in its live exhibits - bees, so the visitors can through direct visual contact reveal the secrets of bee community organisation and marvellous construction solutions of their hives.

Mining department

The collection of mining gives the survey of the mining techniques from the beginnings to the present. The samples of the best known ores are displayed: iron, leid, copper, zinc...and the overview of mines in Croatia from antiquity to the present time. The most important part of this department is the mine, actually a model of a coal and metal shaft. The total length of the mine corridors is 300 meters, and the greatest depth is 6 meters.

Fire Fighting Department

The use of fire is one of the basic evolution acqui-

Julius steam engine, steam fire hose Kernreuter made in Vienna in 1889; transferable fire hose with horse equipment; it was procured by the lottery prize (2900 forints) of waiter Julius Zigeunner who donated it to Voluntary Fire-Fighting Society in Zagreb

sitions that distinguish men from animals. But since the time the man started using the fire he fights against it as a potential danger. Fire protection is as old as fire. Man always fought fire danger by technical achievements of the time. It is the development of fire fighting technique that this department is about. At the beginning burning is explained as chemical process that can be interrupted (by separation of the burning material from the fire, cooling or choking), in the sequel the overview of fire-fighting devices is shown from the beginnings to the present. Special attention is devoted to the most modern solutions for fire alarm and extinguishing under various conditions, as at sea, in tunnels, mines...

Department of the great men of Croatian natural science and techniques

For now it displays the exhibition of Faust Vrančić and demonstration cabinet of Nikoala Tesla with faithful copies of Tesla's most impor-

tant inventions and devices. They are used for demonstration of experiments that Tesla used to show his inventions.

Command table of the water power plant Ozalj I from 1907 (high voltage cell and transformer with forced air-cooling)

Transport Vehicles Department

displays articles related to the development of transport in the air, land and

Motor sledge by Marko Knez; he patented it and built in 1931. A propeller driven by four-stroke five- cylinder petrol engine made the thrust

water. Special attraction is *Samoborček* train, pocket submarine CB 20, personal car Renault NN (1926).

Astronautics Department

accommodates the models of the famous spacecrafts, missiles, carriers and orbit stations that show the beginning of astronautics development.

Energy Transformation Department

has the steam engine from the middle of the 19th century. The department of Croatian Great men of science and technology has demonstration cabinet Nikola Tesla and other scientists and their achievements (First Croatian radio station transmitter, from 1926).

Planetarium

the only one in this part of Europe, housed in a dome, with projection on artificial sky and lecture, gives to the visitors the impression of sky from the north pole to the equator at any time of night and day or season.

Planetarium dome - projection on the artificial sky displaying faithful sky image

⓯ SPORTS AND BUSINESS CENTRE CIBONA
SPORTSKO-POSLOVNI CENTAR CIBONA
Savska cesta 30

The sports and business centre Cibona is situated at Dražen Petrović Square, close to Savska street. It was built in 1987, for the University Games, and consists of a basketball hall and a business tower, one of Zagreb symbols of the end of the 20th century. The basketball hall experienced its record during the first Cibona play in autumn 1987 when Dražen Petrović (1964 -1993) in match with Finnish Kotkan made a record of 62 goals. After his tragic death in 1993, the hall was named after him.

⓰ THE MOSQUE
DŽAMIJA

Gavellina ulica 40
☎ 01/613 71 62
🖳 www.islamska-zajednica.hr
🕐 8 a.m. - 8 p.m.
☞ with prior announcement

The Society of *Brothers of Croatian Dragon* initiated the construction of the mosque in 1912, but the initiative did not live. With the arrival of more Islamic believers

Dražen Petrović (1964 - 1993)

Dražen Petrović was one of the best European basketball players of all times. He was not of age when he played for Yugoslav national team, and beginning with 1984 he participated at three Olympic games and returned with a medal each time. As player of Šibenka and Cibona he won all important national and international trophies and then went to Real in Madrid, afterwards to NBA. During the years in USA he proved his great talent and justified the title of basketball Mozart. Returning from a match in Poland he tragically died in a car accident on the motorway near Bavarian town Ingolstadt.

Cibona tower

to Zagreb, after the foundation of the Kingdom of Serbs, Croats and Slovenes, in 1922 the Muslim religious community was founded, a high regional religious seat. The Muslim community initiated the question of mosque construction, but it was not resolved until 1944 when the Visual Art Gallery (project by I. Meštrović from 1938) was rearranged into the mosque, and Stjepan Planić and Zvonimir Požgaj added three minarets to it. By the decision of town authorities in 1948, the mosque was moved out, and minarets were pulled down. The construction of the present mosque and Islamic centre in Trstik (Folnegovićevo naselje) was finished in 1987. The builders from Sarajevo Džemal Čelić and Mirza Gološ have erected the architectural complex of around 10 000 square meters. It consists of several functional units; place of warship with a minaret (51 m of height), Islamic religious high school

The Mosque

(medresa), library, common social premises, administration building, residential part, other facilities etc. Though its interior and exterior preserve the traditional arrangement and content, the architecture of the complex is in harmony with the modern construction trends.

Sports center Mladost

⓱ SPORTS PARK MLADOST

Jarunska cesta 5
☏ 01/365 85 55

Sports park *Mladost* is near the dike by the Sava river. The crucial object in the whole park is the Swimming and waterpolo centre. There are indoor and outdoor Olympic-size swimmimg pools (25x50 meters), several smaller pools, children's pool, sun bathing space and other facilities. The visitors can use 16 tennis courts with grain surface, basketball playground, volleyball, handball, foot-bal and field hockey. Within the sports park there is also a volleyball hall and athletic courts.

⓲ JARUN SPORT CENTER
REKREACIJSKO-SPORTSKI CENTAR JARUN
See pages 156 -157

⓳ NEW ZAGREB
NOVI ZAGREB
After the World War II, Zagreb made a decisive step on the second, south bank of the Sava river. Many big settlements were erected here: Zaprude, Utrine, Travno, Sloboština, Sopot, Siget and others. One of the first "settlers" of the south bank was Zagreb Fair. It was moved to its present location in 1956 and since then it has developed into one of the biggest fairs in the world. A very important event for the New Zagreb dwellers was in 1979 when tramway crossed the river. This part of Zagreb today houses many important state and town institutions (economy, culture, sports etc).

HAVK Mladost

After the World War II, the waterpolo club was founded in Zagreb, and to the present day has remained the synonim of successful European waterpolo team. They won the European championship for seven times and three times won in the Supercup. Beginning of the club were in the indoor swimming pool near Dom Sportova, where first trophee generations developed. During the "golden years" between 1967 and 1971, Mladost won four European championships and three Yugoslavian. Victories continued after the construction of the new swimming pool in 1987. Soon afterwards the most successful year of the club arrived. In 1989 Mladost won four titles - champions in the domestic Cup, State champions, European champions and finally the Supercup Champions. Since the independence of Croatia, Mladost was six times in a row a state champion and twice a Cup champion.

⑱ JARUN SPORT CENTAR

REKREACIJSKO-SPORTSKI CENTAR JARUN

Jarunska cesta bb

In the southwest part of Zagreb, not far from Sava dike, there is a spacious recreational and sports centre Jarun - an oasis of peace and nature surrounded by crowds and noise. The former channel of the Sava River was arranged for the University Games in 1987, when the lake and the whole complex was given its present appearance. On two Jarun lakes, Big and Small there are five islands connected with bridges and around them are 2500 meters of pebble beaches. The lakes are filled with clear underground water, and the beaches have sanitary facilites and showers. There are also rescue teams, guards and medical service on site. Jarun's special value is the untouched nature of the Island of wildness. There is preserved natural swamp and pond habitat, rich with land and water plants, with hundred bird species and a multitude of various fish, water animals and insects. Jarun has total surface of 235 ha and is attractive to all generations. It provides facilities for walking, bicycling, various outdoor sports, trim-track of 6500 meters of length, roller.skating, etc. Sports facilities are related to impressive 2250 metres long regatta path where international and world rowing, canoe and kayak contests are held. With daily trainings and performances they give Jarun a special, sporting atmosphere.

① 01 383 28 27
🖳 www.jarun.hr

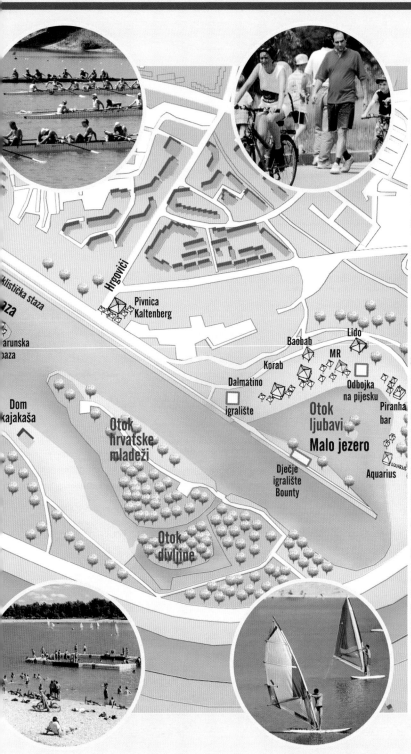

klistička staza

aza

arunska
aza

Hrgovići

Pivnica
Kaltenberg

Baobab

Lido

Korab

MR

Dalmatino

igralište

Odbojka
na pijesku

Piranha
bar

Dom
kajakaša

Otok
hrvatske
mladeži

Otok
ljubavi

Malo jezero

AQUARIUS

Aquarius

Dječje
igralište
Bounty

Otok
divljine

⑳ PARK OF THE NEWLY-WEDS
PARK MLADENACA

Situated between the New Zagreb quarters Siget and Trnsko, The Park of the Newlyweds was the first park created after the World War II. From 1964 to 1978 within the activity *The tree of youth*, all newly-weds, i.e. their witnesses, had to buy a young tree that was planted in the park.

㉑ ZAGREB FAIR
ZAGREBAČKI VELESAJAM

Avenija Dubrovnik 15
☎ 01/650 31 11
🖥 www.zv.hr

Zagreb Fair is one of the largest and most distinguished fairs in this part of Europe. The 1864 was considered the beginning of fair tradition, in the present sense of the word, when the first international exhibition was held in Zagreb. In 1909 the Zagreb Zbor was founded as predecessor of the present Zagreb fair. The fair was at first held in Martić street, and in 1936 was moved to a new location, Savska street, at the place of present Students' Centre. In 1956 the fairgrounds crossed the river and settled at the present place in New Zagreb. Then its strong development began. Today, Zagreb Fair accommodates numerous economy

Zagreb Fair

performances, specialised exhibitions, conferences and conventions.

㉒ THE ZAGREB HIPPODROME
HIPODROM ZAGREB

Ulica Radoslava Cimmermana 5
☎ 01/653 65 52
🕐 7 a.m. - 8 p.m.

The Zagreb Hippodrome is situated on Kajzerica, between Sava and Zagreb Fair. By its surface it is among the largest in Europe. It houses the *Zagreb Horseriding Club*, and next to it,

Horseriding club *Pony Express* giving the opportunity of recreational horse riding. During the past few years, on several occasions the Hippodrome was the place of gathering of huge number of people. On September 11th, 1994, Pope John Paul II held the mass for the believers of the town and its broader surroundings, and in summer 1998 the legendary British pop group *The Rolling Stones* held their concert at the Hippodrome.

New Zagreb

Town Vicinity

❶ MEDVEDNICA

One of the favourite excursion places of Zagreb citizens is the park of nature Medvednica, with its highest peak Sljeme (1033m). It is reachable by cablecar or on foot by marked trails, about two hours to the top. There are several objects with hotel servic-

Mountain hut on Medvednica

es, but the most popular are smaller mountain huts offering food and drink. During winter Sljeme is the favourite destination of skiers and other lovers of winter sports. From time to time one of the best skiers of all times Janica Kostelić and her brother Ivica could be seen on Sljeme ski runs.

Veternica

🕐 Sun 10 a.m. - 3 p.m.

On the west slopes of Medvednica, there is one of the biggest caves in Croatia - Veternica. It is on the fourth place by length in Croatia (6 816 m). During summer the cool breeze is coming from its opening because there is air current due to difference in the density of outer air and the cave air. Underground corridors are a rich paleontological and antropological site, and they run in length of 380 m.

Medvedgrad

The remnants of Medvedgrad are at the slopes of Medvednica and could be reached by road from Lukšić or Šestine. The medieval fortified town was erected in the middle of the 13th century, as one of the most important fortifications in this part of Europe. Thus it joined Kaptol and Grič as defence against possible new Tatar invasion. It is placed in an excellent strategic location, protected also by natural rocks. It was abandoned during the 16th century and since then was left to decay until the end of the 20th century when it was renovated and protected.

Medvedgrad

The church of Holy Mary of Sljeme, the Queen of Croats

The parish church situated in the woods of Medvednica, erected according to the design of Juraj Denzler, due to contributions of excursionists and hikers. It is made of green Sljeme stone, entirely integrated with the environment by its mass, composition and material. It has a square groundplan, with the shrine shaped in elliptic apse and the bell tower growing from the monumental rustical stone wall. Wooden constructions are made of trees cut from the building site. The chapel is the reflection of specific concept of con-

The church of Holy Mary of Sljeme, the Queen of Croats

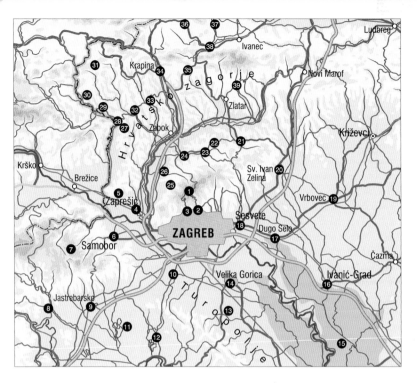

nection between traditional building values and modern approach and shows the ultimate achievement of Croatian modern architecture. The majority of interior work was done by the sculptor Radoje Hudoklin. His works are the relief of *God's Mother with Jesus on her hands* above the altar and the wooden ceiling of the shrine with figures of Holy Mary with the child and the four saints - protectors of Croatia with coats-of-arms of Croatian towns and regions. The sculptor Vanja Radauš made the marble antependium whose composition reminds of domestic Romanesque patterns. The painter Gabrijel Stupica made two frescos:

the right shows the gift of the newly built church as the sign of Croat's reverence, and the left shows Jesus surrounded by the great men of Croatian history up to the 18th century.

❷ REMETE

The village Remete, today integral part of Zagreb, was named after the monastery of the order of St. Pauline that was mentioned in the 13th century. It worked until 1786 when Emperor Joseph II closed it. In 1772 the monastery church of St. Mary was given baroque features and after the big 1880 earthquake renovated according to the design of

Hermann Bolle. On the baroque portal from the 18th century, there is an outstanding grid of cast iron, and in the interior the wooden sculpture of the Holy Mary of Remete, placed on the altar, attracts the attention. In this church are the tombs of famous Croats.

Church in Remete

❸ Šestine

Šestine is situated at the north outskirts of Zagreb. They are named after the custom that village people had to give the sixth of their harvest to the Medvedgrad nobility. (šestina - the sixth part) There is the church of St. Mirko in Šestine with multicoloured roof, built in 1622 and extended in 1909. By the church is the graveyard with the tomb of Ante Starčević. Šestine are well known for its national folk costume with the outstanding *škrlak*, black felt male hat with narrow rim, decorated with many-coloured ribbon, usually in colours of Croatian national flag. It is popular to wear, as a part of male and female costume, big red umbrella from Šestine with rims of several stripes of different colours.

❹ Zaprešić

Zaprešić is situated in the lowland area surrounded by Medvednica and three rivers, Sutla, Sava and Krapina, 18 kilometres from Zagreb. It was mentioned as a parish in 1334, and in the 15th century the name Zapresečje was mentioned for the first time. Its name means the region behind the hill, the wood. The town and its vicinity are full of historical and cultural monuments, with out-

View to St. Mirko's church

standing castles and numerous valuable and interesting churches and chapels. There are also some valuable natural features and monuments. There is ornithological refuge on the Sava river and in the region of Dubravice the protected Eco-resort of the Čret woods. In the Gmajne woods is a unique site of the carnivorous plant, rosike. On the east side is the Nature Park Medvednica, with an attractive place *Stone wedding*.

❺ Manors Around Zaprešić

Jelačić's New Manor

☎ 01/ 331 05 40
🖥 www.matijaskurjeni.hr
☞ with prior announcement

The new manor is only a kilometre from Zaprešić.

Jelačić's New Manor

First owners were counts Zrinski, but its masters later changed. The manor was substantially altered in the course of time, and its present appearance dates from the middle of the 19th century. In 1852, the notable Croatian ban Josip Jelačić bought it and built a neo-gothic chapel of St. Joseph next to it. The park houses and the neo-gothic family tomb made of white stone were built in 1884 according to the design of Hermann Bollé. In 1992 the remains of ban Jelačić were buried there. The special value of New manor is in its preserved and partially reconstructed production facilities with the round threshing machine from the 17th century, the oldest of the kind in Croatia. The three floor granary was in 1987 turned into the Matija Skurjeni Gallery. It houses the permanent exhibition of the prominent naiive painter, Matija Skurjeni, and historical photo-exhibition *Jelačić's New Manor*.

Januševec

Januševec manor, 6 kilometres west of Zaprešić, is the finest classicist style manor in Croatia. It has a rectangular ground plan, and the central round hall with 11 m high dome, 8 m in diameter. The general Vrkljan, minister of the Archduchesse of Parma, Marie Louise, the second Napoleon's wife, built the manor in 1830. It changed its owners a lot later, and in May 1945 was seriously damaged in an explosion. There is a nice park by the manor.

Lužnica Manor

Lužnica

Lužnica is an one-floor baroque manor, 6 kilometres west of Zaprešić. It has three wings, U shaped ground plan. The central wing is pointed out with cantilever, and the corners have cylindrical towers. Above the main entrance is a spacious balcony. The manor front, above the windows, is decorated with relief busts. The manor chapel has a rococo style altar.

❻ SAMOBOR

Samobor is a little town in a fertile valley of the Sava River, at the footings of Samobor Mountains.

Laduč Manor

Laduč

Laduč manor is 7 kilometres west of Zaprešić. It is an one-floor building erected in 1882. Rich two wing stairs with stone balustrades lead to the first floor. The ceiling on the first floor is painted with valuable decorations. In front of the manor is the French type garden.

It is a genuine town-museum. Each house, square or street tells its history. The ruins of the medieval burg above the present town witness the rich history as well as numerous exhibits in the Town Museum. King Bela IV gave to Samobor the charter and the status of free royal trading place. Samobor is the most developed tourist place in Zagreb County, and favourite destination of many Zagreb citizens and other guests. It is especially notable for its food and drink and attractive festivals, carnival festivities in particular. In the town vicinity there is an interesting Grgos cave and old iron, tin and gypsum mines in Rude. Some other attractive destinations are the Fairy Pits, Eco-centre Slani dol, *Suban* - the medicinal herb garden in Manja Vas etc.

Samobor

❼ ŽUMBERAK - SAMOBOR MOUNTAINS

The Nature Park Žumberak - Samobor Mountains is situated west of Zagreb. It attracts numerous visitors by its natural beauties, his-

Okić

torical and cultural heritage and recreational opportunities. Picturesque villages are 800 m above sea level. The mountain interspersed with deep stream valleys is heavily wooded with meadows and pastures. There are nice water mills, some originally reconstructed, on the numerous streams and small rivers. In the Park there are natural resorts as the protected landscape of the deep canyon of Slapnica stream, protected landscape of Okić town with surroundings and wood vegetation resort on Japetić. Numerous diverse plant and animal species live on Žumberak and Samobor Mountains. Eco-centre Slani Dol would be the best starting point for sightseeing, the seat of the Park's management. Near Krašić, in Medven *kurija*,

with water mill, there is Park's information centre, and appropriate access from the south side of Žumberak. Hiking trails are marked, and there are some mountain huts along.

❽ KRAŠIĆ

Picturesque Krašić is situated at the footings of Žumberak Mountain, at its lowest slopes, 52 kilometres from Zagreb. It was mentioned in documents for the first time in 1249, and the parish church in 1334. The Krašić region gave two cardinals, two Zagreb bishops. The Blessed Alojzije Stepinac (1898 - 1960) was born in Brezarić, but spent his childhood in Krašić where he held his first mass after returning from his studies in Rome. He also spent here his last years of life. Cardinal Franjo Kuharić (1919 - 2002) was born in Pribić, a village 3 km eastwards from Krašić. The Krašić surrounding is full of natural beauties, and the valley of Kupčina River,

Parish church in Krašić

bordered with oak woods is especially attractive. Near Krašić, in Mirkopolje there are golf courts.

❾ JASTREBARSKO

Jastrebarsko is a nice town 30 km southwest of Zagreb, at the edge of the nice Žumberak Mountains, at the footings of wine-growing district of Plešivica. The town was mentioned for the first time in 1249, and in 1257 king Bela IV gave it the status of free royal trading place. Four-wing manor with two rounded towers

The counts Oršić Manor

and inner courtyard with arcade porch started to be built at the beginning of the 16th century. It was the property of the Erdödy family. By the manor, there is a baroque parish church of St. Nicholas from the second half of the 18th century, renovated in 1922. St. Mary church is decorated with row of niches on the main portal. The town surroundings are attractive. In nearby Mladina, there is famous moto-cross track. Gentle Plešivica is famous for its high quality wines and attractive "wine-road". In the nearby Slavetić, 13 km northwest of Jastrebarsko, there is the manor of counts Oršić. It is a burg, later altered into a manor (15 - 18th century).

⑩ BREZOVICA

Brezovica as settlement is mentioned already in 1522. The place has beautiful baroque church of St. Mary's Assumption, with two slender bell towers, built by counts Drašković in 1756. During the 18th century the Drašković family constructed the baroque manor with two cylindrical towers at the corners of the main front and with central prominent cantilever. In the main hall there are wall paintings from 1776, representing the events from the Seven year war, in which the owner of the manor, Kazimir Drašković had participat-

Brezovica manor

ed. There is a nice park around the manor, and not far from Brezovica is a special resort of wood vegetation.

⑪ CRNA MLAKA

In the central part of the swamp and wood area

Crna mlaka

along the Kupa River, there is famous ornithological refuge Crna mlaka, rich in diverse bird species. At the beginning of the 20th century, from the permanently flooded area the woods were cut and the ponds were built. In the central part a nice park was arranged with diverse trees and bushes. In the middle of the park, its first owner, Kornelius Zwilling erected a nice, spacious Vienna secession style manor, and called it Ribograd (fish town). Crna mlaka is rich in diverse flora and fauna, but the most valuable is the

settlement of around 235 bird species, the eagle in particular.

⑫ PISAROVINA

Among Vukomeričke gorice, the river Kupa and Draganić woods, there is Pisarovina. The landscape's features are lowlands, gentle hills interspersed with old oak woods and rivers. At the east and north are the slopes of Vukomeričke gorice, and from Donja Kupčina by a macadam road you can reach the attractive Ornithological refuge Crna mlaka. The first known name, Piezarewo from 1328 is

Wooden house in Pisarovina

considered to be the predecessor of Pisarovina. Four kilometres southward from Pisarovina, the settlement of Jamnička Kiselica is situated, known for its rich springs of mineral water, popular *Jamnica*. The mineral spring of extraordinary quality was discovered in 1825, and the water was marketed since 1891. It is one of the best quality mineral waters that combine well with wine and juice.

⓭ TUROPOLJE

Lowland area between the left bank of the Sava River and Vukomeričke gorice. The wooden chapels and noblemen *kurije* (houses) are of special value. They are rightly called wooden Turopolje beauties. They are made of oak tree, and existed already in the Middle Ages. They represent the highest achievement of national baroque architecture in the north Croatia region. Turopolje is generally rich in woods, with especially attractive Veliki Turopoljski lug.

Wooden church in Turopolje

⓮ VELIKA GORICA

The largest Turopolje settlement was mentioned for the first time in 1228. In the centre of the town there is the so-called Turopolje's town, one floor building of rectangular basis, with ground-floor porch, built around 1765. It was the seat of the Turopolje municipality, and the assemblies were held on the first floor. Today the building houses the Museum of Turopolje, founded in 1960. It has archaeological, ethnographic and cultural and historical collection. Near Velika Gorica,

in Pleso, there is Zagreb Airport. The region is full of rivers and their affluents creating a lot of lakes and marshy areas, the most known being Čiče. Not far from Velika Gorica, in Šćitarjevo, there is a valuable archaeological site - antique Andautonija. It was the former seat of the Illyrian tribe Andautonii, and the Roman municipality of the Upper Pannonia, as numerous finds from the 1st to 4th centuries prove.

⓯ LONJSKO POLJE

The Nature Park Lonjsko polje is situated between the Sava River and Moslavačka gora, partially along the Lonja River, not far from the town of Kutina. It is exceptionally rich in animal and plant species. Here are the important duck nests, and there are also some rare

European species of eagle, egret and blue-grey heron and black stork. This is the place of the largest carp hatchery in Europe. There are some indigenous species of swine, wild boar, horse (hrvatski posavac), deer, doe, otter, beaver, wild cat. The wooden houses from Posavina are valuable monuments of architectural heritage.

⓰ IVANIĆ GRAD

Forty kilometres from Zagreb, by the rivers Sava and Lonja, not far from the slopes and wine-growing hills of Moslavačka gora. It was mentioned for the first time in 1246. Some finds, however, indicate the earlier existence of Roman settlement in the region. At that time the main Roman Pannonian roads ran from Andautonia towards Mursa and fur-

Čigoč - stork village

Dugo Selo

ther. Today, Ivanić Grad is the cultural and economic centre of the region, with long and rich tradition. The Naftalan spa, the second of the two known springs of special healing oil naftalan is situated in the town. The region around Ivanić Grad, Kloštar Ivanić and Križ with more than 50 settlements and rich in rivers and lakes, is called Otok Ivanić (Island Ivanić). South of the town, there are woods named Žutica, world famous Nature Park Lonjsko polje with rare birds wading in the marsh.

❶⑦ DUGO SELO

Dugo Selo was mentioned for the first time in 1209, in the deed of donation by king Andrew II, as Terram sancti Martini, that is The Land of St. Martin. Its present name was recorded for the first time in 1622. Beside the historical and cultural monuments, the region is

charming for its natural beauties. On the hilly Martin Breg there are vineyards and orchards and summerhouses. In Božjakovina, 6 kilometres northeast of Dugo Sela, there is a valuable mansion of the count family Drašković with the park dating from the 18th century and protected as the horticultural monument. On the Prozorje hill, there are ruins of St. Martin's church. The parish church of St. Martin in the village was erected in 1900 according to the design of Hermann Bollé.

❶⑧ SESVETE

Sesvete is a large suburb settlement in the east part of Zagreb area. It is named after the monumental church of All Saints. It is a baroque building with a dome, erected in the middle of the 18th century. It is painted with baroque wall paintings. The main portal has two bell towers, and the windows have nice iron cast grids. In the centre of Sesvete there is the outstanding baroque kurija housing the Regional museum.

❶⑨ VRBOVEC

Vrbovec is situated in the fertile valleys of the Lonja River, Česma River and Glogovnica River, some 40 km northwest of Zagreb. The area is rich in woods, and the zoological resort Varoški lug is of special value. There are many artificial lakes in the area, ideal for the fish growing and sports fishing. There are also good hunting opportunities. Vrbovec is well known for its original dishes, prepared according to *grandma's cuisine*. There is a manifestation dedicated to those old dishes, *Kaj*

Church of St. Vid in Vrbovec

su jeli naši stari (What did our old folks eat). Vrbovec and its vicinity have a lot of monuments of the historical and cultural inheritance. The parish church of St. Vid is the old building in baroque-like style, with baroque altars, big wooden crucifix, chalice from 1722 and other. The parish office from the 18th century is an outstanding building among style houses. There is the baroque chapel of Three Holy Kings in the graveyard and the mausoleum of the De Piennes family.

⓴ SVETI IVAN ZELINA

Gentle hills of Zelina are full of vineyards so the whole area is known for its quality wines, with the outstanding indigenous *kraljevina*. The

Church of Marija Bistrica

attractive Zelina wine road passes here, the second in the Zagreb County. The first traces of life found here date from the bronze era and the settlement Pyrri was here under the Roman rule. But the first document mentioning Zelina dates from 1185, signed by Croatian and Hungarian king Bela III, which confirms to Zagreb canons the right to Zelina land. From that period the extremely interesting ruins of the old town of Zelingrad have been preserved that was mentioned for the first time at the end of the 13th century. In Sveti Ivan Zelina there is a valuable church of St. John the Baptist. In the rearranged medieval church there is a preserved, richly decorated baroque pulpit from 1726 and the rococo baptistery from 1761. The present appearance of the church dates from 1720.

ⓤ MARIJA BISTRICA

The Church of Marija Bistrica is one of the best known pilgrimage places in Croatia. In 1334 it was mentioned as the parish church of St. Peter, and in the second half of the 19th century Hermann Bollé altered it in the Romanesque historicism style spirit. In the church, there is a votive wooden gothic statue of Mary with the Child, standing on the moon with human head. The statue is the original work of domestic master from around 1500. The reverence of Holy Mother from Bistrica as the lady-patron dates from the 16th century, from the time of Turkish invasions, when her statue was saved. Several hundreds of pilgrims visit the church yearly, and the Pope John Paul II visited it as well. The Way of the Cross is arranged on the hill

behind the church decorated with statues by Croatian artists.

ⓦ GORNJA STUBICA

Gornja Stubica, on the northwest slopes of Medvednica, in Hrvatsko Zagorje, is famous for the peasants' revolt in 1573. By the parish church of St. George and original old village house, there is a several hundred years old linden, the monument of nature. According to the legend, it was the place where plans were hatched and the revolt agreed. The town has the Peasants' Revolt Museum, founded in 1973 on the occasion of 400 anniversary of the revolt. The museum is housed in the baroque manor of the Oršić family, architectural monument of the first category that makes a remarkable whole together with its parks. The permanent exhibition of the museum shows the period from the construction of the burgs until the serfdom abolishment by ban Jelačić. The monument to the Peasants' Revolt and their leader, Matija Gubec is an integral part of the

The old linden at dusk

Statue of Matija Gubec

museum complex, the work of Antun Augustinčić. Within the manor, there is the preserved baroque chapel of St. Francis Xavier, with the 18th century frescoes, housing the permanent exhibition of the sacral art.

㉓ DONJA STUBICA

Donja Stubica was mentioned for the first time in 1209. It has a baroque-like parish church of the Holly Trinity altered in 1881, after the earhquake. The bell towers top is the kind of the top of the old Zagreb cathedral bell-tower. The church has the figural decorated priest seats in late gothic style. There is also a renaissance tombstone with relief figure of Franjo Tahi, the cruel squire who, by his behaviour, provoked the peasants' revolt in 1573 led by Matija Gubec.

㉔ STUBIČKE TOPLICE

Stubičke Toplice is situated at the footings of the north slopes of Medvednica, in Hrvatsko zagorje. It has thermal pools and the spa, working intermittently since 1776. The spa building with the pool was erected in 1811, and up to 1814 the pools, pavilions and a neo-gothic church were built. At the time, they were among the most modern and finest spas in this region. The water temperature at the spring is between 43 and 69.5 Celsius degrees and is rich in minerals, calcium and magnesium. It is effective in curing of rheumatism, ishialgia, post traumatical conditions and other illnesses and diseases. The spa is one of the favourite destinations of Zagreb citizens and they are known for the excellent offer of domestic dishes from Zagorje.

㉕ GORNJA BISTRA

In Gornja Bistra, some twenty kilometres north of Zagreb, there is the monument of the zero category,

Park in Gornja Bistra

the baroque manor of the Oršić family from the 18th century. It is a one-floor building of harmonious proportions, with U-shaped groundplan. In the central, oval hall there are illusionist mythological paintings, dating from 1778. The park is around the manor and today the manor houses children's hospital.

㉖ JAKOVLJE

Jakovlje manor was built in the 18th century, at the footings of the north slopes of

Entrance to Jakovlje manor

Medvednica. It was extended and altered on several occasions, and its final appearance dates from the period after the 1880 earthquake. Then the central part of the manor got the new neo-historicism style decoration on the portal. Around the manor, there is a park, tree-lined walk of horse-chestnut trees and a vegetable garden. The park, erected probably in the second half of the 19th century has a part with outdoor statues.

㉗ MONUMENT TO CROATIAN ANTHEM

In Zelenjak, not far from Klanjec, there is a unique monument in the world. That is the monument to the Croatian national anthem, *Lijepa naša*. According to the legend, it was at this place, at the footings of the hill with the ruins of the gothic-renaissance style town of Cesargrad that Antun Mihanović wrote the anthem *Lijepa naša domovino* in 1835 published in *Danica* magazine. Some ten years later Josip Runjanin set those verses to music.

㉘ KLANJEC

Klanjec is a picturesque town by the Croatian and Slovenian border, on the river Sutla. The place has a three-wing Franciscan monastery, founded in the 16th century, and the parish church of St. Mary. The church has two side chapels. In the church there are intarsin benches from 1774, baroque altars, vessels, paint-

Scene from the Gallery in Klanjec

ings and library. In the crypt there are tin sarcophagus of E. Erdödy, the unique monument from the baroque period. At the main town square there is a monument to Antun Mihanović, the writer of the Croatian national anthem *Lijepa naša*. Klanjec has the Antun Augustinčić Gallery, founded in 1970 when Antun Augustinčić (1900 – 1979), one of the most prominent Croatian sculptors, donated his whole work to his birthplace Klanjec. The present permanent exhibition consists of two mutually dependent parts: the interior exhibition has especially plastic portraits and public monuments while the park of statues is around the gallery. The gallery develops the publishing activity beside the museum and organises occasional exhibitions.

㉙ KUMROVEC

Picturesque village, 59 km far from Zagreb, situated on the slope by the river Sava. It has extremely valuable and attractive ethno-village. Some 40 houses and farming houses from the end of the 19th and the beginning of the 20th centuries have been preserved and renovated. They make rural unity named *Old*

Old village in Kumrovec

village. Here is also the native house of Josip Broz Tito, the leader of the antifascist battle and the president of the former Yugoslavia that is turned into a museum. The house was built in 1860 and was the first brick house in the village. By the house there is a bronze statue of marshall Tito, work of the famous sculptor Antun Augustinčić from 1948.

㉚ MILJANA

Not far from Kumrovec, Miljana is situated, one of the most picturesque and finest manors in Croatia. It belonged to the Ratkay family who started to build it in the 17th century. Since the construction lasted for almost three centuries, it was subjected to alterations and mixtures of styles and compositions, and its colour changed as well: it was white, grey, black and blue. From 1979 to 1982 it was renovated, getting the appearance from its final phase. The manor has valuable rococo wall paintings with allegorical and landscape scenes.

㉛ VELIKI TABOR

☎ 049/343 052
🕐 10 a.m. - 5 p.m.
  (April, 1 - September, 30)
  9 a.m. - 3 p.m.
  (October, 1 - March, 31)

Veliki Tabor, medieval town three kilometres east of Desinić, in Hrvatsko Zagorje, the best preserved medieval fortification in Croatia. It was erected at the beginning of the 16th century. In the 17th and 18th century it was rearranged into a castle. It is the highest category monument and the representative example of late medieval fortification architecture. It is built on a hill, as if taking care of the whole Hrvatsko Zagorje. The town has mostly kept its original appearance. The defence walls have preserved late gothic and renaissance style details, carved coat-of-arms and carved signs, *bifora, erkeri*, two floor arcade porches in the courtyard. The castle generated many stories and legends, more than any other ancient building. Through the history it changed the owners, and between the two World Wars it was the propriety of the famous painter, Oton Iveković.

㉜ TUHELJSKE TOPLICE

Tuheljske Toplice in Hrvatsko Zagorje, known as bathing place and spa already in Roman times, and because of the specific smell of sulphor it was popularly called "stinking spa". Bathing is possible in summer and winter because the water temperature is 32.5 degrees Celsius. It helps in treatments of arthrosis, respiratory diseases, gynaeocological problems, ishias, neuralgy and others. Here is also a nice baroque manor *Mihanović, kurija* altered into a representative catering object. In Tuhelj, the settlement 4 kilometres of Tuheljske toplice, there is the interesting St. Mary's Church, one nave late gothic building.

Pools in Tuheljske toplice

㉝ KRAPINSKE TOPLICE

Krapinske Toplice, settlement, spa and thermal baths 17 kilometres southwest of Krapina, in Hrvatsko zagorje, has the hyperthermal mineral radioactive water springs. It was known in Roman times, and the modern spa started to be built in 1772. In the middle of the last century, in 1956, the hospital department for rheumatic diseases and rehabilitation was founded. Water and healing mud are used in treatments of rheumatism, gout, ishias, muscular problems, chronical inflamations, heart and nerves diseases, post heart-attack and post-operational rehabilitation etc. Only a kilometre west of Krapinske Toplice, there is a one-floor classicist style manor Klokovec.

View to Veliki Tabor fortification

34 KRAPINA

Krapina, picturesque town in the heart of Hrvatsko Zagorje, mentioned for the first time in 1193. It was a fortified town in 1330 of which only remnants have been preserved. In the middle of the 14th century it was free royal trading place, and by the end of the 15th century it was the seat of the Croatian ban. Krapina is best known by the remnants of pre-hestoric men od Neanderthal type, found by Dragutin Gorjanović Kramberger in 1899, in the cave on the Hušnjakovo hill. Apart from bones of twenty pre-historic men, the objects they made were also found: points, bone axe and others. Today, in front of the cave there are reconstructions of pre-historic men and animals in natural size. The permanent exhibition, i. e. the Evolution museum has been opened. The town has also the native museum of Ljudevit Gaj, who was born here and in 1891 and has got his statue.

35 TRŠKI VRH

In Trški Vrh, the settlement a kilometre northwest of

The site on Hušnjak hill near Krapina

Krapina, there is a spacious votive church of Mary of Jeruzalem from 1761. It is situated on a high plateau, enclosed with square shaped cincture whose construction was completed in 1773. It has integrated rounded chapels that do not look like towers and the building for the clergy. The inside of the cincture has arcades. There is bell tower with baroque shapes spreading from the main portal. The Church interior is richly furnished. There are decorative illusionist wall paintings in rococo style, and nice and valuable altars. In one of the cincture's chapels, there is the damaged stone statute of the Holy Mary with the child dating from the period between 1410 and 1420.

36 TRAKOŠĆAN

① 042/796 281
① 9 a.m. - 6 p.m.
☞ with prior announcement

Trakošćan is the most popular and most visited castle in this part of Croatia. It is the

monument of the highest category. It is not known for sure who and when built it, but it is assumed that it was erected in the 14th century, as a fortress. In the castle basis one could recognise the features of the simple Romanesque type *castels* from 12-13 centuries. It was

Trakošćan Castle

extended and additionally built on several occassions. In the 16th century it was managed by the emperor Maximilian II who in 1569 appointed ban and bishop of Zagreb Joseph II Drašković to manage the castle. Later it became the permanent property of the Drašković family, but in the middle of the 17th century for several years it was the propriety of Nikola Zrinski. Its present appearance dates from the 19th cen-

Detail from the church in Trški Vrh

tury, when it was renovated in neo-gothic style. With its beautiful garden, park-forest and large artificial lake, the castle is really an impressive view.

37 KLENOVNIK

In Klenovnik, the settlement 9 kilometres northwest of Ivanec, there was a medieval fortified burg that in 1244 king Bela IV gave to Mihalj, the Varaždin prefect. The new square renaissance castle was built in 1616 by counts Drašković. Later the caslte was extended and altered, and in 1927 it was rearranged into the healing centre. Some rooms have valuable wall paintings from the 19th century. Lavish castle chapel has a stucco ceiling, three baroque altars, a pulpit and the tomb of the Drašković family.

38 LEPOGLAVA

Lepoglava situated in the valley of the Bednja River is the historical town in Hrvatsko Zagorje, known for its rich cultural heritage. There is a notable monastery of the St. Pauline Order with the Church of the Impeccable Conception of the Holy Virgin Mary from 1400. It repre-

sents one of the substantial cultural monuments in the continental part of Croatia. The construction began after the arrival of the monks of the St. Pauline order, "the white friars", and it was the counts Celjski that invited them to Lepoglava. In the course of almost four centuries, until the abolishment of their order, the monks took care of cultural education of the people, leaving unerasable trace. The complex of St. Pauline Order consists of church, monastery with the inner courtyard and buildings that in front of the main portal enclosed the outer courtyard. The baroque-like church of st. Mary is the one nave building with bell-tower at the side. It has four side chapels, and two halls in front of the entrance. In the middle of the 19th century the monastery area was rearranged into the prison that was finally moved out in 2001.

The front of Lepoglava church

39 BELEC

Belec has the most beautiful baroque church in Croatia. The parish church of St. Mary of Snow was erected in the second half of the 17th century, and its present appearance dates between 1739 and 1741, when it was rearranged and extended. It is

Altar in the Belec church

one nave church, with polygonal shrine and sacristy on the north. On the left and right of the nave are two side chapels, and by the west portal the bell-tower erects. The church is enclosed with picturesque cincture. In the interior there is an open porch with arches and arcades. The church interior is among the most valuable achievements of the baroque art in Croatia, decorated with illusionist wall paintings and lavish altars. The main wooden altar from 1743 is the rich work of the mature baroque. Belec also has the remnants of the burg, Belegrad, that was a part of the chain of burgs at the south side of Ivančica mountain.

TRANSPORT

Due to favourable geographical and traffic position, Zagreb is close to all big European cities. It is well connected with other parts of Croatia as well, by roads, railways and planes. The public transport is also well organised. Those who are going to use their private cars have at their disposal a lot of parking places and parking garages.

Modern motorways lead to Zagreb

ARRIVAL BY ROAD
The main arrival directions by road are: Trieste - Ljubljana - Zagreb, Graz - Maribor - Zagreb, Klagenfurt - Ljubljana - Zagreb, Budapest - Varaždin - Zagreb. The directions from Zagreb lead over Karlovac towards Rijeka, Zadar, Split and other towns at the Adriatic Coast. The roads to the east lead towards Slavonski Brod and Osijek. The majority of roads are modern motorways. The drivers must obey the speed limits and have their seat-belts fastened. Take care not to drive with higher blood alcohol level because the fines are extremely high.

AIR CONNECTIONS
There are regular air flights, direct or, for some longer destinations with the change, that connect Zagreb to all larger European and world cities. Regular flights are operated by national line company Croatia Airlines, but also by meany other world and European companies. The Zagreb airport is 17 km far from Zagreb connected by a good, wide road and it takes only 20 to 25 minutes by car or bus.

ARRIVAL BY TRAIN
The main Railway station is in the centre of the town, on Trg Kralja Tomislava 12. By daily international trains Zagreb is connected to Munich, Vienna, Venice, Budapest, Paris, Geneva, Graz and Moscow.

TAXI
Zagreb Taxi service is fast and efficient but rather expensive. All taxes have meters, which must be reset at the beginning of your jour-

---

Bus station
Avenija Marina Držića bb
① 060 313 333; 060 34 03 40
🖳 www.akz.hr

Pleso Airport
Pleso bb
① 01 626 52 22
🖳 www.zagreb-airport.htnet.hr

Main Railway station
Trg kralja Tomislava 12
① 060 333 444
🖳 www.hznet.hr

Table at Taxi station with the price list

ney. You have to pay 20% charge for the night ride and additional charge for the luggage. Taxi could be ordered by dialing of 970 (taxi radio service).

RENT-A-CAR
There are several rent-a-car agencies in the town. Besides others there are Avis and Hertz, well known multinational companies. Individual

agencies could have their offices at the Zagreb airport as well. Some offer you the possibility of leaving the

Punching machine

Public transport ticket for one ride and a day ticket

car at some other place, or town not necessarily the same where you rented the car.

PUBLIC TRANSPORT
Public transport in Zagreb is performed by buses and trams. The tickets are the same for both. They can be bought at the kiosks or directly from the driver, but in that case they are more

expensive. There are one ride tickets and day tickets, which are valid for the unlimited number of rides during that day. The purchased ticket should be punched in the machine located near the door. Passengers are transported also by a funicular connecting Ilica and the Upper Town. The ticket for it is purchased on entering.

Aircompanies

Adria Airways
Praška ulica 9
☎ 01 487 20 55; 01 487 20 76
🖳 www.adria.si
🕐 8.30 a.m. - 4 p.m.

Aeroflot
Varšavska ulica 13
☎ 01 487 20 55; 01 487 20 76
🖳 www.aeroflot.ru
✉ aeroflot@zg.htnet.hr
🕐 7.30 a.m. - 4 p.m.

Air Canada
Kršnjavoga 1 (Hotel Opera)
☎ 01 482 20 33
🖳 www.aircanada.ca/e-home.htm
🕐 8 a.m. - 4 p.m.

Air France
Kršnjavoga 1 (hotel Opera)
☎ 01 483 71 00
🖳 www.airfrance.com
🕐 9 a.m. - 5 p.m.; ● Sat, Sun

Austrian Airlines
Aerodrom Pleso
☎ 01 626 59 00
🖳 www.aua.com/hr
🕐 8 a.m. - 4 p.m.

British Airways
Ulica kneza Borne 2
☎ 01 455 33 36
🖳 www.britishairways.com
🕐 8.30 a.m. - 5 p.m.; ● Sat, Sun

Bosna Air
Aerodrom Pleso
☎ 01 456 26 72
🖳 www.airbosna.ba
🕐 9 a.m. - 4 p.m.

Croatia Airlines
Trg Nikole Šubića Zrinskog 17
☎ 01 481 96 33; 0800 77 77
🖳 www.croatiaairlines.hr
🕐 8 a.m. - 8 p.m.; Sat 8 a.m. - 2 p.m.

ČSA
Trg Nikole Šubića Zrinskog 17
☎ 01 487 33 01

🖳 www.csa.cz
🕐 8 a.m. - 4 p.m.; Sat 9 am - 12 am.

Delta Airlines
Trg Nikole Šubića Zrinskog 14
☎ 01 487 87 60
🖳 www.delta.com
🕐 8 a.m. - 8 p.m.;
   Sat 9 a.m. - 4 p.m.; ● Sun

KLM
Radićeva ulica 23
☎ 01 487 86 00
🖳 www.klm.com/hr
🕐 8 a.m. - 4 p.m.; ● Sat, Sun

LOT
Trg bana Josipa Jelačića 2/I
☎ 01 483 75 00
🖳 www.lot.com.
✉ lotzag@net.hr
🕐 Sat 9 a.m. - 4 p.m.

Lufthansa
Trg Nikole Šubića Zrinskog 18
☎ 01 487 31 21
🖳 www.lufthansa.com
🕐 8 a.m. - 8 p.m.; Sat 9 a.m. - 2 p.m.

Malaysia Airlines
Strossmayerov trg 7
☎ 01 481 07 77; 01 481 38 77
🖳 www.malaysiaairlineseurope.com
✉ zagto@malaysiairlines.hr
🕘 8.30 a.m. - 4.30 p.m.

Malev
Kršnjavoga 1 (Hotel Opera)
☎ 01 483 69 35; 01 483 69 36
🖳 www.malev.hu
✉ zagreb@malev.hu
🕘 8 a.m. - 4 p.m.

Swiss Airlines
Trg Nikole Šubića
Zrinskog 1/III
☎ 01 481 41 44
🖳 www.swiss.com
🕘 8 a.m. - 4 p.m.

Turkish Airlines
Jurišićeva ulica 12
☎ 01 492 18 54
🖳 www.turkishairlines.com
🕘 9 a.m. - 5 p.m.; Sun 8 a.m. -11 a.m.

Quantas
Kršnjavoga 1
(Hotel Opera, I. kat)
☎ 01 481 40 20
🖳 www.qantas.com
🕘 Mon-Fri 8.30 a.m. - 4 p.m.

Travel agencies

A-Tours
Držićeva ulica 4
(Autobusni kolodvor)
☎ 01 600 86 66
🖷 01 611 31 88

Adriatours
Rooseveltov trg 4
☎ 01 482 63 77
🖷 01 482 69 34
🖳 www.adriatours.hr
✉ adriatours@zg.htnet.hr

Adrijana International d.o.o.
Teslina 13/1
☎ 01 487 22 41; 01 487 22 42
🖷 01 487 22 43
🖳 www.adrijana-international.hr
✉ adrijana@adrijana-international.hr

Astratours
Gajeva 7
☎ 01 481 11 92

🖷 01 481 11 93
✉ turizam@astra-tit.hr

Atlantis Travel
Petrinjska ulica 59
☎ 01 481 11 55
🖷 01 481 89 14
🖳 www.atlantis-travel.hr
✉ atlantis1@zg.htnet.hr

Atlas Airtours d.o.o.
Ulica Zinke Kunc 2
☎ 01 610 20 00
🖳 www.atlasairtours.hr

Azur Tours
Tkalčićeva ulica 14
☎ 01 481 13 89
🖷 01 481 37 37
🖳 www.azurtours.hr
✉ azur-tours@zg.htnet.hr

Ben Tours
Kaptol 11
☎ 01 481 68 68
🖷 01 481 46 77
🖳 www.bantours.hr
✉ ban-tours@zg.htnet.hr

Business Travel International O-Tours
Gajeva ulica 6/I
☎ 01 483 14 44
🖷 01 481 30 10
🖳 www.otours.hr

Croatia Expres
Ulica N. Tesle 4
☎ 01 481 18 42
🖷 01 481 19 20
🖳 www.zug.hr
✉ croatia-express-pa@htnet.hr

Dalmacijaturist
Zrinjevac 16
☎ 01 487 30 73
🖷 01 487 30 75

Diners Club Travel
Berislavićeva ulica 2
☎ 01 487 32 04
🖷 01 481 72 46
🖳 www.diners.hr
✉ diners.travel@diners.hr

Diners Club Travel
Ulica A. Hebranga 25
☎ 01 488 64 05
🖷 01 485 66 06
🖳 www.diners.hr
✉ diners.travel@diners.hr

Ferek Tours
Gajeva ulica 25
☎ 01 492 40 24
🖷 01 492 36 41
🖳 www.ferek-tours.hr
✉ info@ferek-tours.hr

Ferial
Nova Ves 11 (Centar Kaptol)
☎ 01 486 00 11

🖷 01 486 00 10
🖳 www.ferial.hr
✉ ferial-zg@ka.htnet.hr

Fortuna Travel
Gundulićeva ulica 25
☎ 01 485 44 15
🖷 01 485 44 14
🖳 www.fortunatravel.hr
✉ fortuna@zg.htnet.hr

Generalturist
Praška ulica 5
☎ 01 481 00 33
🖷 01 481 04 28
🖳 www.generalturist.com
✉ generalturist@generalturist.com

Globtour Zagreb
Zrinjevac 1/1
☎ 01 481 00 21
🖷 01 481 22 77
🖳 www.globtour.hr

Integral
Pothodnik Glavnog
kolodvora
☎ 01 457 72 33
🖷 01 457 72 58
🖳 www.integral-zagreb.hr
✉ integral-zagreb@zg.htnet.hr

Jammark
Trg kralja Tomislava 17
☎ 01 492 22 50
🖷 01 492 22 51
🖳 www.jammark.hr
✉ info@jammark.hr

Jumbo
Britanski trg 5/I
☎ 01 482 35 00
🖷 01 482 35 01
🖳 www.jumbo-tours.hr
✉ jumbo@zg.htnet.hr

Kompas
Zrinjevac 14
☎ 01 481 15 36
🖷 01 487 87 69
🖳 www.kompas.hr
✉ kompas@kompas.hr
🕘 8 a.m. - 5 p.m.

Kompas Travel
Savska cesta 19
☎ 01 481 18 63
🖷 01 481 18 69
🖳 www.kompas-travel.com
    www.kompasdmc.com
✉ kompasdmc@kompas-travel.com

Kontakt
Gundulićeva ulica 3
☎ 01 483 07 37; 01 483 07 38
🖷 01 483 07 35
🖳 www.kontakttours.hr
✉ kontakt@zg.htnet.hr

Marine Air
Gajeva ulica 55
☎ 01 492 21 40
🖷 01 492 21 41
✉ marineair@zg.htnet.hr

Penta
Ulica A. Hebranga 20
☎ 01 455 32 90
📠 01 455 32 84
🖥 www.penta-zagreb.hr
✉ penta@zg.htnet.hr

Obzor putovanja
Teslina ulica 5
☎ 01 487 31 68
📠 01 616 02 40
🖥 www.croatiaairlines.hr
✉ obzor@croatiaairlines.com

Transagent
Ulica A. Hebranga 10
☎ 01 481 70 02
📠 01 481 70 04
✉ transagent.zagreb@transagent.hr

TUI Centar za putovanja
Praška ulica 10
☎ 01 483 35 02; 01 483 35 03
🖥 www.airtours.hr

TUI Centar za putovanja
Ilica 11/I
☎ 01 492 37 49; 01 492 37 50
🖥 www.airtours.hr

Ulix
Miramarska ulica 26
☎ 01 615 40 90
📠 01 615 40 92
🖥 www.ulixtravel.com
✉ ulix@ulixtravel.com

Vladek
Petrinjska ulica 73
☎ 01 484 12 21
📠 01 484 12 25
🖥 www.nazor.hr
✉ vladek@nazor.hr

Vladimir Nazor d.o.o.
za organizirani odmor djece
i mladeži grada Zagreba
Maksimirska cesta 51
☎ 01 231 01 00
📠 01 231 97 17
🖥 www.nazor.hr
✉ nazor@nazor.hr

Zagrebtours
Zrinjevac 18
☎ 01 487 33 05
📠 01 487 31 25
🖥 www.zagrebtours.hr
✉ zagrebtours@zg.htnet.hr

Rent-a-car

ADB
Gajeva ulica 40
☎ 01 457 75 65
🕐 8 a.m. - 4 p.m.; Sat 8 a.m. - 12 a.m.

An Nova
Pleso bb, Aerodrom
☎ 01 456 22 44
📠 01 456 22 47
🖥 www.an-nova.hr
🕐 7 a.m. - 10 p.m.

Avis
Kršnjavoga 1 (hotel Opera)
☎ 01 483 60 06
🕐 8 a.m. - 4 p.m.; ● Sun

Budget
Ulica kneza Borne 2
(hotel Sheraton)
☎ 01 480 56 90
   01 480 56 88
🕐 7 a.m. - 8 p.m.; Sun 8 a.m. - 12 a.m.

Budget
Pleso bb, Aerodrom
☎ 01 456 22 21
🖥 reservations@budget.hr
🕐 7 a.m. - 9 p.m.

Dollar&Thrifty
Pleso bb, Aerodrom
☎ 01 626 53 33
🕐 7 a.m. - 9 p.m.

Hertz
Pleso bb, Aerodrom
☎ 01 456 26 35
🖥 www.hertz.hr
🕐 7.30 a.m. - 8 p.m.

H&M
Pleso bb, Aerodrom
☎ 01 456 22 63
🕐 7.30 a.m. - 8 p.m.

Ina/Itr
Pleso bb, Aerodrom
☎ 01 456 20 74; 01 456 20 74
🕐 8 a.m. - 7 p.m.; Sun 9 am - 1 am.

M.A.C.K. Concord
Pleso bb, Aerodrom
☎ 01 456 20 74
🕐 7 a.m. - 8 p.m.

National
Pleso bb, Aerodrom
☎ 01 456 25 50
🕐 07-21
🖥 www.nationalcar.hr

Sixt
Pleso bb, Aerodrom
☎ 01 621 99 00; 01 619 99 99
📠 01 621 99 11
🕐 07-21
🖥 www.e-sixt.com

Rent-a-bike

Euro Bike Centar
Gajeva ulica 29a
☎ 01 481 22 75
🕐 08-20; sub 08-15

Metalia Commerce
Vlaška ulica 28
☎ 01 481 41 28
🕐 8 a.m. - 8 p.m.; Sat 8 a.m. - 3 p.m.

Unis Bike centar
Martićeva ulica 11
☎ 01 461 97 78
🕐 8.30 am. - 9 p.m.; Sat 8 am. - 3 p.m.

Public transport

ZET
Ozaljska cesta 105
☎ 01 365 15 55
🖥 www.zet.hr
Tramvaji voze:
4 a.m. - 11.45 p.m
11.35 p.m. - 3.46 a.m.

Autobusi – informacije
Ozaljska cesta 105
☎ 01 660 04 46 – zapad
   01 660 04 45 – istok

Parking (0-24)

Centar Kaptol I-2
Nova Ves 17
☎ 01 486 02 41
🖥 www.centarkaptol.hr

Importanne Centar
Starčevićev trg bb
☎ 01 457 70 76

Importanne Galeria
Iblerov trg bb

Zagrebparking
Ilica 45
☎ 01 484 85 54

Zagrebparking
☎ 01 481 94 47

Zagrebparking
Palmotićeva ulica 25
☎ 01 48 169 01

Taxi

Radio Taxi 970
Ulica Božidara Magovca 55
☎ 01 668 25 05
🖥 www.radio-taxi-zagreb.hr
✉ info@radio-taxi-zagreb.hr
🕐 0-24

MISSIONS IN CROATIA

Large number of countries opened their embassies and various other missions in Zagreb, ranging from economic offices to cultural centres.

Embassies

Albania
Jurišićeva ulica 2a
☎ 01 481 06 79

Australia
Nova Ves 17
Centar Kaptol/III
☎ 01 489 12 00

Austria
Ulcia Jabukovac 39
☎ 01 488 10 50

Belgium
Ulica Pantovčak 125b
☎ 01 457 89 01

Bosnia and Herzegovina
Ulica Pavla Hatza 3
☎ 01 481 94 20

Bulgaria
Novi Goljak 25
☎ 01 482 33 36

Czech Republic
Savska cesta 41/VIII
☎ 01 617 72 46

Chile
Smičiklasova ulica 23/II
☎ 01 461 19 58

Egypt
Tuškanac 58a
☎ 01 483 42 72

Finland
Berislavićeva ulica 2/I
☎ 01 481 16 62

France
Ulica Andrije Hebranga 2
☎ 01 489 36 00

Greece
Opatička ulica 12
☎ 01 481 04 44

Guinea Bissau
Jurjevska ulica 51
☎ 01 466 35 00

India
Boškovićeva ulica 7a
☎ 01 487 32 41

Iran
Ulica Pantovčak 125c
☎ 01 457 89 83

Italy
Medulićeva ulica 22
☎ 01 484 63 86

Japan
Ksaver 211
☎ 01 467 77 55

Canada
Prilaz Gjure Deželića 4
☎ 01 488 12 00

China
Mlinovi 132
☎ 01 463 70 11

Libian National Bureau
G. Prekrižje 51b
☎ 01 462 92 50

Hungary
Ulica Pantovčak 255-257
☎ 01 489 09 00

Macedonia
Petrinjska ulica 29/I
☎ 01 492 29 02

Malaysia
Slavujevac 4a
☎ 01 483 43 47

Netherlands
Ulica Medveščak 56
☎ 01 468 48 80

Germany
Ulica grada Vukovara 64
☎ 01 615 81 05

Norway
Petrinjska ulica 9/1
☎ 01 492 28 29

Peru
Ksaverska cesta 19
☎ 01 467 73 25

Poland
Krležin Gvozd 3
☎ 01 489 94 44

Portugal
Trg bana Josipa Jelačića 5/II
☎ 01 488 22 10

Romania
Mlinarska cesta 43
☎ 01 467 75 50

Russian Federation
Bosanska ulica 44
☎ 01 375 50 38

U.S.A
Thomasa Jeffersona 2
Buzin
☎ 01 661 22 00

Slovakia
Prilaz Gjure Deželića 10
☎ 01 484 89 41

Slovenia
Savska cesta 41
☎ 01 631 10 14

Serbia and Montenegro
Ulica Pantovčak 245
☎ 01 457 90 67

Churches and Religious Communities

Zagreb Islamic community
Gavellina 40
☎ 01 613 71 62

**Croatian Bishops'
Conference**
Kaptol 22
☎ 01 481 18 95

**Serbian Orthodox
Community**
Ilica 7
☎ 01 481 26 16

Zagreb Jewish community
Palmotićeva 16
☎ 01 492 26 92

Malta
Becićeve stube 2
① 01 467 79 99

Holy See
Apostolska nuncijatura
Ksaverska cesta 10a
① 01 467 39 95

Spain
Tuškanac 21a
① 01 4848 950

Sweden
Frankopanska ulica 22
① 01 492 51 00
　　Vize: 01 484 93 33

Switzerland
Bogovićeva ulica 3
① 01 487 88 00

Turkey
Masarykova ulica 3/II
① 01 485 52 00

Ukraine
Voćarska ulica 52
① 01 461 62 96
　　Vize: 01 463 37 28

Great Britain
Ulica I. Lučića 4
① 01 600 91 00
Odjel za vize:
Alexandera von
Humboldta 4
① 01 600 91 22

Consulates

Bosnia and Herzegovina
Hatzova ulica 3
① 01 481 94 20

Brasil
Medulićeva ulica 26
① 01 482 65 37

Danemark
(Generalni Konzulat)
Pavlinovićeva ulica 1
① 01 376 05 36

Finland
Jurjevska ulica 15
① 01 489 90 64

France
(Konzularni Odjel)
Gajeva ulica 12/I
① 01 487 25 08

Indonesia
Preradovićeva ulica 34
① 01 485 60 99

Ireland
Turinina ulica 3
① 01 667 44 55

Malta
Pavlinovićeva ulica 4
① 01 390 05 15

New Zealand
c/o Hrv. matica iseljenika
Trg Stjepana Radića 3
① 01 615 13 82

Portugal
Trg hrvatskih velikana 3/I
① 01 461 44 53

Peru
Ksaverska cesta 19/II
① 01 467 73 25

Thailand
Gundulićeva ulica 18
① 01 483 03 59

Cultural Centres

Austrian Cultural Institute
Gundulićeva ulica 3
① 01 488 12 50

British Council
Ilica 12/I
① 01 481 37 00

French Cultural Centre
Preradovićeva ulica 40
① 01 485 52 22

Goethe Institut
Ulica grada Vukovara 64
① 01 619 50 00

UNESCO
Ilica 207
① 01 378 02 00

Economic Institutions

American Chamber of Commerce in Croatia
Kršnjavoga 1
① 01 483 67 77

Austrian Office for Foreign Trade and Tourism
Ilica 12/II
① 01 488 19 00

Bulgarian Trade Office
Zelengaj 77
① 01 457 85 85

European Bank for Reconstruction and Development (EBRD)
Petrinjska ulica 59/V
① 01 487 87 00

French Office for Economy Affairs
Preradovićeva ulica 35/I
① 01 455 77 22

Croatian Chamber of Commerce Zagreb Chamber
Draškovićeva ulica 45
① 01 460 67 77

Croatian Chamber of Trades and Crafts
Ilica 49
① 01 480 66 66

International Monetary Fond (IMF)
Trg Burze 3
① 01 456 47 27

Zagreb Chamber of Trades and Crafts
Ilica 49
① 01 484 67 41

World Trade Center Zagreb
Avenija Dubrovnik 15
① 01 650 32 32

Orientation in Town

The best way to go through Zagreb is on foot, since the majority of things worth seeing are located on a narrow area of the town centre. The information on important cultural and sports events can be found in daily papers and numerous information boards around the town. Banks and shops do not work on Saturdays afternoon and Sundays, but you can do your shopping in the nearby shopping centres which work on weekends. For all additional information the best place to turn to is the Zagreb Tourist Information Office, whose offices are all over the town.

Greetings

Persons who do not know each other or are not in closer relationship address each other with mister, for man, and Mrs (married woman) or Miss (unmarried woman) for woman. The addressing by title is also frequent, as for example, professor or doctor, and the employees in a company or institution address each other with colleague. Greetings depend on the part of the day: good morning, good day, good evening and, before going to bed, good night. Other greetings are goodbye, see you or hello, and the informal Zagreb greeting is "bok", for both "hello" and "goodby".

Time

Croatia is on Central European Time, as Italy, Austria, Germany. . .

Smoking

In closed public places smoking area is separated

The smoking or non smoking signs are highlighted at public places

but the relation to smoking is rather flexible. You can smoke in every restaurant though some have smoking and non smoking areas.

Working Hours

The majority of shops, especially food shops, work non stop, from morning until 8 or 9 p.m., and some even longer. The majority of shops work shorter on Saturdays, until 2 or 3 p.m., and on Sundays shops on duty are opened, but also a lot of small food shops, especially those around markets. Public offices and services are open on work days from 8 a.m. to 4. p.m.

Electricity

In Zagreb, that is in the whole Croatia, the voltage is 220 V. Plugs are the standard European two-pin variety.

Public Toilettes

Use of public toilettes on bus and railway station , as well as in some large shopping centres, tend to be paid for (2 kunas). In restaurants the use is mostly free of charge, though it is possible you will be asked for a kuna or two. Public toilettes are opened around markets as well, and one is situated at Ban Jelačić Square.

In the centre of town there is a number of public toilettes

PARKING

Public parking facilities are divided into zones,

Parking fee depends on zones

and the price and allowed parking time depends on the zone. It is clearly marked on the tables at the parking facilities.

Parking tickets can be bought at the machines and should be put in the car so that an inspector can see it. If stated, the parking fee could be paid by domestic mobile

networks. There are also many parking garages in the town where payment is arranged at the entrance or departure. Large shopping centres usually have their own garages or car parks. If you park illegaly at the place where parking is not allowed your car could be towed away.

TOURIST INFORMATION

All information the visitors to Zagreb may need could be found at Tourist Information Centres or

Public Holidays in Croatia	
1 January	- New Year's Day
6 january	- Holy Trinity or Epiphany
Easter (variable)	
Easter Monday (variable)	
1 May	- International Labour Day
Corpus Christi (variable)	
22 June	- Anti-Fascist Struggle Day
25 June	- Croatian Statehood Day
5 August	- Homeland Thanksgiving Day
15 August	- Assumption
8 October	- Croatian Independence Day
1 November	- All Saint's Day
25 December	- Christmas
26 December	- St. Stephen

Zagreb Tourist Information Centre.

Tourist Information Centre at Ban Jelačić Square

Tourist Information Centre
Trg bana Josipa Jelačića 11
☏ 01 481 40 51; 01 481 40 52
💻 www.zagreb-touristinfo.hr
🕐 8.30 a.m. - 8 p.m.
 Sat 9 a.m. - 5 p.m.
 Sun 10 a.m. - 4 p.m.

Trg Nikole Šubića Zrinjskog 14
☏ 01 492 16 45
💻 www.zagreb-touristinfo.hr
🕐 Mon, Wedn, Fri 9 a.m. - 5 p.m.
 Tu and Thur 9 a.m.- 6 p.m.

Zagreb Tourist Information Centre
Kaptol 5
☏ 01 481 40 51
💻 www.zagreb-touristinfo.hr
🕐 Mon - Fri 8 a.m. 4 p.m.

Parking is available on the streets as well as in numerous underground garages

Money

Official money in Croatia is Croatian kuna (KN) and all prices are quoted in kunas. Paying in other currencies is not possible although the exchange of foreign currency into kunas is very easy. Money can be exchanged in banks or authorised exchange offices. Exchange offices have rather flexible working hours, and foreign currency could be exchanged at the post offices, tourist offices and hotels.

You can take your cash as the cash machines but buy mobile VIP account as well

Banks

The biggest banks in Croatia, like Zagrebačka banka or Privredna banka have their seats in Zagreb so they have a lot of branch offices in town. All other important banks have their branch offices in Zagreb. Banks are open from 8 a.m. to 7. p.m. on work days, Monday to Friday, and from 8 a.m. to 1 p.m on Saturdays. It is good to know that Zagrebačka banka at the Zagreb Airport works daily from 7 a.m. to 9 p.m., and the exchange office on duty stays open until the last flight. At the Main Railway station there is 24 hour Exchange Office.

Cash Machines

There are a lot of cash machines in Zagreb which operate 24 hours a day. There are no queues in front of them, or rarely, even during "rush" hours so you save your time. The most extensive ATM networks in Zagreb are those of Zagrebačka banka and Privredna banka, who accept all major credit/debit cards: American Express, Diners, EC/MC, Maestro, Visa Electron and Visa.

Purchase

All major credit/debit cards are accepted - visa, MasterCard, American Express, diners and others. You can use them in hotels, shops, gas stations, larger and smarter restaurants. On all entrances the accepted cards are displayed. If you lose yours, you should notify the bank immediately in order to cancel it as soon as possible.

There are a lot of banks in town

The accepted cards are displayed at the entrance

MONEY

The currency is kuna, with one hundred lipa to one kuna. The following bank notes are used: 1000, 500, 200, 100, 50, 20, 10, and 5 kunas. The coins are of 5, 2 and 1 kuna, and 50, 20, 10, 5, 2 and 1 lipa.

The 100 kuna bank note (100 kn)

The 50 kuna bank note (50 kn)

The 200 kuna bank note (200 kn)

The 20 kuna bank note (20 kn)

The 500 kuna bank note (500 kn)

The 10 kuna bank note (10 kn)

The 1000 kuna bank note (1000 kn)

The 5 kuna bank note (5 kn)

COMMUNICATION

The communication system in Zagreb is efficient and highly developed. All kinds of information could be easily got, and those who do not speak Croatian can get papers in their language althouth there are tourist editions. Croatian radio broadcasts the news in foreign languages, and it is easy to find other television channels through a satellite.

Public telephone booth

Croatian Post Office Sign

Office is by the Main Railway Station operating for 24 hours with the 24 hour exchange office.

POSTAL SERVICE

Zagreb post offices are well organised and efficient. You can buy stamps, phone cards and everything else you need for the postal service. You can also use post office fax. Except at the post offices, stamps and phonecards could be bought in newpaper kiosks, and the letters could be sent through post boxes as well. The Main Post

Post box with indicated time of collection

TELEPHONE CALLS

You can make a telephone call from most Croatian Telecom Centers and numerous phone booths. It is cheaper to call from the phone booth than, for example, a hotel, because they will charge you service fee. In the evenings and during the night the phone calls are cheaper as well as on public holidays. For the telephone booths the phonecards used of 50, 100, 200 and 500 impulses and could be bought at the newpaper kiosks, "Duhan" kiosks and post offices. There are three GSM operators in Croatia: HT mobile, with numbers starting with 098, HTmobile with 099 area code, and VIPnet beginning with 091. The Croatia country code is 385, and Zagreb area code is 01. You should dial it only if you call from outside the town or from a mobile phone. If you call from Zagreb, of Croatia, a number in foreign country, you should first dial the international number 00, then the country code, area code and finally the phone number.

INTERNET

There are a lot of internet cafés in Zagreb where you will find all you need. Most hotels also provide internet and e-mail service.

NEWSPAPERS, RADIO, TELEVISION

Zagreb offers many European and world papers as well as magazines and specialised magazines. Croatian Television broadcasts two national programmes. Nova TV and RTL Television also have national coverage. Besides those, there are regional television sta-

Useful telephone numbers

Local directory enquiries 988

Speaking clock 95

To send a telegramme 96

Phone alarm-clock 9100

Weather forecast and road and traffic information 060 520 520

Internet could be used at many places in town

tions at a local level. Almost all hotels have cabel television so you can watch numerous foreign channels. Croatian

radio daily broadcasts the News in English and German. The information of traffic are also regularly broadcast.

Post office

Central Post Office
Jurišićeva ulica 13
① 01 481 10 90
  9832 (opće informacije)
⏱ 7 a.m. - 9 p.m.
  Sun 8 a.m. - 4 p.m.; ● Sun

Post office 10 000
Branimirova 4
⏱ 0-24

Internet

@VIP
Iblerov trg 10
① 091 209 10 91
⏱ 7 a.m. - 11 p.m.;
  Sun 9 a.m. - 11 p.m.

Aquarius net
Držislavova ulica 4
① 01 461 29 19
⏱ 10 a.m. - 11 p.m.;
  Sun 3 p.m. - 11 p.m.

Art Net Club
Preradovićeva ulica 25
① 01 455 84 71
⏱ 9 a.m. - 8 p.m.;
  Sun 9 a.m. -5 p.m.

Charlie Net
Gajeva ulica 4a
① 01 488 02 33
⏱ 8 a.m. - 10 p.m.; ● Sun

Cyber cafe Sublink
Teslina ulica 12
① 01 481 13 29
⏱ 9 a.m. - 10 p.m.;
  Sun 3 p.m. - 10 p.m.

Iskoninternet - KIC
Preradovićeva ulica 5/1
① 01 481 17 58
⏱ 9 a.m. - 10 p.m.;
  Sat, Sun 12 a.m. - 11 p.m.

Net Kulturni klub MAMA
Preradovićeva ulica 18 (dvorište)
① 01 485 64 00
⏱ 10 a.m. - 10 p.m.

VIP
Preradovićev trg 5
① 01 483 00 89
⏱ 8 a.m. - 12 p.m.

Delivery-express mail

City Express
Ulica kneza Mislava 3

① 01 461 03 33; 01 461 88 67
🖶 01 461 88 66
⏱ Mon-Fri 8 a.m. - 7 p.m.;
  Sun 8 a.m. - 1 p.m.

DHL
Turinina ulica 3
① 01 665 11 11
⏱ 7.30 a.m. - 8 p.m.;
  Sat 8 a.m. - 12 p.m.

Fedex
Cebini bb, Buzin
① 01 660 60 00
✉ fedex@mail.inet.hr
⏱ 8 a.m. - 6 p.m.; ● Sat, Sun

Overseas Express
Kovinska ulica 20
① 01 345 33 55; 01 345 31 40
🖥 www.overseas.hr
✉ overseas.express@zg.htnet.hr
⏱ Mon-Fri 8 a.m. - 7 p.m.;

UPS
Avenija Dubrovnik 15
① 01 655 13 01; 01 655 13 02
🖶 01 652 03 38
✉ eur6dxp@europe.ups.com
⏱ Mon-Fri 8 a.m. - 6 p.m.

ACCOMODATION

Accomodation facilities in Zagreb are numerous and diverse, meeting everyone's possibilities.

There are big, high quality hotels, operating within world known chains and small private accommodation facilities. The accommodation category is rated with stars, and the price of overnight stay and other services depend on the hotel category.

Sign of a Youth Hostel

Zagreb hotels are rated with stars

HOTELS

Zagreb has the possibility of accommodation in the very centre. Here are the most luxurious hotels, like Sheraton or Esplanade, but also some cheaper accommodation.

Generally, the hotel service is of good quality and the rooms are neat. The majority of hotels have their own car parkss and some might have underground garage.

RESERVATIONS

The easiest way to book a room is by direct call to the hotel since the reception staff speaks all languages. You could make your reservations through fax or Internet. It is recommended to make a reservation in advance during the Zagreb Autumn Fair, because at this time of the year the town is full of businessmen from all over the world.

PRIVATE ACCOMMODATION

Private accommodation is not so common in Zagreb as it is at the Adriatic coast, but could be easily found. Beside lower prices, this accommodation is rather interesting because it gives better opportunities for meeting the Zagreb way of life.

HOSTELS

For young visitors to Zagreb there are possibilities of hostel accommodation. If you have Youth Hostelling Card you could have an additional stay discount. During summer some of the student halls of residence provide accommodation as well.

CAMPING

Nature lovers are offered camping facilities in the

Camping facilities near Zagreb

vicinity of Zagreb. Detailed information on accomodation and payment could be obtained through the Internet page.

The entrance to the most luxurious Zagreb hotel, Sheraton

Legend:

- 🚻 Disabled-friendly area
- ☎ Room phone
- 🛗 Elevator
- 🅿 Parking
- 🅿 Garage
- 🚭 Non smoking area
- ❄ Room air-conditionning
- 📺 Room TV
- 🏛 Conference hall

HOTELS

NARROW CENTRE

	Wellness	Internet	Pets	Pool

Opera Zagreb
Kršnjavoga 1
☎ +385 1 489 20 00
📠 + 385 1 489 20 01
🖥 www.opera-zagreb.com
★ ★ ★ ★ ☆
VISA · MasterCard · AMERICAN EXPRESS · Diners
Wellness ■ | Internet ● | Pets ■ | Pool ●

Sheraton Zagreb
Ulica kneza Borne 2
☎ +385 1 455 35 35
📠 + 385 1 455 30 35
🖥 www.sheraton.com/zagreb
★ ★ ★ ★ ★
VISA · MasterCard · AMERICAN EXPRESS · Diners
Wellness ■ | Internet ● | Pets ■ | Pool ●

The Regent - Esplanade
Mihanovićeva ulica 1
☎ +385 1 456 66 66
📠 + 385 1 457 79 07
🖥 www.esplanade.hr
★ ★ ★ ★ ★
VISA · MasterCard · AMERICAN EXPRESS · Diners
Internet ● | Pets ■

Dubrovnik
Gajeva ulica 1
☎ +385 1 487 35 55
📠 + 385 1 481 84 77
🖥 www.hotel-dubrovnik.htnet.hr
★ ★ ★ ☆
VISA · MasterCard · AMERICAN EXPRESS · Diners

Palace Hotel Zagreb
Strossmayerov trg 10
☎ +385 1 481 46 11
📠 + 385 1 481 13 58
🖥 www.palace.hr
★ ★ ★ ☆
VISA · MasterCard · AMERICAN EXPRESS · Diners
Pets ■

Arcotel Allegra
Branimirova ulica 29
☎ +385 1 469 60 00
📠 + 385 1 469 60 96
🖥 www.arcotel.at
★ ★ ☆
VISA · MasterCard · AMERICAN EXPRESS · Diners
Wellness ■ | Internet ●

HOTELS

Central
☆ ☆ ☆

Ulica kneza Branimira 3
☎ +385 1 484 11 22
🖷 + 385 1 484 13 04
🖳 www.hotel-central.hr

Jadran
☆ ☆ ☆

Vlaška ulica 50
☎ + 385 1 455 37 77
🖷 + 385 1 461 21 51
🖳 www.hup-zagreb.hr

Ilica
☆

Ilica 102
☎ + 385 1 377 75 22
🖷 + 385 1 377 76 22
🖳 www.hotel-ilica.hr

BROADER CENTRE

Four Points by Sheraton Zagreb
☆ ☆ ☆ ☆

Trg sportova 9
☎ + 385 1 365 83 33
🖷 + 385 1 309 26 57
🖳 www.starwood.com/fourpoints/zagreb

International
☆ ☆ ☆

Miramarska cesta 24
☎ + 385 1 610 88 00
🖷 + 385 1 615 94 59
🖳 www. hotel-international.hr

Laguna
☆ ☆ ☆

Kranjčevićeva ulica 29
☎ + 385 1 382 02 22
🖷 + 385 1 382 00 35

Dora
☆ ☆

Trnjanska cesta 11 E
☎ + 385 1 631 19 00
🖷 + 385 1 631 19 09

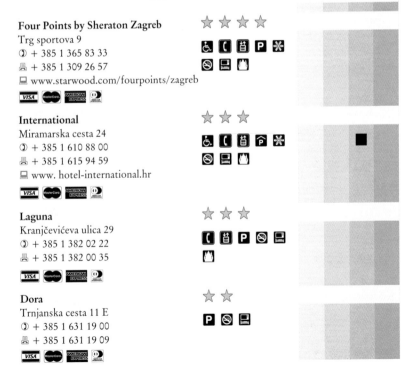

HOTELS

Lido
Malo jarunsko jezero bb
☾ + 385 1 383 28 37
🖨 + 385 1 383 28 38
🖥 www.lido.hr

Sliško
Supilova ulica 13
☾ + 385 1 618 47 77
🖨 + 385 1 618 47 77
🖥 www.slisko.hr

OTHER

Aristos
Cebini 37, Buzin
☾ + 385 1 66 95 900
🖨 + 385 1 669 59 02
🖨 www.hotel-aristos.hr
VISA MasterCard AMERICAN EXPRESS

As
Zelengaj 2a
☾ + 385 1 460 09111
🖨 + 385 1 460 09303
VISA MasterCard AMERICAN EXPRESS

Garni Hotel gaj
Jezerska ulica 24a
☾ + 385 1 381 72 22
🖨 + 385 1 381 72 25
🖥 www.gajgrupa.hr
VISA MasterCard AMERICAN EXPRESS

Golden Tulip Holiday
Ljubljanska avenija bb
☾ + 385 1 349 66 21
🖨 + 385 1 349 66 07
🖥 www.hotel-holiday.hr
VISA MasterCard AMERICAN EXPRESS

Tomislavov dom
Sljemenska cesta
☾ + 385 1 456 04 00
🖨 + 385 1 456 04 01
🖥 www.sljeme.hr
VISA MasterCard AMERICAN EXPRESS

HOTELS

Vienna
★ ★ ★
Zagrebačka cesta 211
☎ + 385 1 386 27 77
🖨 + 385 1 386 28 08
🖳 www.hotel-vienna-zg.com

Villa Tina
★ ★ ★
Bukovačka cesta 213
☎ + 385 1 244 51 38
🖨 + 385 1 244 52 04

Fala
★ ★
II Trnjanske ledine 18
☎ + 385 1 619 44 98
🖨 + 385 1 619 44 98
🖳 www.hotel-fala-zg.hr

Hotel "I"
★ ★
Remetinačka cesta 106
☎ + 385 1 614 12 22
🖨 + 385 1 654 2115

Naš dom
★ ★
Av. Dubrava 176
☎ + 385 1 286 42 59
🖨 + 385 1 298 82 65

Porin
★ ★
Jakuševac bb
☎ + 385 1 660 78 88
🖨 + 385 1 660 78 83

Zagreb
★ ★
Bundek bb
☎ + 385 1 663 73 33
🖨 + 385 1 663 72 29
🖳 www.hup-zagreb.hr

Hotel Hunjka
★
Sljemenska cesta 10
☎ + 385 1 458 03 97
🖨 + 385 1 455 21 85

HOSTELS

Omladinski hostel
Petrinjska ulica 77
① +385 1 484 12 61
🖷 + 385 1 484 12 69
🖳 www.hfhs.hr

Omladinski hotel
Remetinec
Remetinečki gaj
① +385 1 654 25 39
🖷 + 385 1 614 00 39

Youth hostel
Ravnice
Ravnice 38
① +385 1 233 23 25
🖷 + 385 1 234 56 07
🖳 www.ravnice-youth-hostel.hr

STUDENT HALLS OF RESIDENCE

Cvjetno naselje
Odranska ulica 8
① +385 1 619 12 45
🖳 www.step.hr/studentski-domovi/cvjetno

Studentski dom Stjepan Radić
Jarunska cesta 2
① +385 1 363 42 55
🖳 www.step.hr/studentski-domovi/sava

MOTELS

Motel Jägehorn
Ilica 14
① 01 483 35 53
🖳 www.hotel-pansion-jaegerhorn.hr

Motel Plitvice
Lučko bb
① 01 653 04 45
🖳 www.motel-plitvice.hr

CAMPS

Plitvice
Lučko bb
① 01 653 04 46
🖳 www.motel-plitvice.hr

PRIVATE ACCOMMODATION

ADP Glorija
Britanski trg 5
① 01 482 35 67
🖳 www.adp-glorija.com

Mare
Širokobriješka ulica 29
① 01 363 11 91
🖳 www.accommodation-mare.com

Pugna
Radnička cesta 27
① 01 604 09 10

Di Prom
Trnska cesta 25
① 01 655 00 39

Mirna noć
Miroševac 35
① 01 298 51 17

Privatni smještaj Božo Mužar
Jadranska ulica 9
① 091/ 5401 300
🖳 www.free-zg.htnet.hr/muzar/

Evistas
Šenoina ulica 28
① 01 483 95 54
✉ evistas@zg.htnet.hr

Nemoj stati, Never Stop
Žajina ulica
① 01 301 32 82
🖳 www.nest.hr

Vila Marija
Potočka ulica 18
① 01 291 79 28
🖳 www.vila-marija.info

Food

Croatian cuisine is the unique representative of the harmony of interesting and tasty, often seemingly incompatible contradictions. The richness and generosity at Zagreb tables, full of tasty dishes and supporting drinks are recorded in many cookbooks. The first cookbook dates from the 19th century, written by Marija Kumičić. She based her cookbook on the middle class models of the time, Katarina Prato and Sint-Hylaire but did not forget domestic, national dishes.

Prežgana juha (**flour soup**)

Zagreb cuisine is the combination of rich heritage reflecting the troubled history. Citizens of Zagreb were always attentive to what they ate. In the medieval Gradec there were already 90 craftsmen related to food. It is worth mentioning that Zagreb citizens like home-cooked dishes, generating numerous traditional gastronomy events with presentations and ratings in the town and its vicinity. Surveys show that citizens of Zagreb are great admirers of Mediterranean cuisine, probably due to undoubtedly better food selection, than Dalmatians. Modern Zagreb cuisine and

diet habits of its citizens are at the Croatian top from the nutricionists point of view.

Traditional Cakes
The tradition of Zagreb coffee huses and cakeshops is long and rich, thus it is worth trying Zagreb strudels stuffed with cottage cheese, apples or cherries, then *kremšnite* and various cakes.
Paprenjak (spiced buiscits), depicted in August Šenoa's novels who was the descendent of one of the first Zagreb pattiseurs, has become a popular Zagreb souvenir. This goes for *licitar* as well,

Paprenjaci

most frequently heart-shaped, that many find tasty especially accompanied with *medica* and *gvirc*, beverages sold at church feasts made of brewed honey. A nice tasty souvenir from Zagreb could be also *bermet* from Samobor and Samobor *muštarda* (mustard), Zagreb cake or yeast cakes stuffed with nuts, poppy, carot, cottage cheese or jam.

Meat Dishes
Zabreb has its own steak -

Stuffed veal breast

Zagreb steak: its veal stuffed with cheese and ham and then put in breadcrumbs and fried as the Viennese steak. If an opportunity arises do not miss traditional Zagreb *gablec* (mid-morning meal) - wine gulasch or tripes, stewed season vegetables made of leek, sweet or *sauerkraut* with beans accompanied by minced meat or sausages, *sarma* or stuffed paprika - then beef soup or chicken soop with noodles, *krpice sa zeljem* (square pasta with rosted cabbage), blood sausages and bratwurst saussages with potatoes and sauerkraut, cooked smoked pork shank with sour cabbage, cooked hen or beef with horseradish sauce, and cooked ham with freshly grated horseradish..

PURICA S MLINCIMA (TURKEY WITH KIND OF PASTA)

Purica s mlincima is an excellent combination of the wilderness of the New World, that gave us that poultry and Old World where various breads without yeast are baked for centuries. Zagreb is very fond of roasted poultry, especially turkey for special holidays. Though *mlinci* go well with roasted suckling pig as well, as they were once served, and turkey

Pute mit Plinsen

was served with poatotes as other poultry, stuffed with mixture of rolls and giblets, minced veal, mashrooms or cut vegetables, the combination of turkey and *mlinci* with various salads is irreplacable.

Schweinekoteletts und Würste, in eigener Soße gedünstet auf Samoborart

KOTLOVINA (STEWED MEAT)

Kotlovina is indiguous specialty of Zagreb and northwest Croatia. Pork chops and sausages are fried in a very big metal dish and then are stewed in their own juice, wine and spices. Sometimes they are given to some smoked meat and more and more frequently some vegetables to give to special taste - onions, potatoes, tomatoes, paprika . . The most important thing in preparing *kotlovina* is that it should be done outdoors. It was only recently that it moved to the restaurant kitchens from the fairgrounds and roads in front of the inns where it was made and invited the guests.

PISANICE (BEEF FILLET STEAK)

At the times, there was no celebration without roasted beef fillet steak. Since it has been awarded, the *Stubica* fillet steak has become more popular. While beef is usually stuffed wih root vegetables and bacon, that pork fil-

let, and more and more frequently according to nutricionist trends turkey breast, is stuffed with dried plums and soaked in plum brandy. That favourite modern specialty dates from the nobility tables in Zagorje castles.

ŠTRUKLI

Štrukli have become the most famous Croatian specialty in the last twenty years, due to presentation of Croatian cuisine and cooks in the leading world hotel chains. They are also called *zagorski štrukli*, but they are popular throughout Croatia. Although thin pulled dough, undoubtedly taken from Turks during invasions towards Vienna, is stuffed with various stuffings (pumpkin, poppy seeds, apples . . .), the favourites are stuffed with cottage cheese. They can be boiled or baked, added to soup or served as dessert, salty or sweet and they are mostly accepted as small dish, or warm starter, boiled and baked in cream.

Teigtaschen mit Quark gefüllt, auf Zagorjeart

CROATIAN CUISINE

Baltazar
Nova Ves 4
℡ 01 466 69 99
🖥 www.morsko-prase.hr/
   baltazar/baltazar.htm
🕐 12 a.m. - 12 p.m.; ● Sun

Cadena
Karlovačka cesta 201
℡ 01 653 00 16
🖥 www.cadena.hr
🕐 10 a.m. - 12 p.m.;
   Fri and Sat 10 a.m. - 2 a.m.
   ● ned

Ⓟ

Cantinetta
Teslina ulica 14
℡ 01 481 13 15
🖥 www.petrac.hr/cantinetta/
🕐 9 a.m. - 11 p.m.; ● Sun

Dubravka
Margaretska ulica 3
℡ 01 481 25 95
🖥 www.son-ugo-cor.com/
   cro/dubravka.htm
🕐 8 a.m. - 11 p.m.

Dva goluba
Maksimirska cesta 7
℡ 01 232 89 50
🕐 8 a.m. - 12 p.m.

Restaurant Baltazar

Frankopan
Frankopanska, 8
℡ 01 484 85 47
🕐 9 a.m. - 24 p.m.;
   ● Sun

Hrvatski kulturni klub
Trg maršala Tita 10
℡ 01 482 80 84
🖥 www.restauranthkk.hr/
🕐 10 a.m. - 24 p.m.; ● Sun

Kerempuh
Kaptol 3
℡ 01 481 90 00
🖥 www.kerempuh.hr
🕐 6 a.m. - 3 p.m.; ● Sun

Lady Shram
Mesnička ulica 12
℡ 01 485 11 22
🕐 9 a.m. - 11 p.m.;
   Sun 9 a.m. - 5 p.m.; ● Mon

Marijino zvono
Prudi 27
℡ 01 619 50 05
🖥 www.marijino-zvono.hr
🕐 10 a.m. - 12 p.m.; ● Sun

Ⓟ

Miramare
Miramarska cesta 19
℡ 01 611 07 32
🖥 www.miramare.hr
🕐 10 a.m. - 12 p.m.; ● Sun

Ⓟ

Nova Ves - Tinča
Nova Ves 88
℡ 01 466 78 26
🕐 10 a.m. - 12 p.m.;
   Sun 10 a.m. - 11 p.m.

Ⓟ

Obrtnički dom
Mažuranićev trg 13
℡ 01 482 84 98
🕐 8 a.m. - 11 p.m.; ● Sun

Ⓟ

Okrugljak
Mlinovi 28
℡ 01 467 4112
🖥 www.okrugljak.hr
🕐 11 a.m. - 1 a.m.

Ⓟ

Puntijarka
Graščica 40
℡ 01 467 46 00
🖥 www.puntijarka.com
🕐 12 a.m. - 12 p.m.;
   Sun 12 a.m. - 6 p.m.; ● Mon

Ⓟ

Purger
Petrinjska ulica 33
℡ 01 481 07 13
🕐 7 a.m. - 11 p.m.; ● Sun

Stara poštarica
Ogrizovićeva ulica 8
℡ 01 382 00 23
🕐 9 a.m. - 11 p.m.;
   Sat 10 a.m. - 11 p.m.;
   Sun 10 a.m. - 9 p.m.

Stara Sava
Savska cesta 208
℡ 01 363 43 22
🕐 9 a.m. - 12 p.m.;
   Fri-Sun 9 a.m. - 1 a.m.

Ⓟ

Stara vura
Opatička ulica 20
℡ 01 485 13 68
🕐 12 a.m. - 12 p.m.; ● Sun

Ⓟ

Stara zagrebačka škola
Kombolova ulica 2a
℡ 01 660 39 13
🕐 9 a.m. - 12 p.m.; ● Sun

Ⓟ

Stari fijaker
Mesnička ulica 6
℡ 01 483 38 29
🕐 8 a.m. - 11 p.m.;
   Sun 10 a.m. - 10 p.m.

Stari Puntijar
Gračanska cesta 65
℡ 01 467 56 00
🕐 12 a.m. - 12 p.m.

Ⓟ

Starina
Mlinovi 85a
℡ 01 467 43 36
🕐 12 a.m. - 12 p.m.;
   Sun 12 a.m. - 5 p.m.

Ⓟ

Šestinski lagvić
Šestinska cesta bb
℡ 01 467 44 17
🖥 www.crotours.com/
   sestinski-lagvic/
🕐 10 a.m. - 12 p.m.

Ⓟ

Šport
Maksimirska cesta 105
℡ 01 231 82 11
🕐 8 a.m. - 10 p.m.; ● Sun

Trnjanka
Trnjanska cesta 31
℡ 01 611 96 86
🕐 8 a.m. - 12 p.m.

Ⓟ

Veseli kutić
Lovćenska ulica 2
℡ 01 467 43 40
🕐 09-24

Vinodol
Teslina ulica 10
01 481 14 27
www.vinodol-zg.hr
10 a.m. - 12 p.m.

Zagorcu
Frankopanska ulica 13
01 463 05 38
10 a.m. - 12 p.m.; ● Sun

Zagrebački bijeli
Kranjčevićeva ulica 4
01 366 83 37
9 a.m. - 11 p.m.;
Sat, Sun 9 a.m. - 12 p.m.
P

Zagrebački plavi - Plavi 9
Zvonimirova ulica 83
01 231 69 66
8 a.m. - 11 p.m.

Zelenjak
Zelenjak 35
01 463 55 56
10 a.m. - 23.30 p.m.;
Sun 10 a.m. - 6 p.m.

Croatian regional cuisine

Istria

Altamira
Palmotićeva ulica 19
01 481 02 21
11.30 a.m. - 12 p.m.;
Sat 6 p.m. - 12 p.m.; ● Sun

Kod Pavela
Gračanska cesta 46
01 467 50 36
12 a.m. - 12 p.m.; ● Mon
P

Slavonia

Slavonski dukat
Radnička cesta 22
01 618 48 04
www.slavonski-dukat.hr/
10 a.m. - 12 p.m.; ● Sun

Vallis Aurea
Tomićeva ulica 4
01 483 13 05
9 a.m. - 11 p.m.; ● Sun

Grill

Gušti
Markuševačka cesta 22
01 467 60 00
11 a.m. - 12 p.m.;
Sat, Sun 11 a.m. - 2 a.m.
P

Kaptolska klet
Kaptol 5
01 481 48 38
9 a.m. - 12 p.m.

Mačak
Lastovska ulica 83
01 615 72 88
8 a.m. - 11 p.m.
P

Medvednica
Bukovačka ulica bb
01 242 12 63; 01 525 04 01
7.30 a.m. - 12 p.m.

NK Sava
Gredice 157
01 363 37 77
1 p.m. - 11 p.m.

NK Trnje
Ulica kardinala Šepera bb
01 615 12 22
11 a.m. - 11 p.m.;
Sun 12 a.m. - 8 p.m.
P

Pod gričkim topom
Zakmardijeve stube 5
01 483 36 07
11 a.m. - 12 p.m.;
Sun 11 a.m. - 5 p.m.

Pod mirnim krovovima
Fijanova ulica 7
01 231 62 69
10 a.m. - 12 p.m.

Sconto Gastro
Vlaška ulica 68
01 455 55 56
08-23

Stari kotač
Petrovaradinska ulica 20
01 388 27 68
8 a.m. - 11 p.m.
P

Game

Jägerhorn
Ilica 14
01 483 38 77
www.hotel-pansion-jaegerhorn.hr
10-24

Seafood

As (hotel As)
Zelengaj 2a

Restaurant Okrugljak

01 460 91 11
9 a.m. - 12 p.m.
P

Atlanta
Tkalčićeva ulica 65
01 481 38 48
12 a.m. - 12 p.m.

Bonaca
Trakošćanska cesta 41
01 363 45 09
www.restoranbonaca.hr
11 a.m. - 12 p.m.; ● Sun

Dubravkin put
Dubravkin put bb
01 483 49 70
10 a.m. - 11 p.m.

Gallo
Hebrangova ulica 34
01 481 40 14
www.gallo.hr
12 a.m. - 12 p.m.

Gašpar
Nova ves 4
01 466 69 99
12 a.m. - 12 p.m.; ● Sun

Hippodrome
Cimermanova ulica 5
01 652 29 02
12 a.m. - 12 p.m.;
Sun 12 a.m. - 20 p.m.
P

Jadran
Zvonimirova ulica 124
01 231 67 45
12 a.m. - 12 p.m.; ● Sun

Karaka
Hebrangova ulica 12
☎ 01 481 71 50
🕐 11 a.m. - 11 p.m.; ● Sun

Korčula
Teslina ulica 17
☎ 01 487 21 59
🕐 9 a.m. - 11 p.m.;
   Sun 9 a.m. - 5 p.m.

Korkyra
Ulica B. Adžije 26
☎ 01 364 61 01
🕐 9 a.m. - 11 p.m.;
   Sun 9 a.m. - 11 p.m
Ⓟ

Leut
Aleja Matije Ljubeka bb,
Jarunsko jezero
☎ 01 383 15 95
🕐 10 a.m. - 12 p.m.

Lido
Jarun bb
☎ 01 383 28 37
🖥 www.lido.hr
🕐 9 a.m. - 2 a.m.
Ⓟ

Lopud
Kaptol 10
☎ 01 481 87 75
🕐 10 a.m. - 11 p.m.; ● Sun

Marinero
Kninski trg 7
☎ 01 619 83 27
🖥 www.marinero.hr
🕐 9 a.m. - 11 p.m.;
Ⓟ

Primošten
Stupnička ulica 14
☎ 01 619 11 95
🕐 12 a.m. - 11 p.m.

Zlatna školjka
Martićeva ulica 51
☎ 01 461 73 22
🕐 8 a.m. - 10 p.m.;
   Sat and Sun 11 a.m. - 9 p.m.

INTERNATIONAL CUISINE

Axa Azzuro
Dežmanova ulica 1
☎ 01 481 23 91
🕐 12-24

Big Mamma
Ulica Ive Horvata 35b
☎ 01 661 06 20
🕐 10 a.m. - 12 p.m.
Ⓟ

Fontana (hotel Sheraton)
Ulica kneza Borne 2
☎ 01 455 35 35

Restaurant Gašpar

🖥 www.sheraton.com/zagreb
🕐 6.30 a.m. - 12 p.m.
Ⓟ

Galant
Buzin, Cebini 37
☎ 01 662 37 60
🕐 7 a.m. - 11 p.m.

Galerija
Petrinjska ulica 9
☎ 01 492 13 22
🕐 8 a.m. - 11 p.m.;
   Sun 10 a.m. - 10 p.m.

Gospodarski klub
Ulica grada Vukovara 78
☎ 01 610 70 45
🕐 10 a.m. - 6.30 p.m.; ● Sat, Sun
Ⓟ

Kaptol (hotel Opera)
Kršnjavoga 1
☎ 01 489 20 00
🖥 www.opera-zagreb.com
🕐 7 a.m. - 12 p.m.
Ⓟ

Klub hrvatskih književnika
Trg bana Jelačića 7/1
☎ 01 481 22 90
🕐 12 a.m. - 12 p.m.; ● Sun

Klub Maksimir
Oboj 1
☎ 01 234 11 89
🕐 12 a.m. - 2 a.m.; ● Sun
Ⓟ

Kokot
Tomićeva ulica 3
☎ 01 485 25 95
🕐 9 a.m. - 12 p.m.; ● Sun

Marcellino
Jurjevska ulica 65a
☎ 01 467 71 11
🕐 12 a.m. - 12 p.m.; ● Sun
Ⓟ

Opatija
Bukovačka cesta 160b
☎ 01 244 52 66
🕐 11 a.m. - 12 p.m.; ● Mon

Paviljon
Trg kralja Tomislava 22
☎ 01 481 30 66
🖥 www.restaurant-paviljon.com
🕐 12 a.m. - 12 p.m.
Ⓟ

Strossmayer (hotel Palace Zagreb)
Strossmayerov trg 10
☎ 01 481 46 11
🖥 www.palace.hr
🕐 6 a.m. - 11 p.m.
Ⓟ

Taverna Grič (hotel Golden Tulip Holiday)
Ljubljanska avenija bb
☎ 01 349 66 21
🖥 www.hotel-holiday.hr
🕐 9 a.m. - 11 p.m.
Ⓟ

Taverna Šestine (hotel 4 Points by Sher. Zg.)
Trg sportova 9
☎ 01 365 84 47
🕐 6 a.m. - 11 p.m.

Villa Tina (hotel Villa Tina)
Bukovačka cesta 213
☎ 01 244 51 38
🕐 12 a.m. - 12 p.m.
Ⓟ

Italian

Angelo D´Oro
Ulica Kruge 48
☎ 01 611 28 89
🖥 www.ipo.com.hr/angelodoro
🕐 10 a.m. - 11 p.m.; ● Sun
Ⓟ

Bigy
Pokornog 12
① 01 239 55 55
  01 239 56 66
⌨ www.pizzeria.hr/bigy
🕘 9 a.m. - 12 p.m.;
  Sun 11 a.m. - 11 p.m.

Boban
Gajeva ulica 9
① 01 481 15 49
⌨ www.boban.hr
🕘 10 a.m. - 12 p.m.

Canzona
Ulica Ivana Šveara 9
① 01 461 77 77
🕘 9 a.m. - 11 p.m.;
  Sun 12 a.m. - 11 p.m.

LR
Palmotićeva ulica 13
① 01 481 03 34
🕘 12 a.m. - 4 p.m. and
  7 p.m. - 12 p.m.; ● Sun

Ristorante *Rossini*
Vlaška ulica 55
① 01 455 10 60
🕘 11 a.m. - 12 p.m.;
  Sat 11 a.m. - 11 p.m.; ● Sun

**Piccolo Mondo
(hotel Dubrovnik)**
Gajeva ulica 1
① 01 487 35 55
⌨ www.tel.hr/hotel-dubrovnik
🕘 11 a.m. - 11 p.m.

Placa
Radićeva ulica 42
① 01 481 33 90
⌨ www.placa.hr
🕘 10 a.m. - 11 p.m.; ● Sun

Panino
Nova Ves 17
(Kaptol centar)
① 01 466 90 13
⌨ www.panino.hr
🕘 8 a.m. - 11 p.m.
Ⓟ

Trattoria Fellini
Savska cesta 90
① 01 617 75 45
⌨ www.fellini.hr
🕘 9 a.m. - 11 p.m.;
  Sat 12 a.m. - 11 p.m.; ● Sun

Trattoria Fellini
Jurišićeva ulica 1/I
① 01 482 02 00
🕘 9 a.m. - 11 p.m.;
  Sat 12 a.m. - 11 p.m.; ● Sun

Indian

Maharadja
Opatovina 19
① 01 481 43 05
🕘 12 a.m. - 11 p.m.

Chinese

China Garden
Ulica Nikole Andrića 29
① 01 663 77 88
⌨ www.china-garden.hr
🕘 12 a.m. - 12 p.m.
Ⓟ

China House
Rapska ulica 63a
① 01 618 75 00
🕘 11.30 a.m. - 11 p.m.
Ⓟ

Huatian
Ulica Kneza Mislava 1
① 01 4613 666
🕘 8 a.m. - 12 p.m.

Peking
Ilica 114
① 01 3776 361
🕘 12 a.m. - 12 p.m.

Japanese

Takenoko sushi bar
Nova Ves 17 (Kaptol centar)
① 01 486 05 30
⌨ www.takenoko.hr
🕘 12 a.m. - 1 a.m.;
  Sun 12 a.m. - 6 p.m.

Mexican

Caramba
Frankopanska ulica 6
① 01 484 85 70
🕘 11 a.m. - 12 p.m.

Desperado (Lenuci)
Trg Nikole Šubića Zrinskog 15
① 01 487 30 91
⌨ www.lenuci.com
🕘 11 a.m. - 11 p.m.;
  Fri, Sat 11 a.m. – 12 p.m.
  ● Sun

Mex cantina
Savska cesta 154
① 01 619 21 56
⌨ www.mex-cantina.hr
🕘 9 a.m. - 12 p.m.;
  Sun 12 a.m. - 12 p.m.
Ⓟ

Phoenix
Jurišićeva ulica 19
① 01 481 44 11
🕘 11 a.m. - 11 p.m.;
  Sun 12 a.m. - 11 p.m.

Cuban

Havana club
Perkovčeva ulica 2
① 01 482 61 03
🕘 12 a.m. - 11 p.m.; ● Sun

OTHER EATING PLACES

Konoba

Konoba Antica
Kaptol 27
① 01 481 21 87
🕘 12 a.m. - 11 p.m.; ● Sun

Konoba Čiho
Ulica Pavla Hatza 15
① 01 481 70 60
🕘 10 a.m. - 12 p.m.;
  Sun 12 a.m. - 12 p.m.

Konoba Dida
Petrova ulica 176
① 01 233 56 93
🕘 9 a.m. - 11 p.m.;
  Sun 9 a.m. - 10 p.m.

Konoba Gračanka
Gračanska cesta 48
① 01 467 40 89
🕘 12 a.m. - 11 p.m.; ● Mon
Ⓟ

Konoba Maškalin i Lata
Hebrangova ulica 11a

① 01 481 82 73
🕘 12 a.m. - 11 p.m.; ● Sun

Beer house

Kaptolska klet
Kaptol 5
① 01 481 48 38; 01 481 43 30
🕘 7 a.m. - 11 p.m.

Pivnica 10
Avenija Dubrovnik 19
① 01 655 46 85
🕘 8 a.m. - 2 a.m.;
  Sat, Sun 5 p.m. - 12 p.m.

Pivnica Centar
Trg Ante Starčevića bb,
Importane centar
☎ 01 457 74 70
🕐 7 a.m. - 12 p.m.; ● Sun

Pivnica Tomislav
Trg kralja Tomislava 18
☎ 01 492 22 55
🕐 7 a.m. - 11 p.m.

Pivnica Kaltenberg
Ljubljanica 7
☎ 01 369 44 33
🕐 Mon-Fri 8 a.m. - 11 p.m.
    Sat anf Sun 9 a.m. - 11 p.m.

Pivnica Medvedgrad
Savska cesta 56
☎ 01 617 71 19
🕐 10 a.m. - 12 p.m.

Pivnica Mlinarica
Jandrićeva ulica 36
☎ 01 467 36 07
🕐 8 a.m. - 11 p.m.;
    Sun 9 a.m. - 11 p.m.

Pivnica Pinta
Radićeva ulica 3
☎ 01 483 08 89
🕐 9 a.m. - 11 p.m.;
    Sun 10 a.m. - 11 p.m.

Pivnica Stara Tkalča
Tkalčićeva ulica 70
☎ 01 481 32 35
🕐 9 a.m. - 1 a.m.

Pizzeria

Bas
Ulica Ivana Kukuljevića 1
☎ 01 482 12 22
🕐 7 a.m. - 11 p.m.;
    Sun 9 a.m. - 11 p.m.

Baschiera
Selska cesta 215
☎ 01 369 89 99; 01 369 78 17
🕐 11 a.m. - 1 a.m.;
    Fri, Sat 11 a.m. - 2 a.m.
    Sun 11 a.m. - 1 a.m.

Bravo
Jablanska ulica 30
☎ 01 386 16 61
🕐 9 a.m. - 11 p.m.;
    Fri, Sat 9 a.m. - 12 p.m.
    Sun 9 a.m. - 11 p.m.

Gentleman
Kranjčevićeva ulica 11a
☎ 01 231 64 38
🕐 8 a.m. - 11 p.m.;
    Sun 12 a.m. - 11 p.m.

Lav - Lavica
Vlaška ulica 23
☎ 01 481 26 99
🕐 8 a.m. - 11 p.m.

Home delivery

Dragaš
Kranjčevićeva 2
☎ 01 364 87 16
    01 366 83 33
🕐 10 a.m. - 12 p.m.

Vege Hop
Nova cesta 166
☎ 01 301 54 33
🕐 Mon-Fri 10 a.m. - 6 p.m.;
    Sat 10 a.m. - 3 p.m.

Mama Mia
Ilica 63
☎ 01 484 60 93
🕐 9 a.m. - 11 p.m.;
    Sun 12 a.m. - 11 p.m.

Maslina
Stupnička ulica 14
☎ 01 619 12 25
🕐 9 a.m. - 11 p.m.

Napolitana
Preradovićeva ulica 34
☎ 01 485 61 05
🕐 7 a.m. - 11 p.m.;
    Sun 10 a.m. - 11 p.m.

Pizzeria 2
Nova Ves 2
☎ 01 466 88 88
🕐 10 a.m. - 1 a.m.

Pizzeria 6
Medulićeva ulica 6
☎ 01 484 62 48
🕐 9 a.m. - 11 p.m.;
    Sun 12 a.m. - 11 p.m.

Stara Sava
Savska cesta 208
☎ 01 363 43 22
🕐 9 a.m. - 12 p.m.;
🅿   Fri-Sun 9 a.m. - 1 a.m.

Viva
Kranjčevićeva ulica 69
☎ 01 364 06 40
🕐 10 a.m. - 11 p.m.;
    Sun 12 a.m. - 11 p.m.

Zagi
Zrnetićeva ulica 9
☎ 01 345 65 55
🕐 7 a.m. - 11 p.m.

Fast Food

Bonita
Cesarčeva ulica 2
☎ 01 481 38 35
🕐 0-24

Borut E-3
Trg kralja P. Krešimira IV 6
☎ 01 461 41 12
🕐 9 a.m. - 5 p.m.; ● Sun

Diogenes
Opatovina 19
☎ 01 481 43 05
🕐 12 a.m. - 11 p.m.

Rubelj Grill
Dolac 2
☎ 01 481 87 77
🕐 8 a.m. - 11 p.m.

Frankopanska 2b
☎ 484 92 57
🕐 8 a.m. - 11 p.m.

💻 www.rubelj-grill.hr

Fino & Friško
Splavnica 2
☎ 01 481 61 85
Varšavska ulica 1
🕐 7 a.m. - 10 p.m.; ● Sun

Ham Ham
Varšavska ulica 8
☎ 01 483 00 23
🕐 9 a.m. - 11.30 p.m.; ● Sun

Hamby
Draškovićeva ulica 5
☎ 01 461 65 55
🕐 0-24; ● Sun

Hamby
Ilica 1, passage
☎ 01 481 70 45
🕐 0-24

Kokopeli
Jurišićeva ulica 19
☎ 01 481 91 86
🕐 7.30 a.m. - 8 p.m.;
    Sat 7.30 a.m. - 3 p.m.
    ● Sun

McPicek
Cesarčeva ulica 2
☎ 01 481 30 03
🕐 7 a.m. - 10 p.m.; ● Sun

Nepoznata životinja
Miramarska cesta 26
☎ 01 611 91 87
🕐 7 a.m. - 11 p.m.;
    Sat 9 a.m. - 8 p.m.; ● Sun

Mali Phoenix
Jurišićeva ulica 19
☎ 01 481 44 11
🕐 11 a.m. - 11 p.m.

Pingvin Sandwich Bar
Teslina ulica 7
☎ 01 481 14 46
🕐 9 a.m. - 5 a.m.;
    Sun 9 a.m. - 2 a.m.

Slon
Starčevićev trg 1, Importane
☎ 01 457 74 25
🕐 0-24

Sandwich bar Martin 1
Starčevićev trg 1, (Importane)
☎ 01 457 70 54
🕐 7 a.m. - 9 p.m.

Pizza Cut Duck
Teslina ulica 17
① 492 02 83
🕐 9 a.m. - 12 p.m.;
   Sun 5 p.m. - 12 p.m.

Tosteria Sunce
Bogovićeva ulica 1b
① 01 481 09 79
🕐 8 a.m. - 11 p.m.;
   Sun 9 a.m. - 11 p.m.

Subway
Gajeva ulica 1
① 01 483 53 98
🕐 8 a.m. - 11 p.m.;
   Sun 9 a.m. - 11 p.m.

McDonald´s
Maksimirska cesta 2
① 01 230 35 05
🕐 Mon-Thu 8 a.m. - 12 p.m.
   Fri and Sat 8 a.m. - 1 a.m.;
   Sun 9 a.m. - 12 p.m.

Trg Grgura Ninskog 3
① 01 457 31 70
🕐 Mon-Thu 8 a.m. - 12 p.m.
   Fri and Sat 8 a.m. - 1 a.m.;
   Sun 9 a.m. - 12 p.m.

Avenija Dubrava 143
① 01 298 72 17
🕐 Mon-Thu 8 a.m. - 1 a.m.
   Fri and Sat 8 a.m. - 3 a.m.;
   Sun 9 a.m. - 1 a.m.

Jurišićeva ulica 3
① 01 481 37 08
🕐 Mon-Thu 8 a.m. - 12 p.m.
   Fri and Sat 8 a.m. - 1 a.m.;
   Sun 9 a.m. - 12 p.m.

McDrive, Heinzelova ulica 65
① 01 230 36 97
🕐 Mon-Thu 8 a.m. - 1 a.m.
   Fri and Sat 8 a.m. - 3 a.m.;
   Sun 9 a.m. - 1 a.m.

McDrive, Jadranska avenija bb
① 01 659 03 26
🕐 Mon-Thu 8 a.m. - 1 a.m.
   Fri and Sat 8 a.m. - 3 a.m.;
   Sun 9 a.m. - 1 a.m.

McDrive, Pile I broj 2
① 01 615 70 25
🕐 Mon-Thu 8 a.m. - 1 a.m.
   Fri and Sat 8 a.m. - 3 a.m.;
   Sun 9 a.m. - 1 a.m.

McDrive, Rudeška cesta 87a
① 01 388 17 77
🕐 Mon-Thu 8 a.m. - 1 a.m.
   Fri and Sat 8 a.m. - 3 a.m.;
   Sun 9 a.m. - 1 a.m.

Macrobiotics, vegetarian

Din Don
Iblerov trg
(Importane galerija)
① 01 461 91 35
🕐 9 a.m. - 10 p.m.;
   Sun 12 as.m. - 10 p.m.
P

Magea - centar za biotički opstanak čovjeka
Martićeva ulica 31/I
① 01 455 06 90
🖥 www.magea.hr
🕐 Mon-Fri 12 a.m. - 5 p.m.

Makronova centar - Zdravljak Nova
Ilica 72/I
① 01 4847 114
🕐 12 a.m. - 10 p.m.; ● Sun

Sirion
Derenčiniva 1
① 01 455 30 88
🕐 12 a.m. - 6 p.m.;
   Sat 12 a.m. - 3 p.m.; ● Sun

Venera
Vlaška ulica 125
① 01 466 41 75
🕐 8 a.m. - 11 p.m.;
   Sun 12 a.m. - 11 p.m.

Cake shops

Centar
Jurišićeva ulica 24
① 01 481 06 21
🕐 8 a.m. - 11 p.m.

Horak
Ilica 160
① 01 370 16 80
🕐 7 a.m. - 9 p.m.;
   Sun 10 a.m. - 9 p.m.

Ivica i Marica
Tkalčićeva ulica 70
① 01 481 73 21
🕐 9 a.m. - 11 p.m.; ● Sun

Millenium
Bogovićeva ulica 7
① 01 481 08 50
🕐 7 a.m. - 12 p.m.

Slastičarnica Vincek

Mimoza
Trg hrvatskih velikana 1
① 01 461 22 76
🕐 07-21; ned 10-18

Orient
Maksimirska cesta 34
① 01 231 53 23
🕐 09-21; sub 09-17; ● ned

Princess
Gajeva ulica 6
① 01 481 10 37
🕐 08-22

Srebrnjak
Domjanićeva ulica 1
① 01 466 47 73
🕐 08-22; ● ned

Vincek
Ilica 18
① 01 483 36 12
🕐 08.30-22; ● ned

Zagreb
Masarykova ulica 4
① 01 487 28 46
🕐 07-23; ned 09-23

RESTAURANTS IN THE TOWN VICINITY

National cuisine

Gabreku 1929.
Starogradska ulica 46
Samobor
① 01 336 07 22
🕐 12 a.m. - 12 p.m.; ● Sun
AMERICAN EXPRESS · VISA · D · MasterCard

Grešna gorica
Taborgradska cesta 3
Desinić
① 049 343 001

🖥 www.gresna-gorica.com
🕐 9 a.m. - 10 p.m.

Pri staroj vuri
Giznik 2
Samobor
① 01 336 05 48
🕐 11 a.m. - 11 p.m.;
   Sun 10 a.m. - 6 p.m.
AMERICAN EXPRESS · VISA · D · MasterCard

Samoborska pivnica
Obrtnička cesta 1
Samobor

① 01 336 16 23
🕐 9 a.m. - 11 p.m.
   Fri and Sat 9 a.m. - 12 p.m.
   Sun 9 a.m. - 11 p.m.
AMERICAN EXPRESS · VISA · D · MasterCard

Fish

Babylon
Ulica Dr. Franje Tuđmana 5, Sv. Nedjelja
① 01 337 15 00
🖥 www.babylon.hr
🕐 12.00 - 24.00
AMERICAN EXPRESS · VISA · D · MasterCard

Zagreb Wines

The vineyards are for centuries successfully grown in Zagreb and its vicinity and quality wines are produced, in the past popular at the Vienna court. Today, the most important brand producers are in Zelina wine-growing district around the town of Sveti Ivan Zelina and in the district of Plešivica mountain, above Jastrebarsko. The popular wine roads exist in those regions.

Plešivica Wine Road

Plešivica Wine road starts in Jastrebarsko and descends at the other side towards Samobor. There are some 30 cellars on the attractive amfitheatrical slopes, where you can taste some good wine. Beside the old sorts, for example the indigineous kraljevina, plavec žuti, šipelj, lipovina, ranfol, the best world sorts are increasingly grown - chardonnay, rajnski rizling, pinot, traminac, zeleni silvanac, white sauvignon etc. The directions of cellars are marked.

Portuguese wine

The old red wine sort spread in Central Europe, portugizac, has recently become popular again. Each year there is a festival of that wine in Zagreb which is especially valuated as young wine, and the first bottle is ritually opened on first November Saturday, similar to beaujoulais festivals. The outstanding producers are D. Režek, R. Braje, Mladina, F. Gregorić and K. Režek.

Champagne wines

Plešivica vineyards successfully produce champagne wines, in classical, so-called champaign method, whose production was initiated by Franjo Jambrović. Today, the most notable champagne producers are families Tomac and Šember, who arranged attractive taste facilities in Donja Reka and Donji Pavlovčani. The Tomac family has very picturesque champaigne wine cellar, and their champaignes Tom and Classic are the most valued. The classical champaigns are produced in Šenkovec, near Zagreb, named Šenpjen and Lidija rose, by Lidija Volovec.

Šenpjen, Croatian champaigne wine made by classical champaigne method

Chardonnay

The Tomac family is very successful in production of top quality chardonnay - named Premier - that was awarded on the world contest in France. It ripes in barrique, special oak barrels of 225 litres. It is very strong, with expressive aroma, harmonious and elegant. Their rajnski rizling is also appreciated. Stjepan and Zdenko Šember were awarded an international prize for their dry chardonnay and muscat chardonnay, as well as for graševina. Very elegant and highly rated chardonnaye wines, grown sur lie, that is care on yeasts in barriques belongs to the family of notable Croatian enolo-

Guests tasting the wine in the Tomac family cellar

gist Velimir Korak, in Plešivica. They produced the first officially registered *ice wine* in the district, and their rajnski rizling wines are of international quality.

Sauvignon

Notable enologist Drago Režek grows the excellent sauvignon, and in his tasting cellar one could taste quality chardonnay, zeleni silvanac, crni pinot and Portuguese. His relatives, Krešo and Zdravko Režek must be also mentioned as producers of very good sauvingon and rajnski rizling.

Bermet

The old cellar of Mladina company is a tourist attraction, where wines of 15 sorts ripe. The notable winegrowers are Haramija, Žganjer, Vučinić, Nežić, Kolarić, Gregorić, Jagunić, Kurtalja, Sirovica. In Samobor, the Filipec family produces special, aromathic wine bermet made of red wine and various aromathic herbs, primarily wormwood according to secret family recipes.

Premier - top quality wine by the Tomac family, one of the best Croatian chardonnays

Specialty - aromathic wine bermet

ZELINA WINE ROAD

The second important wine road in Zagreb county runs through the Zelina winegrowing district, that administratively covers the places in Zagreb vicinity. There are attractive vineyards around the picturesque hills, and the village of Nespeš is the most notable for its wines. In the past the wine from its cellars was traditionally taken to Zagreb market.

White pinot

Stjepan Jarec became very distinguished primarily due to his white pinot wines. To the wine label he has recently added his son-in-law's family name, Kure. It is very elegant, harmonious wine with fruit and flower aromas and pleasant sugar remains, drinkable, rounded. His barrique chardonnay is also successful.

Kraljevina

Kraljevina Jarec-Kure was often

declared the best at the opular regional wine exhibition in Zelina, the oldest in Croatia. This district is considered the homeland of indigenous sort of kra-ljevina. It is light, less alcoholic wine, tipically summer-like, fresh with higher acids.

Baština

The winegrowers and wine-merchants from Kos-Jurišić family are also prominent in the production of diverse quality wines (graševina, grey pinot, kerner, chardonnay, kraljevina) as well as their relatives Kos, Željko and Mirko, who produce shampaigns as well. Here is also the veteran Blaž Jarec, the families of Stjepan and Zdravko Puhelek, the Žigrović family, the Smrndić family and the Čegec family. In Zagreb, the Faculty of Agronomy develops interesting wine production on their field Jazbina. The wines of high quality inspired by literary heritage, Dora Krupićeva, Zlatarevo zlato, Crni vitez and Crna kraljica, are made of graševina, traminac, merlot, cabernet sauvignon, black pinot, frankovka and zweiglet.

Wine lovers especially appreciate white pinot by the Jurec-Kure family

Café bars

Alcatraz
Preradovićeva ulica 12
℡ 01 485 52 84
🕐 7 a.m. - 11 p.m.;
  Sun 9 a.m. - 11 p.m.

Amadeus
Trg Dražena Petrovića 3
℡ 01 484 30 58
🕐 7 a.m. - 11 p.m.;
  Sun 11 a.m. - 11 p.m.

Armani
Vlaška ulica 115
℡ 01 466 41 13
🕐 7 a.m. - 11 p.m.;
  Sun 8 a.m. - 11 p.m.

Assisi
Opatovina 49
℡ 01 481 05 00
🕐 7 a.m. - 11 p.m.;
  Sun 10 a.m. - 11 p.m.

Babaloo
Trg J. F. Kennedya 6
℡ 01 230 08 67
🕐 7 a.m. - 11 p.m.;
  Sun 9 a.m. - 9 p.m.

Baredo
Varšavska 5a
℡ 01 487 28 89
🕐 7 a.m. - 1 a.m.;
  Sun 10 a.m. - 1 a.m.

Boing
Schlosserove stube 2
℡ 01 455 17 39
🕐 8 a.m. - 12 p.m.;
  Sun 9 a.m. - 12 p.m.

The most popular Zagreb
café-bar Charlie

Bolero
Martićeva ulica 71
℡ 01 461 67 73
🕐 7 a.m. - 0 p.m.; ● Sun

Booksa
Martićeva 14d
℡ 01 461 61 24
🕐 9 a.m. - 11 p.m.; ● Mon

Carpe Diem
Opatovina 23
℡ 01 492 12 96
🕐 7 a.m. - 1 a.m.

Charlie
Gajeva 4
℡ 01 481 10 39
🕐 7 a.m. - 11 p.m.;
  7 a.m. - 11 p.m.

Cvjetni trg
Bogovićeva ulica 5
℡ 01 481 08 76
🕐 7 a.m. - 11 p.m.;
  Sun 8 a.m. - 11 p.m.

Congo
Bukovačka cesta 25
℡ 01 233 92 79
🕐 7 a.m. - 11 p.m.;
  Sun 8 a.m. - 11 p.m.

Coprnjica
Strossmayerovo šetalište bb
℡ 01 483 10 42
🕐 Mon-Sun 8 a.m. - 1 a.m.

Crna kraljica
Radićeva ulica 6
℡ 01 481 92 51
🕐 7 a.m. - 11 p.m.;
  Sun 8 a.m. - 11 p.m.

Cup ´98
Petrinjska ulica 4
℡ 01 481 98 81
🕐 7 a.m. - 11 p.m.

Čvenk
Radićeva ulica 23
℡ 01 485 16 75
🕐 8 a.m. - 11 p.m.;
  Sun 8 a.m. - 1 a.m.; ● Sun

Dominato
Iblerov trg bb
℡ 01 461 99 96
🕐 7 a.m. - 11 p.m.;
  Sun 9 a.m. - 11 p.m.

Duh
Vlaška 68
℡ 01 461 70 14
🕐 pon-sub 07-23; ● Sun

Downtown
Teslina ulica 4
℡ 01 481 19 21
🕐 8 a.m. - 11 p.m.; ● Sun

Escobar
Iblerov trg bb
℡ 461 44 88
🕐 8.30 a.m. - 10 p.m.

Europa 92
Varšavska ulica 3
℡ 01 487 28 94
🕐 Mon-Sat 7 a.m. - 11 p.m.;
  Sun 8 a.m. - 11 p.m.

Fiškal
Trnjanska cesta 25
℡ 615 97 25
🕐 7 a.m. - 11 p.m.

Frankopan
Frankopanska ulica 8
℡ 01 484 85 47
🕐 pon-sub 07-23;
  Sun 8 a.m. - 11 p.m.

Fun
Trg J. F. Kennedya 6b
℡ 01 230 00 68
🕐 7 a.m. - 11 p.m.

Golf caffe
Preradovićeva ulica 2
℡ 01 483 83 13
🕐 7 a.m. - 11 p.m.;
  Sun 9 a.m. - 11 p.m.

Golfland
Tomašićeva ulica 13
℡ 01 461 43 28
🕐 7 a.m. - 11 p.m.; ● Sun

Hemingway
Iblerov trg bb
℡ 01 461 97 36
🕐 7 a.m. - 11 p.m.;
  Sun 9 a.m. - 9 p.m.

Henrik
Gundulićeva ulica 39
℡ 01 485 61 71
🕐 Mon-Fri 7 a.m. - 10 p.m.;
  Sat 7 a.m. - 8 p.m. ● Sun

Hollywood
Starčevićev trg bb
℡ 01 57 70 03
🕐 5 a.m. - 1 a.m.

Joes' bar
Branimirova ulica 29
℡ 01 469 60 00
🕐 7 a.m. - 1 a.m.

K&K
Jurišićeva ulica 3
℡ 01 481 35 58
🕐 8 a.m. - 11 p.m.; ● Sun

Knez Mislav
Ulica kneza Mislava 7
℡ 01 461 50 40
🕐 7 a.m. - 11 p.m.

Kolding
Berislavićeva ulica 8
℡ 01 487 24 88
🕐 8 a.m. - 1 a.m.;
  Sun 9 a.m. - 1 a.m.

Krešimir
Berislavićeva ulica 7
℡ 01 487 23 73
🕐 7 a.m. - 11 p.m.;
  Sun 9 a.m. - 11 p.m.

Kvazar
Opatovina 39
℡ 01 481 41 74
🕐 9 a.m. - 1 a.m.

Lea
Vlaška ulica 62
℡ 01 461 70 86
🕐 7 a.m. - 11 p.m.

Lokin
Maksimirska cesta 111
℡ 01 233 86 86
🕐 7 a.m. - 11 p.m.

Lukyll
Starčevićev trg bb
① 01 457 77 77
🕐 08-21; ● ned

Maraschino Bar
Margaretska ulica 1
① 481 26 12
🕐 8 a.m. - 11 p.m.

Medvedgrad
Radićeva ulica 6
① 01 481 92 51
🕐 7 a.m. - 11 p.m.;
   Sun 8 a.m. - 3 p.m.

Milka
Ilica 7
① 01 481 05 97
🕐 7 a.m. - 10 p.m.; ● Sun

Mocca
Ilica 1a
① 01 481 28 39
🕐 7 a.m. - 11 p.m.;
   Sun 7 a.m. - 9 p.m.

Pikaro
(Mexican Tequila Bar)
Zvonimirova ulica 137
① 01 230 10 08
🕐 7 a.m. - 11 p.m.

Paladium
Prolaz Tkalčićeva 5
① 01 487 37 35
🕐 9 a.m. - 11 p.m.

Press Club
Perkovčeva ulica 2
① 01 482 61 03
🕐 8 a.m. - 11 p.m.; ● Sun

Savski kutić
Savska cesta 118
① 01 619 10 31
🕐 7 a.m. - 4 a.m.;
   Mon, Tue 7 a.m. - 2 a.m.
   ● Sun

Segafredo
Radićeva ulica 3
① 01 483 09 64
🕐 8 a.m. - 11 p.m.; ● Sun

Servus
Tkalčićeva ulica 12
① 01 481 37 48
🕐 7 a.m. - 1 a.m.

Spunk
Ulica Hrvatske bratske
zajednice bb
① 01 615 15 28
🕐 7 a.m. - 12 p.m.;
   Fri-Sat 7 a.m. - 3 a.m.
   Sun 6 a.m. - 12 p.m.

Studio 13
Dežmanova ulica 3
① 01 484 74 95
🕐 7.30 a.m. - 11 p.m.;
   Sun 9 a.m. - 10 p.m.

Sun Set
Preradovićeva ulica 34
① 01 485 54 08
🕐 7 a.m. - 11 p.m.; ● Sun

Sunce
Bogovićeva ulica 18
① 01 481 09 79
🕐 7 a.m. - 11 p.m.;
   Sun 9 a.m. - 11 p.m.

Tip Top
Gundulićeva ulica 18
① 01 483 03 49
🕐 7 a.m. - 11 p.m.

Tolkien´s
Vranicanijeva ulica 6
① 01 485 20 50
🕐 9 a.m. - 11 p.m.;
   Fri-Sat 9 a.m. - 12 p.m.
   Sun 9 a.m. - 11 p.m.

Zodiac
Tkalčićeva ulica 43
① 01 481 33 49
🕐 8 a.m. - 1 a.m.

Zrin
Berislavićeva ulica 3
① 01 487 27 38
🕐 7 a.m. - 11 p.m.;
   Sun 9 a.m. - 11 p.m.

Žirafa
Maksimirska cesta 68
① 01 232 35 23
🕐 7 a.m. - 11 p.m.; ● Sun

Coffee houses

Boban
Gajeva ulica 7

① 01 481 15 57
🕐 7 a.m. - 11 p.m.

Dubrovnik
Gajeva ulica 1
① 01 487 35 55
🕐 7 a.m. - 11 p.m.

Gradska Kavana
Trg bana Josipa Jelačića 9
① 01 481 30 05
🕐 7.30 a.m. - 10.30 p.m.

Lisinski
Trg Stjepana Radića 4
① 01 612 11 14
🕐 7 a.m. - 12 p.m.;
   Sun 12 a.m. - 12 p.m.

Mala kavana
Trg bana Josipa Jelačića 5
① 01 481 68 33
🕐 8 a.m. - 11 p.m.

Palainovka
Ilirski trg 1
① 01 485 13 57
🕐 8 a.m. - 12 p.m.

Žabica
Opatička ulica 1
① 01 481 32 50
🕐 9 a.m. - 11 p.m.

Movie Theatres

A1
Iblerov trg bb
(Importanne galerija)
① 01 461 91 33; 01 461 91 39

Broadway Tkalča
Nova Ves 11
(Centar Kaptol)
① 01 466 76 86

Central
Petrinjska ulica 4
① 01 481 05 36; 062 100 100

CineStar Zagreb
Branimirova ulica 29
① 01 468 66 00

Croatia
Katančićeva ulica 3
① 01 481 37 11

Europa
Varšavska ulica 3
① 01 487 28 88; 062 100 100

Forum
SD Stjepan Radić
Jarunska 2
① 01 301 14 48

Grič
Jurišićeva ulica 6
① 01 481 07 93
   062 100 100

Jadran
Ilica 42
① 01 484 75 53
   062 100 100

KIC Art
Preradovićeva ulica 5
① 01 481 07 14

Kinoteka
Kordunska ulica 1
① 01 377 17 53

Kustošija
Vatrogasna cesta 1
① 01 377 61 17

Studentski centar
Savska cesta 25
① 01 459 36 11
   01 459 36 13

Zagreb
Trg Petra Preradovića 4
① 01 483 07 07; 062 100 100

SHOPPING

Shopping in Zagreb could be a real pleasure. Shops offer selection similar to that of Europe. But the quantity of products may vary so do not wait for a second chance, but buy what you like immediately. Zagreb shopping street is Ilica and the surrounding streets. They are full of great variety of shops.

SHOPPING CENTRES

There are a lot of shopping centres, specialised shops and boutiques in Zagreb, and in the past few years several modern, attractive shopping centres have been opened: Importanne centre, Importanne Gallery, Kaptol centre, Branimir centre and others. Beside numerous shops those centres offer other facilities like restaurants, cinemas etc.

TIPPING

It is customary in Zagreb to give tips in restaurants and similar services (to tourist, museum and other guides). The tipping ranges between 5 and 10 percent of the service amount. The prices in stores and shops are fixed and tipping is not customary. In the restaurants there are menus in several languages, and the waiters (staff) know the basic profession vocabulary in foreign languages, most often in English and German.

MARKETS

Most people buy fresh fruit and vegetables and dairy products at the markets. The largest and the most popular Zagreb market is Dolac, but there are several other smaller but well provided markets (Kvaternik Square, Branimir street, Britain Square, Utrine, Trešnjevka and others). They open early in the morning, every day, except state holiday, and on Sundays they close at noon.

SOUVENIRS AND GIFTS

There is a wide range of products that can be taken as a souvenir or gift: there are clothes, pillows (vanjkuš), calendars, books, monographs and pictures, top quality wines and cakes. Souvenirs with "Zagreb touch" are: casting of Dora Krupićeva, characther from the popular novel by August Šenoa, The Goldsmith's Treasure; *licitar*, pleter, ceramics, castings of works by great Croatian sculptor Ivan Meštrović, plaster houses with Zagreb motives, dove, objects made of crystal glass, knitted articles and homemade articles, casting of the famous Baška Tablet, fruit brandies, ball-point pens, Samobor appetizer bermet and Samobor mustard, ties, books and monographs of Zagreb, wine . . all that and much more could be bought in numerous specialised or ordinary shops in the centre of the town.

An den Türen der Geschäfte gibt es ein Schild mit der Information über die Möglichkeit der Rückerstattung der Mehrwertsteuer

TAX REFUNDS

Foreign tourists who spent more than 500 kunas in shopping have the right to tax refunds. In the shop you have to ask for a tax refund form that should be filled and stamped. The refund is claimed in kunas within 6 months either directly in the shop where the goods were purchased or by mail to the shop address with the bank account number to which the amount should be returned.

Shopping Centres

Centar Kaptol
Nova Ves 11
① 01 486 02 41
🕐 Mon-Sat 9 a.m. - 9 p.m.
Thu 9 a.m. - 11 p.m.
💻 www.centarkaptol.hr

City Centar Varteks
Trg bana J. Jelačića 8
① 01 489 31 05
🕐 Mon-Fri 9 a.m. - 9 p.m.;
Sat 9 a.m. - 5 p.m.

Importanne Centar
Starčevićev trg 1
① 01 45 77 076
🕐 Mon-Sat 9 a.m. - 9 p.m.
💻 www.importanne.hr

Importanne Galleria
Iblerov trg 10
① 01 46 19 503
🕐 Mon-Sat 9 a.m. - 9 p.m.
💻 www.importanne.hr/

Nama
Ilica 4
① 01 45 52 233
🕐 Mon-Fri 8 a.m. - 7.30 p.m.
Sat 8 a.m. - 1 p.m.

Rotonda
Jurišićeva ulica 19
① 01 48 17 785
🕐 Mon-Sat 8 a.m. - 9 p.m.
Sat 8 a.m. - 3 p.m.

Art Galleries

Art galerija Miriam
Jurišićeva ulica 6
① 01 481 21 55
🕐 Mon, Wed, Fri 5.30 a.m. - 9 p.m.
Tue, Thu, Sat 9.30 a.m. - 1.30 p.m.

Darak
Cesarčeva ulica 5
① 01 481 65 66
🕐 8 a.m. - 8 p.m.; Sat 8 a.m. - 2 p.m.

Galerija Arho-Ogledala mašte
Tkalčićeva ulica 13/II
① 091 588 05 13
🕐 9 a.m. - 8 p.m.; Sat 9 a.m. - 2 p.m.

Galerija Badrov - Foto art galerija
Trg žrtava fašizma
① 01 457 25 75
🕐 10 a.m. - 14 p.m.; 4 a.m. - 8 p.m.;
Sat 9 a.m. - 2 p.m.

Galerija Beck
Habdalićeva ulica 2
① 01 485 19 34
🕐 Mon 10 a.m. - 1 p.m.;
Sat 11 a.m. - 1 p.m.
Tue-Fri 10 a.m. - 1 p.m.;
5.30 a.m. - 8 p.m.

Galerija Deči
Radićeva ulica 19
① 01 483 09 44
🕐 9 a.m. - 1 p.m.; 4.30 a.m. - 8 p.m.;
Sat 9.30 a.m. - 2 p.m.

Dars
Radićeva ulica 44
① 01 481 33 89
🕐 10 a.m. - 1 p.m.

Galerija Forum
Teslina ulica 16
① 01 481 07 14
🕐 Mon-Fri 10 a.m. - 2 p.m.;
4 a.m. - 8 p.m.; Sat 10 a.m. - 2 p.m.
💻 www.kic.hr
✉ kic@net.hr

Galerija Grubić
Radićeva ulica 44
① 01 481 33 70
🕐 10 a.m. - 1 p.m.; 5 a.m. - 8 p.m.;
Sat 10 a.m. - 1 p.m.

Galerija Harmica
Trg bana Josipa Jelačića 6
① 01 481 68 35
🕐 8 a.m. - 8 p.m.; Sat 8 a.m. - 3 p.m.

Galerija Klovićevi dvori
Jezuitski trg 4
① 01 485 19 26
🕐 Tue-Sun 11 a.m. - 7 p.m.
💻 www.galerijaklovic.hr
✉ klovicevi-dvori@zg.htnet.hr

Galerija Mala
Trg bana Josipa Jelačića 6
① 01 481 69 54
🕐 9 a.m. - 9 p.m.; Sat 9 a.m. - 2 p.m.

Galerija Miroslav Kraljević
Šubićeva ulica 29
(ulaz iz Martićeve)
① 01 459 26 96
🕐 Mon-Fri 10 a.m. - 1 p.m.;
5 p.m. - 7 p.m.
💻 www.miroslav-kraljevic.hr
✉ branko.franceschi@ina-np-sir.tel.hr

Galerija Nova
Teslina ulica 7
① 01 487 25 82
🕐 Mon-Fri 11 a.m. - 1 p.m.;
5 p.m. - 8 p.m.; Sat 11 a.m. - 1 p.m.

Galerija Oktogon
Ilica 5
① 01 481 26 74
🕐 8 a.m. - 8 p.m.; Sat 8 a.m. - 2 p.m.

Galerija Spektar
Remetinečki gaj 12
(Centar za kulturu
Novi Zagreb)
① 01 614 01 89
🕐 9 a.m. - 6 p.m.; Sat 10 a.m. - 2 p.m.

Galerija Spot fotokluba Zagreb
Ilica 29/III kat
① 01 483 33 59
🕐 Mon-Fri 9 a.m. - 3 p.m.

Galerija Studentskog centra Sveučilišta u Zagrebu
Savska cesta 25
① 01 459 36 02
🕐 Mon-Fri 10 a.m. - 6 p.m.;
Sat 10 a.m. - 3 p.m.

Galerija ULUPUH
Tkalčićeva ulica 14
① 01 481 37 46
🕐 Mon-Fri 10 a.m. - 1 p.m.;
5 p.m. - 8 p.m.; Sat 10 a.m. - 1 p.m.
💻 www.ulupuh.hr
✉ galeria-ulupuh@zg.htnet.hr

Likum Urlich Gallery
Ilica 40
① 01 484 73 71
🕐 8 a.m. - 8 p.m.; Sat 8 a.m. - 2 p.m.

Mala Arta
Ilica 72
① 01 484 71 16
🕐 9.30 a.m. - 8 p.m.;
Sat 9.30 a.m. - 2 p.m.

Nadbiskupski duhovni stol
Spomen zbirka blaženog
Alojzija Stepinca
Kaptol 31
(dvorište katedrale)
① 01 481 17 81
🕐 10 a.m. - 1 p.m.;
1.40 p.m. - 4 p.m.;
Sat 9 a.m. - 2 p.m.

Pot Pouri
Miškecov prolaz
① 01 487 27 56
🕐 9 a.m. - 8 p.m.; Sat 9 a.m. - 2 p.m.

Museums

Lovački muzej
Nazorova ulica 63
① 01 483 45 60; 01 483 45 59
🕐 Wed, Fri, Sat 8 a.m. - 1 p.m.
Tue, Thu 12 a.m. - 5 p.m.
💻 www.hrvatski-lovacki-savez.hr
✉ hrvlosavez@hrvatski-lovacki-savez.hr

Memorijalna zbirka Jozo Kljaković
Rokov perivoj 4
① 01 482 42 70
🕐 Mon-Fri 9 a.m. - 1 p.m.;
3 p.m. - 7 p.m.

Muzej i radionice Franje Schneidera
Trg maršala Tita 11
① 01 482 66 55
🕐 Wed 10 a.m. - 1 p.m.; 4 p.m. - 7 p.m.

Stan arhitekta Viktora Kovačića
Massarykova ulica 21
① 01 485 59 11
🕐 Thu 10 a.m. - 5 p.m.
🖥 ww.mdc.hr/mgz

Tiflološki muzej
Draškovićeva ulica 80/II
① 01 481 11 02
🕐 Mon-Fri 8.30 a.m. - 4.30 p.m.

Zbirka Richter
Vrhovec ulica 38a
① 01 485 18 08
🕐 11 a.m. - 4 p.m.
🖥 www.mdc.hr/msu

Antiques

Agram
Miškecov prolaz 2
① 01 487 27 78
🕐 9 a.m. - 7.30 p.m.;
    Sat 9 a.m. - 2 p.m.

Antique shop
Jurišićeva ulica 5
① 01 481 35 49
🕐 9 a.m. - 8 p.m.;
    Sat 9 a.m. - 3 p.m.

Galerija Kaptol
Kaptol 13
① 01 481 48 16
🕐 9.30 a.m. - 8 p.m.;
    Sat 9.30 a.m. - 2 p.m.

Galerija Link
Radićeva ulica 20
① 01 481 32 94
🕐 10 a.m. - 2 p.m.; Fri 5 p.m. - 8 p.m.;
    Sat 9 a.m. - 2 p.m.

Kerubin
Kamenita ulica 15
① 01 485 16 98
🕐 9 a.m. - 12 a.m. 3 p.m. - 6 p.m.;
    Sat 9 a.m. - 12 a.m.

Sakač
Kršnjavoga 1 (Hotel Opera)
① 01 489 21 36
🕐 10 a.m. - 1 a.m. 6 p.m. - 9 p.m.;
    ● Sun

Souvenirs

Dar Mar
Jurišićeva ulica 19
① 01 481 93 73
🕐 9 a.m. - 8 p.m.; Sat 9 a.m. - 2 p.m.

Galerija Bil Ani
Radićeva ulica 37
① 01 485 23 45
🕐 9 a.m. - 8 p.m.

Nautika Širok
Cesarčeva ulica 5
① 01 481 65 65
🕐 9 a.m. - 7.30 p.m.;
    Sat 9 a.m. - 2 p.m.

Pandora
Tkalčićeva ulica 5
① 01 487 37 50
🕐 9 a.m. - 8 p.m.;

Souvenirs at Tourist Information Centre

Sat 9 a.m. - 2 p.m.

SOHO
Petrićeva ulica 2
① 01 487 35 67
🕐 9 a.m. - 9 p.m.;
    Sat 9 a.m. - 3 p.m.

Širok
Bakačeva ulica 8
① 01 481 65 52
🕐 8 a.m. - 8 p.m.;
    Sat 8 a.m. - 2 p.m.

Bookstores

Algoritam
Gajeva ulica 1
① 01 481 86 72
🕐 8.30 a.m. - 9 p.m.;
    Sat 8.30 a.m. - 3 p.m.

Ljevak
Trg bana Josipa Jelačića 17
① 01 481 29 92; 481 29 63
🕐 8 a.m. - 8 p.m.;
    Sat 8 a.m. - 3 p.m.

Moderna vremena
Teslina ulica 16
① 01 481 07 42
🕐 9 a.m. - 9 p.m.;
    Sat 9 a.m. - 3 p.m.

More comics - strip knjižara
Ulica Frane Petrića 5
① 01 481 28 06
🕐 10 a.m. - 9 p.m.;
    Sat 9.30 a.m. - 2.30 p.m.

Profil
Iblerov trg bb
(Importanne galerija /-1)
① 01 467 02 11
🕐 9 a.m. - 9 p.m.

Studio
Masarykova ulica 20
① 01 487 25 98
🕐 9 a.m. - 8 p.m.;
    Sat 9 a.m. - 2 p.m.

Superknjižara
Rooseveltov trg 4
① 01 487 57 34
🕐 8 a.m. - 8 p.m.;
    Sat 8 a.m. - 2 p.m.

Tamaris
Trg bana Josipa Jelačića 3
① 01 488 26 80
🕐 9 a.m. - 9 p.m.

Cosmetics and beauty products

Alessandro
Vlaška ulica 63
① 01 467 09 04
🕐 8 a.m. - 9 p.m.;
    Sat 9 a.m. - 3 p.m.

City Centar Varteks
Trg bana Josipa Jelačića 8
① 01 489 31 50
🕐 8 a.m. - 8.30 p.m.;
    Sat 9 a.m. - 5 p.m.

Drogerie Markt
Ilica 5
① 01 487 35 97
🕐 8 a.m. - 8 p.m.;
    Sat 8 a.m. - 3 p.m.

Fulmin
Ulica N. Tesle 6
① 01 481 14 54
🕐 8 a.m. - 8 p.m.;
    Sat 8 a.m. - 3 p.m.

Iris
Trg bana Josipa Jelačića 1
① 01 4888 31 51
🕐 8 a.m. - 8 p.m.;
    Sat 8 a.m. - 8 p.m.

Lush
Petrinjska ulica 4
① 01 481 05 49
🕐 9 a.m. - 8 p.m.;
    Sat 9 a.m. - 3 p.m.

Martimex
Nova Ves 17
① 01 486 01 08
🕐 9 a.m. - 9 p.m.;

Nivea
Jurišićeva ulica 8
① 01 481 08 06
🕐 9 a.m. - 8 p.m.;
    Sat 8 a.m. - 3 p.m.

Clothing

Benetton
Bogovićeva ulica 9
① 01 481 24 14
🕐 8 a.m. - 8 p.m.;
    Sat 8 a.m. - 3 p.m.

Camel
Masarykova ulica 2
① 01 481 29 46
🕐 8 a.m. - 8 p.m.;
    Sat 8 a.m. - 3 p.m.

Diesel
Frankopanska ulica 4
① 01 4848-511
🕐 9 a.m. - 8 p.m.;
    Sat 9 a.m. - 3 p.m.

Escada
Gundulićeva ulica 15
① 01 487 55 77
🕐 10 a.m. - 10 p.m.;
    Sat 10 a.m. - 3 p.m.

Gai Mattiolo
Trg bana Josipa Jelačića 4
① 01 481 68 03
🕐 9 a.m. - 8 p.m.;
    Sat 9 a.m. - 3 p.m.

Heruc Galerija
Ilica 26
℡ 01 483 35 69
🕐 8 a.m. - 8 p.m.;
    Sat 8 a.m. - 3 p.m.

Image Haddad
Ilica 6
℡ 01 483 10 35
🕐 8 a.m. - 8 p.m.;
    Sat 8 a.m. - 3 p.m.

Lacoste
Iblerov trg
Immportane galerija
℡ 01 455 74 84
🕐 9 a.m. - 9 p.m.

La Perla
Gundulićeva ulica 3
℡ 01 483 07 24
🕐 8 a.m. - 8.30 p.m.;
    Sat 8 a.m. - 3 p.m.

Levi´s
Trg bana Jelačića 8
℡ 01 487 03 45
🕐 9 a.m. - 8.30 p.m.;
    Sat 9 a.m. - 5 p.m.

Lisca
Nova Ves 17
℡ 01 486 02 02
🕐 9 a.m. - 9 p.m.

Mango
Ilica 20
℡ 01 483 39 16
🕐 9 a.m. - 8 p.m.;
    Sat 9 a.m. - 4 p.m.

Marks & Spencer
Nova Ves 11
℡ 01 486 02 10
🕐 10 a.m. - 9 p.m.

Martin Arbanas
Preradovićeva ulica 7
℡ 01 487 21 61
🕐 9 a.m. - 8 p.m.;
    Sat 9 a.m. - 2 p.m.

Max Mara
Petrinjska ulica 7
℡ 01 492 28 13
🕐 9 a.m. - 8 p.m.;
    Sat 9 a.m. - 3 p.m.

Modni salon Kathy Balogh
Radićeva ulica 22
℡ 01 481 32 90
🕐 10 a.m. - 6 p.m.;
    Sat 10 a.m. - 2 p.m.

Parfume shop

Nebo
Immportane Centar,
Starčevićev trg bb
℡ 01 455 02 14
🕐 9 a.m. - 9 p.m.

Parah
Jurišićeva ulica 19 (Rotonda)
℡ 01 481 77 68
🕐 9 a.m. - 8 p.m.;
    Sat 9 a.m. - 3 p.m.

Pierre Cardin
Ulica N. Tesle 10
℡ 01 481 14 64
🕐 8 a.m. - 8 p.m.;
    Sat 8 a.m. - 3 p.m.

Plavi cvijet
Ulica N. Tesle 14
℡ 01 481 13 09
🕐 8 a.m. - 8 p.m.;
    Sat 8 a.m. - 3 p.m.

Skinny
Immportane Centar,
Starčevićev trg bb
℡ 01 455 01 79
🕐 9 a.m. - 9 p.m.;

Triumf
Jurišićeva ulica 12
℡ 01 481 09 04
🕐 8 a.m. - 8 p.m.;
    Sat 8 a.m. - 3 p.m.

MUSEUMS AND GALLERIES IN THE VICINITY

Galleries

Antun Augustinčić Gallery
Trg Antuna Mihanovića 10
Klanjec
℡ 049 550 343
🕐 9 a.m. - 5 p.m.
🖳 www.augustincic.hr

Krapina Town Gallery
Magistratska ulica 25
Krapina
℡ 049 370 810
🕐 9 a.m. - 1 p.m.
🖳 www.krapina.net

Galženica
Trg Stjepana Radića 5
Velika Gorica
℡ 01 622 11 22
🕐 9 a.m. - 7 p.m.;
    Sat and Sun 10 a.m. - 2 p.m.

Museums

Veliki Tabor Castle
Desinić
℡ 049 34 30 52
🕐 10 a.m. - 6 p.m.
🖳 www.veliki-tabor.hr

Trakošćan Castle
℡ 042 796 281
🕐 9 a.m. - 6 p.m.
🖳 www.mdc.hr/trakoscan/
✉ dvor-trakoscan@vz.tel.hr

Ethno - museum Old village Kumrovec
℡ 049 553 107
🕐 9 a.m. - 7 p.m.
🖳 www.mdc.hr/kumrovec/

Ethno park Ozalj
Trška cesta bb, Ozalj
℡ 047 731 170
Native museum Ozalj should be call for visit

Evolution museum - Hušnjakovo
Šetalište V. Sluge bb, Krapina
℡ 049 371 491
🕐 10 a.m. - 5 p.m.
🖳 www.krapina.com

Marton Museum
Jurjevska ulica 7
Samobor
℡ 01 332 64 26
🕐 Sat and Sun 9 a.m. - 1 p.m.;
    3 p.m. - 6 p.m.

The Samobor Museum
Livadićeva ulica 7
Samobor
℡ 01 336 10 14
🕐 Tue-Fri 9 a.m. - 3 p.m.
    Sat and Sun 9 a.m. - 1 p.m.

The Peasants' Revolt Museum - Oršić Manor
Gornja Stubica
℡ 049 587 888
🕐 9 a.m. - 6 p.m.
🖳 www.mdc.hr/msb

Museum of Turopolje
Trg kralja Tomislava 1
Velika Gorica
℡ 01 622 13 25
🕐 Tue-Fri 10 a.m. - 6 p.m.
    Sat and Sun 10 a.m. - 1 p.m.
🖳 www.muzej-turopolja.hr

Native museum Ozalj
Ulica Zrinskih i
Frankopana 2
Ozalj
℡ 047 731 170
🕐 9 a.m. - 3 p.m.;
    Sat and Sun 11 a.m. - 5 p.m.
🖳 http://ozalj.netfirms.com

ENTERTAINMENT

Zagreb may not be glittering as other big European cities but you will certainly not be bored. It has all that other big European and world cities have - top quality restaurants, some opened until early morning hours, bars and discos, casinos and striptease-bars. There is something to satisfy everyone's taste.

CONCERTS AND THEATRES

There are many interesting events in Zagreb during the whole year. Theatre and concert season in Zagreb actually does not finish. During summer, Zagreb citizens and visitors could go to the Upper Town and listen to the concerts from the cycle Evening on Grič. The concerts are held either in the atrium of the Museum Gallery at the Jesuit square or in St. Catherine's church or in St. Mark's Church. Or they could opt for the concerts in the Zagreb cathedral named The Organs of the Zagreb cathedral During winter, Vatroslav Lisinski concert hall attracts you by its programme. In summer theatre preformances are held outdoors, at the stage on Opatovina (the old part of the town) or somewhere else. In the Croatian National Theatre there are three companies: opera, ballet and drama. The opera company is famous in Croatia and abroad, going on numerous tours and performing classical programme as well as contemporary opera works. The Ballet company is successfull as a whole as well as are its individual dancers. In traditional playing two unavoidable companies are notable: the Zagreb Philharmonic, the orchestra of the international reputation and the Zagreb Quartet, the oldest Croatian chamber ensemble, takes the priceless credit for promotion of Croatian chamber music in the world. They also contributed to the development of musical life in Zagreb.

COFFEE HOUSES, CAFES AND CLUBS

During winter everything is indoor but in summer Zagreb shows its Mediterranean spirit and atmosphere. At night particualr streets or parts of the town, full of cafes overcrowded with guests looking for fun and amusement. Those who like to challenge their luck could run some risk in the casinos within the notable Zagreb hotels or some other casino. Zagreb coffee houses and their more modern versions, cafes, undoubtedly give to town some additional charm. Socializing and lingering over a cup of coffee in a coffee house has really a long tradition in Zagreb. Many like to go to several newly arranged coffee houses at the Ban Jelačić Square, while younger generations prefer cafes. Guests preferring music could relax in some of the numerous Zagreb discos or clubs, of which some are extremely popular. There are also jazz

Concert hall during the concert

International Folklore Festival is event that gathers original folklore groups from all over the world

or swing clubs with rich programme or some candle lit restaurant with rhythm of valse, tango, rumba or samba.

Festivals

During various traditional festivals there is special atmosphere in town because the whole town lives in their atmosphere then. In spring and early summer two world festivals with 20 year tradition are held in Zagreb: World festival of animated films on even years only and Biennial of Contemporary Music - international festival of avant garde music on odd years only. Last days of May or the beginning of June are the time for the Festival of the Zagreb Philharmonic. There is also the contemporary Dance Festival and Eurokaz - international modern theatre festival. Special attraction to numerous tourists in Zagreb is the International Flower Exhibition - Floraart. For the lovers of folk dances there is International Folklore Festival taking place on the last days of July and gathering original folklore groups from all over the world. Then the town becomes a unique stage. Many people say that Zagreb autumns are the loveliest and it is difficult to decide whether to stay in town or go to some picturesque village in the vicinity to pick the grapes. Because, with picking comes the good food and fun accompanied by original folklore group or *tamburaši*.

Theatres

Dječja scena Ribica
Park Ribnjak
☎ 01 481 47 34

Dječje kazalište Dubrava
Cerska ulica 1
☎ 01 291 04 87

Dramsko kazalište Gavella
Frankopanska ulica 8
☎ 01 484 85 52

Gradsko kazalište Komedija
Kaptol 9
☎ 01 481 45 66

Gradsko kazalište Trešnja
Mošćenička ulica 1
☎ 01 363 85 56

Gradsko kazalište Žar ptica
Bijenička cesta 97
☎ 01 234 72 27

Hrvatsko narodno kazalište
Trg maršala Tita 15
☎ 01 482 85 32

Kazalište Mala scena
Medveščak 2
☎ 01 468 33 52

OFF Theater Bagatella
Bednjanska ulica 13
☎ 01 617 04 23

Satiričko kazalište Kerempuh
Ilica 31
☎ 01 483 33 47

Scena Vidra
Draškovićeva ulica 80
☎ 01 481 01 11

Teatar Exit
Ilica 208
☎ 01 370 41 20

Teatar ITD
Savska cesta 25
☎ 01 484 34 92

Zagrebačko kazalište lutaka
Ulica baruna Trenka
☎ 01 369 54 57

Zagrebačko kazalište mladih
Teslina ulica 7
☎ 01 487 25 54

Concert Halls

Hrvatski glazbeni zavod
Gundulićeva ulica 6
☎ 01 483 08 22

Preporodna dvorana palače narodnog doma
Opatička ulica 18
☎ 01 461 18 08

Koncertna dvorana Vatroslava Lisinskog
Trg Stjepana Radića 4
☎ 01 612 11 66

Clubs

Attack
Trnjanski nasip bb
(Tvornica Jedinstvo)
☎ 01 619 51 34
🕐 4 p.m. - 8 p.m.

Aquarius
Ulica Matije Ljubeka bb, Jarun
☎ 01 364 02 31
🖥 www.aquarius.hr
🕐 9 p.m. - 4 p.m.

Baobab
Aleja mira bb
☎ 01 383 15 86
🖥 www.club–baobab.com
🕐 Sun-Tue 9 p.m. - 2 a.m.;
    Wed-Sat 9 p.m. - 4 a.m.

Best
Horvaćanski zavoj bb
☎ 01 369 16 01
🖥 www.bestclubbing.htnet.hr
🕐 Fri, Sat 10 p.m. - 7 a.m.

Brazil Net Club
Maksimirska cesta 98
☎ 234 52 78; 098 917 36 88
🕐 9 p.m. - 4 p.m.

Cab club
Ilica 55
☎ 01 484 63 49
🕐 Fri, Sat 10 p.m. - 4 a.m.

Gap club
Ulica F. Andrašeca 14
☎ 01 309 61 23
🕐 10 p.m. - 4 a.m.
P

GJURO II
Medveščak 2
☎ 01 468 33 67
🕐 9 p.m. - 2 a.m.

Hard Rock Café
Gajeva ulica 10
☎ 01 487 25 48
🕐 9 p.m. - 1 a.m.

Iguana
Tkalčićeva ulica 46
☎ 481 19 16
🕐 9 p.m. - 11 p.m.

Jabuka
Jabukovac 28
☎ 01 483 43 97
🕐 Tue-Sun 10 p.m. - 2 a.m.

KSET
Unska cesta 3
☎ 01 612 97 58
🕐 8 p.m. - 12 p.m.

Lake City
Jarunska obala bb
☎ 01 301 14 94
🕐 8 p.m. - 4 a.m.

Lapidarij
Habdelićeva ulica 1
☎ 01 485 19 36
🕐 8 p.m. - 4 a.m.

Tkalčićeva street with
its cafee bars

Masters
Maksimirska cesta 138
☎ 01 291 60 22
🕐 8 a.m. - 4 a.m.
P

**Rock Club & Bikers Bar
Maximum**
Park Ribnjak 26
☎ 098 288 809
🕐 10 a.m. - 2 a.m.;
    Sun 6 p.m. - 2 a.m.

Močvara
Trnjanski nasip bb
☎ 01 615 96 67
☎ 01 615 96 68
🖥 www.mochvara.hr
🕐 8 p.m. - 4 a.m.;
    Sat and Sun 10 p.m. - 4 a.m.

No. 1
Nova Ves 2
☎ 01 466 61 89
🕐 9 a.m. - 4 a.m.

OTV Club
Vukovarska avenija 68
☎ 01 611 04 24
🕐 10 p.m. - 4 a.m.

Pauk
Jarunska cesta 2
☎ 01 301 14 48

Purgeraj
Park Ribnjak 1
☎ 091 545 60 97
🕐 Mon-Thu, Sun 9 a.m. - 2 p.m.
    Fri, Sat 9 a.m. - 4 a.m.

Route 66
Paromlinska ulica 47
☎ 01 611 87 34
🕐 7 a.m. - 11 p.m.;
    Mon-Fri 10 p.m. - 4 a.m.

Saloon
Tuškanac 1a
☎ 01 483 48 35
🕐 10 p.m. - 5 a.m.; ● Sun and Mon

Sokol klub
Trg maršala Tita 6
☎ 01 482 85 10
🖥 www.sokolklub.hr
🕐 10 p.m. - 4 a.m.

Tantra 23
Gajeva ulica 1
☎ 01 481 88 31
🕐 8 p.m. - 4 a.m.

Tvornica kulture
Šubićeva ulica 2
☎ 01 465 50 07
🕐 7 a.m. - 11 p.m. cafee-bar;
    10 p.m. - 4 a.m. club

Cocktail bars

Argentina
Tkalčićeva ulica 9
☎ 01 487 37 36
🕐 7 a.m. - 12 p.m.

Cadenca
Gundulićeva ulica 11
☎ 01 487 20 92
🕐 7 a.m. - 10 p.m.

Hemingway
Tuškanac 1
☎ 01 483 49 56
🖥 www.hemingwy.hr
🕐 9 a.m. - 4 a.m.

Indy´s
Vranicanijeva ulica 4
☎ 485 20 53
🕐 9 a.m. - 11 p.m.

Khala
Nova Ves 11
(Centar Kaptol)
☎ 234 56 78
🕐 10 a.m. - 2 a.m.

Latina
Savska cesta 23a
☎ 01 484 37 75
🕐 7 a.m. - 11 p.m.;
    Sun 9 a.m. - 11 p.m.

Lira
Teslina ulica 5
☎ 098 313 033
🕐 7 a.m. - 12 p.m.

Mango
Schlosserove stube 2
☎ 01 461 72 55
🕐 8 a.m. - 2 a.m.;
    Sat and Sun 8 a.m. - 4 a.m.

Papaya
Schlosserove stube 2
☎ 01 455 06 60
🕐 8 a.m. - 2 a.m.;
    Sat and Sun 8 a.m. - 4 a.m.

Praćka
Dalmatinska ulica 14
☎ 01 484 79 54
🕐 8 a.m. - 4 a.m.

Thalia
Teslina ulica 7
☎ 01 487 25 60
🕐 8 a.m. - 11 p.m.

Žabac
Jarunska cesta bb
☎ 01 369 57 92
🕐 Mon-Wed 7 a.m. - 1 p.m.
  Thu, Fri 7 a.m. - 1 a.m.
  Sat 7 a.m. - 3 a.m.;
  Sun 8 a.m. - 11 p.m.

Jazz clubs

BP - jazz club
Teslina ulica 7
☎ 01 481 44 44
🕐 10 a.m. - 2 a.m.;

**Klub hrvatskih
glazbenika - SAX**
Palmotićeva ulica 22
☎ 01 487 28 36
🕐 9 a.m. - 4 a.m.;

Gay

Bijoux
Mrazovićeva ulica 9
☎ 091 533 77 57
🕐 12 a.m. - 10 p.m.;
  11 p.m. - 10 a.m.
  (reservations ☎)

Glob@l Club
Ulica Pavla Hatza 14
☎ 01 487 61 46
🕐 11 a.m. - 4 a.m.;
  Sat 8 a.m. - 3 a.m.;

Uslužni obrt David
Marulićev trg 13
☎ 01 533 65 07; 01 533 77 57
🕐 2 p.m. - 10 p.m.;
  Fri 2 p.m. - 12 p.m.
  Sat and Sun 4 p.m. - 12 p.m.

Casino

Royal
Trg športova 9
(Hotel Panorama)
☎ 01 365 83 33
🕐 4 p.m. - 7 a.m.

Vega Casino
Ulica kneza Borne 2
(Hotel Sheraton)
☎ 01 461 18 86
🕐 Thu-Sat 8 a.m. - 7 a.m.;

Atlanta
Draškovićeva ulica 15a
Tel: 01 461 04 94
🕐 9 p.m. - 6 a.m.

Automat Club
Miramarska cesta 24
☎ 01 615 00 26
🕐 8 p.m. - 4 a.m.

California
Ulica kneza Mislava 1
☎ 01 291 76 11
🕐 10 p.m. - 2 a.m.

Casino City
Mihanovićeva ulica 1
☎ 01 450 10 00
🕐 7 p.m. - 4 a.m.

International
Miramarska cesta 24
☎ 01 610 88 00
🕐 9 p.m. - 5 a.m.

Metro
Ulica Grgura Ninskog bb
☎ 01 457 71 34
🕐 0-24

Pubs

**Bulldog Belgian
Beer Café**
Bogovićeva ulica 6
☎ 01 481 63 93
🕐 8 a.m. - 11 p.m.

Dublin Pub
Maksimirska cesta 37
☎ 01 236 04 93
🕐 8 a.m. - 1 a.m.

Bulldog Belgium Beer Caffe

**Fantasy Club in
Tolkien`s Pub**
Katarinin trg 3
☎ 01 485 17 76
🕐 8 a.m. - 11 p.m.;
  Fri, Sat 8 a.m. - 12 p.m.
  Sun 8 a.m. - 11 p.m.

Godot Pub
Savska cesta 23
☎ 01 484 37 75
🕐 7 a.m. - 11 p.m.;
  Sun 8 a.m. - 12 p.m.

Hole in One
Vlaška ulica 42
☎ 01 483 52 80
🕐 8 a.m. - 12 p.m.;
  Fri, Sat 8 a.m. - 1 a.m.
  ● Sun

Kaptol Pub
Kaptol 4
☎ 01 481 34 78
🕐 8 a.m. - 12 p.m.

Londoner Pub
Nova Ves 11
(Centar Kaptol)
☎ 01 486 02 31
🕐 8 a.m. - 4 a.m.;
  Sun 9 a.m. - 4 a.m.

Movie Pub
Savska cesta 141
☎ 01 605 50 45
🕐 7 a.m. - 2 a.m.;
  Sat 9 a.m. - 2 a.m.
  ned 6 a.m. - 2 p.m.

Old Pharmacy Pub
Hebrangova ulica 11a
☎ 01 492 19 12
🕐 9 a.m. - 11 p.m.; ● Sun

Oliver Twist
Tkalčićeva ulica 60
☎ 01 481 22 06
🕐 9 a.m. - 4 a.m.

Tartan Pub
Tkalčićeva ulica 36
☎ 01 481 36 07
🕐 8 a.m. - 11 p.m.

Billliard

Biljarski klub M
Ilica 17
☎ 01 483 35 55
🕐 8 a.m. - 11 p.m.;
  Sat 9 a.m. - 11 p.m.
  Sun 10 a.m. - 11 p.m.

Genius
Paromlinska ulica 7
☎ 01 611 05 40
🕐 7 a.m. - 11 p.m.

Ponti
Masarykova ulica 3/1
☎ 01 485 58 54
🕐 10 a.m. - 11 p.m.; Sat 10
  a.m. - 1 a.m.
  Sun 4 a.m. - 12 p.m.

Comedy club

Tiger Lilly
Tuškanac (Hemingway)
☎ 01 461 13 23
🖥 www. Comedy-club.net

EMERGENCY AID

Ambulance

Personal safety at public places in town is high, and violent criminal is rather rare. Safety is a police matter and they are always ready to help. Of course, the tourists must take care of some precautions in order to avoid potential inconveniences, as in any large city in the world. Thus, never leave your valuable things and money unserveilled. Watch your luggage especially if you are on a crowded place. If you lose your documents, go to the police immediately. Health standards in town are high and there is no danger of any diseases, the tap water is drinkable everywhere.

HEALTH SERVICE

Health care institutions in Zagreb, emergency ward, clinics, hospitals are all accorded to European standards. In case of any accident of illness you would be treated with care. There are also many private doctors and clinics where you can have high standards medical service. Apart from the ordinary pharmacies there are many herbal pharmacies where you can buy domestic and imported natural products . All medication and products could be freely bought except those that expressly state the medical recipe.

Pharmacy neon sign

always have a doctor on duty who could assist the patient. In case of child emergency the best choice would be Klaićeva Children's Hospital. Dental problems would be best solved in Stomatological Polyclinics in Perković street (just behind the Journalist's Centre).

EMERGENCY AID

All hospitals in Zagreb work for 24 hours and

SERVICE TO PEOPLE WITH SPECIAL NEEDS

The disabled people are taken care of and Zagreb tries to make thir moving through town easier as well as their acess to public institutions.There are designated disabled parking areas, and many buildings, especially those recently built

have the access adapted to disabled persons. The rules of good behaviour tell us that disabled persons have advantage in public transport, banks, post offices, cinemas etc. The Main railway station, as well as the airport and bigger hotels and restaurants are wheelchair-friendly.

ROAD ASSISTANCE

If your car gets broken or you had an accident, Croatian Autoclub - HAK will assist you. Its services are available during the day at number 987. If you are using mobile, prefix the number with 01. They will fix your car, if possible, at the site. HAK regularly reports on traffic conditions, traffic crowds and alternative directions.

Emergency numbers	
Police	92
Fire	93
Emergency medical help	94
Emergency rescue	985
Road assistance	987
General information	981

Hospitals (0-24)

KB Sestre milosrdnice
Vinogradska ulica 29
① 01 378 72 20

Dječja bolnica
Klaićeva ulica 16
① 01 460 01 11

KB Dubrava
Avenija Gojka Šuška 6
① 01 290 24 44

KBC Rebro
Kišpatićeva ulica 12
① 01 238 88 88

Klinička bolnica Merkur
Zajčeva ulica 19
① 01 243 13 90

Klinika za plućne bolesti "Jordanovac"
Jordanovac 104
① 01 234 82 22

KBC klinika za ženske bolesti i porode
Petrova ulica 13
① 01 460 46 46

Traumatologija
Draškovićeva ulica 19
① 01 461 00 11

Ortopedija
Šalata 2-4
① 01 481 99 11

Zarazna bolnica
Mirogojska cesta 8
① 01 460 32 22

Pharmacy (0-24)

Ilica 43
① 01 484 84 50

Ilica 301
① 01 375 03 21

Grižanska ulica 4
Zagrebačka Dubrava
① 01 299 23 50

Avenija V. Holjevca 22
Siget
① 01 652 54 25

Ozaljska ulica 1
Trešnjevka
① 01 309 75 86

Stomatologija
Perkovčeva ulica 3
① 01 482 84 88
🕐 Mon-Fri 10 p.m. - 6 a.m.;
Sun 0-24

Road assistance

HAK
Opće informacije
① 01 464 08 00
🕐 0-24

Ured - Draškovićeva ulica 25
① 01 461 29 37; 01 461 29 38
🖥 www.hak.hr

Uvjeti na cestama
① 01 4640 800

Garages

AC Siget
Siget 17
① 01 6526 874
🕐 6.30 a.m. - 7 p.m.;
Sat 7 a.m. - 12 a.m.; ● Sun

Auto Will
Ljubljanska avenija 100
① 01 386 98 00
🕐 7.30 a.m. - 5 p.m.;
Sat 7.30 a.m. - 12 a.m.
Opel

Autokuća Baotić
Maksimirska cesta 282
① 01 2900 005
🕐 8 a.m. - 5 p.m.;
Sat 8 a.m. - 1 p.m.; ● Sun
Mercedes

Automaksimir
Kraljevićeva ulica 24
① 01 233 76 87
🕐 7.30 a.m. - 5 p.m.;
Sat 7.30 a.m. - 2 p.m.

Autokuća Matoković
Vinogradska ulica 68
① 01 376 87 71
🕐 Mon-Fri 8 a.m. - 4 p.m.
Nissan

Automehanika
Koturaška cesta 41
① 01 617 04 01
🕐 Mon-Fri 7.30 a.m. - 3.30 p.m.
Hyundai

CS Zagreb
Tratinska ulica 32
① 01 3821 902
🕐 7.30 a.m. - 3.30 p.m.;
● Sat, Sun
Citroen

Mechanic
Zvonimirova ulica 25
① 01 4553 758
🕐 7.30 a.m. - 6 p.m.;
● Sat, Sun
Alfa Romeo, Zastava,
Fiat

Mechanic
Lopašićeva ulica 12
① 01 4611 622
🕐 7.30 a.m. - 3.30 p.m.;
● Sat, Sun
Daewoo, Honda, Lada

Renauto
Draškovićeva ulica 49
① 01 461 35 05
🕐 8 a.m. - 8 p.m.;
Sat 9 a.m. - 1 p.m.
Renault

Servis američkih vozila
Remetinečka cesta 131
① 01 6555 500
🕐 8 a.m. - 4 p.m.
GM, Jeep, Chrysler

Child care

Uspinjača
Tkalčićeva ulica 27
① 01 481 37 26
🕐 9 a.m. - 5 p.m.

Frizer za djecu
TAF for kids
Marićev prolaz
① 01 487 38 54
🕐 9 a.m. - 8 p.m.;
Sat 9 a.m. - 2 p.m.

Playroom

Igraonica centar Kaptol
Nova Ves 17
① 01 486 02 03
🕐 9 a.m. - 9 p.m.

Ribica
Martićeva ulica 24
① 01 455 55 36

Suncokret
Sortina ulica 1c
① 01 655 17 05

Cloth repair

Cahun
Pod zidom 8
① 01 481 49 75
🕐 9 a.m. - 7 p.m.;
Sat 9 a.m. - 2 p.m.; ● Sun

Cik - Cak
Masarykova ulica 10
① 01 482 00 00
🕐 8 a.m. - 8 p.m.; ● Sun

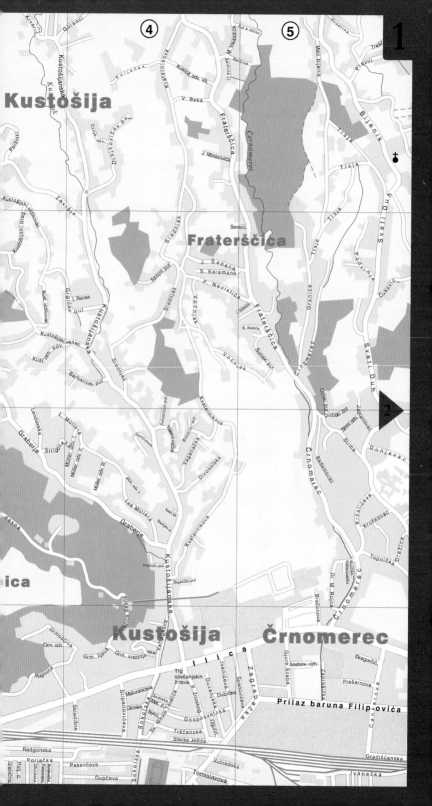

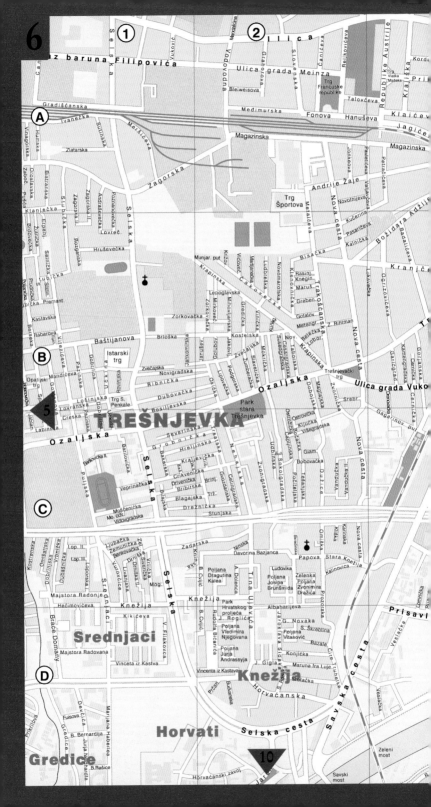

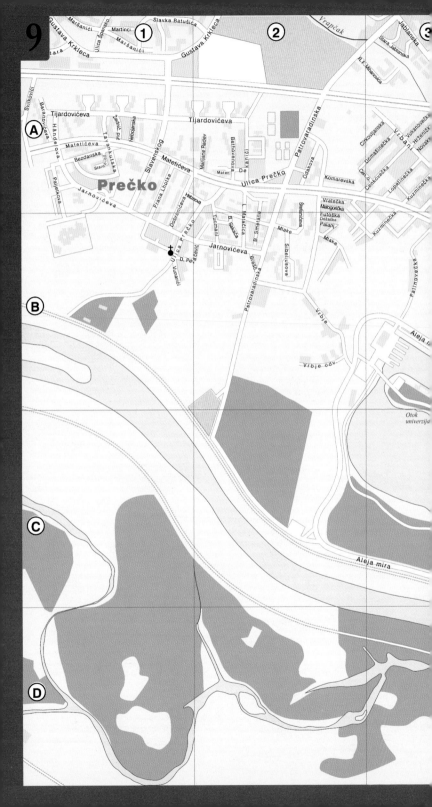

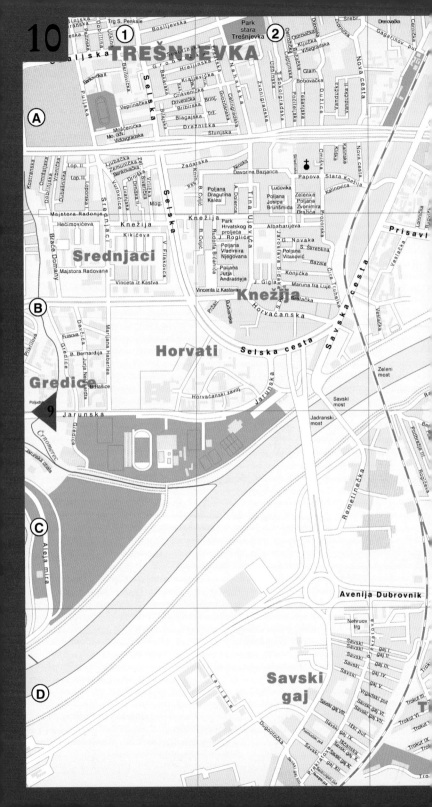

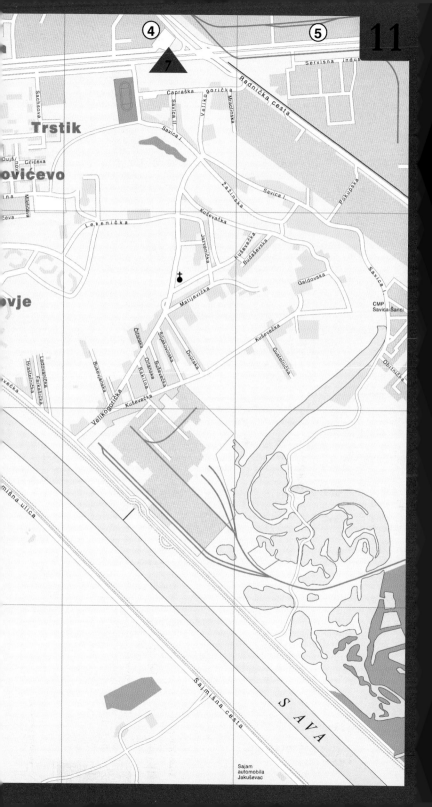

NETWORK OF DAILY TRAM LINES WITH BUS LINES

MIHALJEVAC
102 Britanski trg
233 Markuševec

JANDRIĆEVA
104 Dom umirovljenika

PETROVA ULICA
201 Kaptol
202 Kozjak

KAPTOL
105 Britanski trg
106 Mirogoj - Krematorij
201 Petrova ulica
226 Remete - Svetice

MANDALIČINA
129 Vrhovec
129 Šestinski Dol

BRITANSKI TRG
101 Gornje Prekrižje
102 Mihaljevac
103 Kraljevec
105 Kaptol

RELJKOVIĆEVA
146 Malešnica-Stenjevec

ČRNOMEREC
109 Dugave
119 Podsused
120 Gajnice
121 Karaznik
122 Susedgrad
123 Podsusedsko Dolje
124 Gornji Stenjevec
125 Gornje Vrapče
126 Gornja Kustošija
127 Mikulići
128 Lukšići
130 Borčec
131 Bizek
134 Prečko
135 Graberje
136 Spansko
137 Perjavica
172 Zaprešić
176 Gornja Bistra
177 Poljanica - Gornja Bistra

LJUBLJANICA
113 Jarun
114 Prečko
115 Spansko
116 Podsused
117 Stenjevec

TRG MAŽURANIĆA
118 Voltino

SAVSKI MOST
108 Glavni kolodvor
110 Botinec
111 Donji Stupnik - G.Stupnik
112 Lučko - Gornji Stupnik
132 Goli Breg
133 Sveta Klara - Čehi
159 Strmec Odranski
160 Lipnica
161 Kupin. Kralj.- Štrpet
162 Ašpergeri - Kupinec
163 Donji Trpuci
164 Horvati
165 Klinča Sela
168 Ježdovec
169 Kupinec
315 Lukavec

PREČKO
114 Ljubljanica
134 Črnomerec

JANKOMIR
107 Žitnjak

REMETINEC
222 Žitnjak

ZAPREŠIĆ
172 Zagreb (Črnomerec)
174 Zejinci
175 Pojatno - Gornja Bistra
181 Novi Dvori - "Inker" - Veliki Vrh
182 Sibice

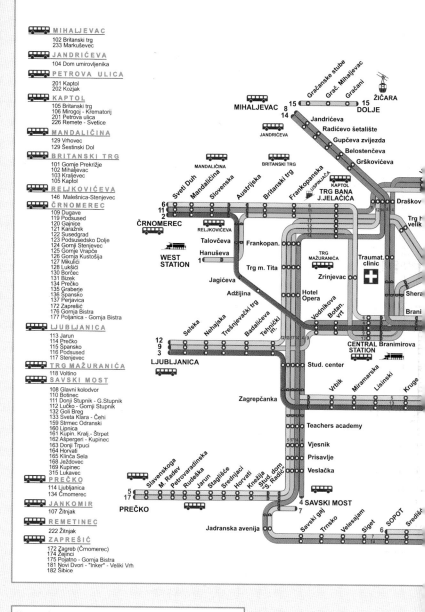

Lines no. 3 and 8 are not operational on saturday, sunday and holiday